CUCKOO IN THE NEST

Nat has been a stand-up comedian for five years and still isn't famous (sorry mum). She's also a writer and sketch performer. You won't recognise her from TV but if you meet her pretend you do. People have said a lot of things about her, here's a favourably edited selection:

(On the book)

'*An emotional exfoliation that will have you howling like a dog that's lost its favourite toy*' (Russell Kane)

'*Utterly unique, ludicrously funny*' (GQ)

'*Warm, insightful and downright hilarious*' (Isy Suttie)

'*The boomerang generation's funniest voice*' (Shappi Khorsandi)

(On stand-up)

'*Disgustingly talented*' (The Guardian)

'*Wincingly funny*' (The Observer)

'*Fiery newcomer*' (The New Statemsan)

'*A perfect blend of smart and silly*' (Spoonfed Comedy)

'*An original thinker . . . A distinctive comedy voice*' (Chortle)

Nat has written for Channel 4, BBC One, BBC 3, *The Times*, *GQ Magazine* and Radio 4.

NAT LUURTSEMA
CUCKOO IN THE NEST

28 and back home with mum and dad.
Living the dream . . .

HODDER &
STOUGHTON

First published in Great Britain in 2012 by Hodder & Stoughton
An Hachette UK company

1

A CIP catalogue record for this title is available from the British Library

ISBN 978 1 444 73714 1
eBook ISBN 978 1 444 73717 2

Typeset by Hewer Text UK Ltd, Edinburgh
Printed and bound by CPI Group (UK) Ltd, Croydon, CR0 4YY

Hodder & Stoughton policy is to use papers that are natural, renewable and recyclable products and made from wood grown in sustainable forests. The logging and manufacturing processes are expected to conform to the environmental regulations of the country of origin.

Hodder & Stoughton Ltd
338 Euston Road
London NW1 3BH

www.hodder.co.uk

For Mum, Dad and Michael

I will give you each a copy of this book
with certain pages folded down.
Skip past those, they are not for you.

If you stop making eye contact with me
I'll know you disobeyed me.

CONTENTS

Chapter 1

PLAN A

In June last year, at the age of twenty-eight, I moved into my parents' house for a month while I sorted out a new flat. Now, I love mum and dad, I'd fling myself in front of a bus for them, although not if asked. But I hadn't lived with them for years because a) I am an adult b) their house is uncomfortably clean and c) despite being made by them and from them, I am nothing like them and this irritates us all.

Returning to the family nest was an unappealing option, but the alternative was a month spent catnapping on bus journeys, washing in the rain and hiding the fact that I never went home. I was hardly known for my hedonistic ways so suggesting all-night clubbing every night of the week would lose me friends quicker than a BNP facial tattoo. I had to call that Plan B.

A few months earlier, I lived in a nice flat in north London. Nice but extremely small. My boyfriend Craine[1] and I lived in such close proximity we had started to cleave to each other's contours like fleshy jigsaw pieces. I had to stick a leg out the front door to wriggle into my jeans. Numbers 1, 2 and 5 had already caught me in my pants, it was only a matter of time before 3, 4 and 6 joined

---

1 Tom Craine, but I call him Craine, as I like to give my love life a quasi-military air. Formal but no guns.

the Bum Club and I wouldn't be able to look anyone in the eye when I put the bins out. Despite the squash, Craine and I rarely argued but I suspect it was because there wasn't room to gesticulate. If you folded your arms, you got wedged and only buttered elbows set you free.

In a bold move I decided that we would move out. We would simply find another flat, I explained to Craine, look, there are loads of buildings in this city and we only need one. I gave a month's notice, during which time Phase Two of the master plan really let me down. We started house hunting, then house searching, then surrendered to house rummaging with unattractive whimpering noises. There was nothing for us to live in. I started eyeing up skips.

With hindsight, I think that this was the Real World I'd heard so much about. I didn't care for it much, the novelty soon wore thin. Obviously I had *heard* of the recession, I was aware of it but so far it hadn't troubled me. It wasn't like I spent my days slurping champagne and laughing on yachts; champagne and boats make me queasy, I'd be a sick-spattered millionaire. I just didn't engage with things that bored me. I am a stand-up comedian – I tell jokes for bits of money, I don't have home contents insurance, I'll never have a pension and yes, I'll probably die in a gutter, but at least I won't be bored. If anything, I bet spending my eighties as a penniless tramp will be a little too 'interesting'.

But despite all my evasive manoeuvres, Real Life had found me and touched me with its boring clammy finger. Apparently the recession had affected house prices which meant that people weren't selling so people who would've bought their first homes were forced to rent and the misery was trickling down from home-owners to people with aspirations and down to us scum with no such hopes. We just wanted to hire a room, with a sink, perhaps a bit of electricity, but we found nowhere that satisfied this extravagant brief. Nowhere we could live without daily tears and smothering ourselves in anti-bacterial fluid.

I'm sure at this point there will be readers poking this book into their toaster, furious at my stubborn insistence on living in the most over-priced, over-crowded city in the country.

'There's your problem Nat, you div!', you're probably yelling at my singeing pages. I acknowledge that point, but I will always be a suburban dweeb dazzled by the Big City. Plus, London contains my friends and my work and without those I'd be at a bit of a loose end. So dig me out of the toaster and let's move on.

I spent a month with estate agents leading me around grotty, smelly little grief pits, until I felt like a doctor in an STI clinic, reacting tactfully to strangers showing me disgusting things.

'Okay, what's this? Window mould? Actually on the glass? That's all right, it happens to most men, it's nothing to be ashamed of. And how nice, a door swinging off its hinges, no it's . . . it's welcoming. "Come in," it says. "Heck, I've done half the work for you!" And . . .? A triangular kitchen that ends in a point so sharp you can't open the washing machine door wider than a sock? Right. Well no, I haven't seen this before but I'm open-minded. In fact, my mind's probably open wider than your kitchen appliances! I'm sorry, that was rude of me.'

I reconsidered the appeal of nooks, crannies and alleys. I'm a quiet sleeper, maybe I could stow away somewhere? Craine snores but forget him; it was every woman for herself now. I started eavesdropping on the bus: 'Did you say your aunt got six years for GBH? So sad. And now tell me, New Friend, did she begin this crowbar-twirling frenzy from a one- or two-bed? Zone 2 or 3?'

Looming over all this was the horrible threat of having to slink back to our parents' homes. That was all right for Craine, his parents lived in a lovely house in Bath, where he had a gorgeous view of the Cotswolds from his bedroom window (that's the hills, not the fit neighbours opposite). Plus, his relationship with his parents was very different to the one I had with mine.

Craine is the youngest of four brothers, by thirteen years; he's a bonus ball baby! It doesn't matter what he does, because all his brothers have achieved things like homes, careers and children so polite you could eat your dinner off them. (You shouldn't but if you did, they'd be really decent about it.) This leaves Craine free to do anything with his life. Which is lucky because he's a stand-up comedian too.

'Oh well,' his dad once said to me gamely, 'he's not hurting anyone . . .'

I'm the oldest child of a meagre two. It's a more high-pressure role. I'm the one that has to pioneer and make all the mistakes first. And I've really taken that obligation seriously over the years.

The Craines Senior are very different from my parents, being replete with religion and good manners, but they're equally idio-syncratic. For example, if you find yourself dining at the Craine house, don't squeeze the ketchup bottle too hard. For reasons of economy, his dad waters down the sauce with vinegar so it is unexpectedly runny and an over-enthusiastic squeeze results in a pile of ketchup queuing patiently by your plate. I thought the money saved in making the ketchup go farther was probably squandered on the extra detergent needed for the tablecloth, but I never voiced this opinion; Mr Craine is a man of keen intellect and a firm stance on the merits of wetchup.

If you manage to take the ketchup situation in your stride, you'd be a fool to relax – you're not out of the woods yet, my friend! The runny ketchup has probably dampened your love of ketchup, while piquing your interest in the supporting act, vinegar. But try and enjoy the vinegar and you'll notice that shaking it on a pile of chips leads to nothing but wet chips. That's right, the vinegar has been watered down with water. Again for reasons of economy and again, I suspect, any savings gained are reabsorbed into the stockpile of inedible chips.

If you left the dinner table at this point and decided to cleanse yourself of a confusing ten minutes, that would be understand-able, but rash: for squeezing the pump on the handwash will send soapy liquid shooting aggressively over your shoulder. It's also watered down! (With a runny liquid I supposed was water but could have been vinegar. I never felt curious enough to taste it.)

I loved this combination of economy and eccentricity in the Craine household and always wanted to join in. I suggested that, what with water in the vinegar and vinegar in the ketchup and either or both of these in the washing-up liquid, the Craines should just have Generic Kitchen Juice, for washing, seasoning, baking and any other needs. Mother Craine looked rightly repulsed but Father Craine's eyes took on a gleam of inspiration. I felt that he should just swing around a thurible of the stuff like a madcap Catholic, soaking guests and leaving them free to squeeze it out of their hair when needed. I'm sure his only objection to this was low-church religious ideology and vinegar in the eye.

So Craine was going to return to his idyllic life in Bath where, he assured me, it wasn't perfect, because 'all the tourists can get really annoying'. I slapped down this whinge, pointing out that tourists were proof that a place was nice. Trust me, picking through tourists was not a daily hassle in Watford, where my parents lived. But Craine promised that he would visit me A LOT. And I promised I would visit him EVEN MORE.

'No, no', he said, 'I want to come and see YOU!'

A tender squabble less about love than the fact that no one's parents are as annoying as your own.

At this point, I had a fairly amazing relationship with Craine and an ok-ish one with my mum and dad. Not perfect, I didn't visit as often as I should and maybe those times were only when my car broke down or another tax year approached and yet again I'd forgotten to find out how tax works. Every year I thought, 'This'll be the year!' But you know, it never was . . .

It didn't help that my parents had long ago convinced themselves that I was a moron, and I was reluctant to leave behind a life of giddy freedom to return to a house where I was treated like a lunatic child. Years ago they decided: 'Natalie may be good at school but she's an idiot otherwise,' and like the obedient mollusc I am, I grew into this persona until it fit like a stained glove. I swear I'm fairly competent most of the time, but the moment I'm back in the family home, all the jokes about my ineptitude make me paranoid and incapable. I blame their expectations of my idiocy for my . . . well, acts of idiocy. I guess they could claim that their expectations are founded on my years of idiocy, but at this point it would all get a bit Catch-22.

It had got to the stage where I was not allowed to cook in my parents' kitchen, sit on their pale-coloured sofa or perform a variety of everyday tasks. I wasn't even allowed to walk with a pen because, 'You know what you're like'. It was a very clever ruse this, to sigh and say, 'You know what you're like'. Any attempt to defend myself sounded like a lack of self-awareness.

They said if I walked around with a pen I'd draw on the walls. Accidentally, I assume, not because they thought inside me was a troubled six-year-old scrawling 'basterd' behind the doors. Nor, I think we'll have to accept, did they hold my comedic genius in such high esteem that they feared the muse would seize me and I'd start ecstatically scribbling jokes over the wallpaper.

Their concerns were obviously nonsense; I'm an adult woman with winter coats and my own furniture. I even had a credit card, once (until loved ones tore it from my grasp). But when mum and dad told me I wasn't allowed to hold a pen when I walked, I couldn't put one foot in front of the other without lurching at the walls with pen-filled hands. And that was all their fault.

Complaining was pointless, because this was the system we'd always followed; they'd say I was an idiot, while they were infallible and I'd go along with the charade because it made me feel safe. (Following the same instincts, I'd rather microwave a gluey supermarket croissant than savour a nice buttery, flaky, fresh one because that's what I'm used to: home is suffocating on wet dough.)

To maintain the delicate status quo, I would ignore the rare occasions when my parents were wrong. Like when mum polished the hallway floor until it gleamed, which was very pleasing to the eye. So pleasing that it felt churlish to point out that she'd buffed up a death trap. The floor was so slippery, when I stepped on it I invariably skidded into the cupboard under the stairs, which is not my favourite place. They keep the potatoes in there. Their anaemic little roots give me the creeps and the genius who named them 'eyes' didn't help.

Despite these peace-keeping efforts, I didn't know if I could face returning to a house where I wasn't allowed to use the oven, where conversations began, 'You know that film? With the man? Come on, you do!' (In an aggrieved tone that said *I* was the one being difficult.) Where dad felt compelled to list a burp's probable nature based on earlier meals. It was a characteristically methodical approach to life but I didn't know WHY in the name of sweet noseless relief he thought we wanted his bodily functions to come with footnotes.

I could only speak for myself, but I'm sure I've never seen him belch and hungered for further information, or stood vigil outside the toilet, pleading for intel. Dad has an archaeologist's mind, eager to investigate and interpret. Sadly, without qualifications or a dig-site he is forced to look within.

Still, it was undeniably time for Plan A, so I called home:
'01923 . . .'
'Dad, you don't have to say your phone number, I just dialled it.'
(Deeply suspicious tones) 'Who is this?'
'I'm clearly a woman and I'm calling you "Dad". Come on.'
'Oh hello. (Silence.) Well, I'll get your mother . . .'
Winning the hearts and minds, I congratulated myself as I heard him stomp off. Now to point this charm offensive at mum.
'Natalie?'
'All right Muvver.'
I should flag up a small peculiarity in our house. My mum has a typical Watford accent, with tones of her East End heritage

popping out in Cockney phrases: 'Pfft. I should coco!' 'Right. I bet you . . . should.' From dad you get a Dutch accent defending its territory against an invading Watford influence. It's not a happy blend. You won't hear this accent on your Sat Nav any time soon: 'Left at the . . . eh, tiny garden grass disc, oh shiser, thingummy, ROUNDABOUT! Bollocks, missed it.'

I grew up sporting a chirpy Watford voice that took a light beating when I won a scholarship to the nearby private school. I then dragged it to Oxford University, where it got utterly annihilated. I returned after one term with an upper-class accent that my family genuinely struggled to understand, though they admired it greatly. It was impressive, just a bit impractical – like I'd returned home with a peacock under my arm. 'Everyone, this is Jeremiah. He's going to live in the bath.'

So, I enunciate like a lady advertising pantyliners until I go home, then all my inner Watford bubbles to the surface. The moment I put the key in the door I slide down two or three socioeconomic groups. I don't mind having two voices, I just can't talk to mum before a gig or my vowels get confused and it takes an emergency call to a posh mate to straighten them out, or risk the Artful Dodger hopping onstage. So for the duration of my stay you need to imagine my voice box demonically possessed by the Queen and Babs Windsor. Two gals I'd like to think would rub along cheerfully enough in this unlikely event.

But back to the charm offensive, where I was possibly leaning harder on the second word than the first.

'Natalie? I was watching *Neighbours*.'

'You're always bloody watching *Neighbours*. You know those two episodes a day are the same right? You're not that forgetful yet, are you? Anyway, less of this boring chat . . . Craine and I haven't found a new flat yet.'

'No?! But you're both so efficient and organised and not stupid in any way.'

'I'll ignore that.'

'I'll just say it again.'

'Can I come home and stay for a little bit? Just a little bit, a month or so. I'm sure we'll find somewhere soon.'

(An admirably small silence while she quietly chewed her fists.)

'Of course! That'll be lovely!'

Mum often says things like, 'That'll be lovely' when faced with situations that clearly won't be. As if by saying it, through sheer determination and big smiles, she can twist reality. This was particularly evident on bad family camping holidays. 'Well, isn't this FUN!' she'd beam brightly, as we huddled in a tent flattened by rain so apocalyptic it felt clear that God did exist and he hated us.

That was fine; if mum wanted to ignore the truth, I was happy to join in. It *would* be lovely! We'd spend lots of time together! Playing board games, going for long walks, maybe a bit of badminton, heck why not? Lovely. Fun!

I have a younger brother, Michael, who wisely moved abroad and sidesteps much of this shit. He once said that he left to get out of my shadow and be his own man, neither statements I took seriously as I could smell the *Dawson's Creek* on them. Michael lives on a small island in Thailand and his life may or may not be evolving into a limerick. I'm withholding judgment 'til Barbra Streisand gives him a diamond.

We're very different people. I take a particularly firm stance on people who travel abroad to 'find themselves', arguing that it's pretty optimistic to assume your 'self' is waiting for you on a tropical beach, as it's just as likely to be sitting expectantly in Slough. But no one ever checks Slough first, do they? My brother poo-pooed the Slough theory and went Travelling. Or 'Unemployment, the World Tour' as I privately dubbed it.

That quip (though thigh-shiveringly hilarious) wasn't accurate; as usual I had sacrificed Truth on the altar of LOLs. Michael was a diving instructor, a cushy job but nothing that a clown like me could disparage. He went Travelling four years ago and mid-travel, at the furthest point away from us, he stopped. This might not surprise you, given the unlovable family traits I've already paraded before you, with the misplaced pride of a toddler with a newly christened potty, but it horrified us.

When he stopped moving, we pointed out that in order to be Travelling you really need to keep moving. It's that sort of a verb. Semantics didn't dislodge him, he simply said 'I live here now' and we said, 'No, but . . . because . . . oh.'

Mum fumed: 'If I'd known this was going to happen I'd never have let him out the bloody house.'

We resorted to cheap tactics, declaring ourselves Trick or Treating at Death's door, but the webcam betrayed our ruddy fibbing faces. So for the time being we let him stay in his house on stilts in the sea and on the boat in which he sailed to work whilst frequently reminding him that 'quality of life' was highly over-rated, despite the happiness he thought he felt.

We occasionally revived the campaign to bring him home: 'Mum found a lump! In the duvet, but still . . .' Or we'd swear that dad was developing brain problems (stick him on the phone for five minutes, the evidence stacked up), but Michael wouldn't budge. Strangely enough, lumpy beds and dad babbling about a man he once knew (. . . or was it a shop?) weren't enough to tempt him off his beach. And so, for now, I was stuck dealing with mum and dad alone.

While my brother looks like dad and thinks like mum (it's less horrific than it sounds), I'm untraceable to either of them. We'd always agreed that I was the cuckoo in the nest, an anomaly some joker sneaked into a family too polite to return me. I wouldn't take any blame for this, they were my creators, if the end product displeased them they had only themselves to blame. Who breeds their own nemesis? Idiots and those bugs whose children eat them.[2] The only thing we appeared to have in common was a big chin. (We don't share it. A big chin each.)

2 I may have dreamt this 'fact'.

Dad is half Dutch, half Indonesian, a blend that sounds exotic but the reality looks like an Asian Mr Bean. He emigrated from the Netherlands to England when he was eighteen; on a visit to the Moederland we spotted why: Dutch women are huge! They took my understanding of 'leggy' and popped heels on it. We joke that dad emigrated in a bid to find a woman small enough for him. He doesn't find this as funny as we do, as the bid failed and mum, Michael and I are all very tall. I guess it's not that fun to be mocked for your height by three gangling bastards, one you wed, two you made, all of whom should treat you nicer.

Inexplicably, dad went straight from the Netherlands to Watford, an unremarkable medium-sized commuter town in Hertfordshire. When I asked why, he sighed dreamily and said, 'I'd always heard so much about it . . .'

'Like what?' I demanded: 'Rumours of its ring road? Folk tales about its really big Yates's?'

Still it worked out for the best, as Watford is where he met my mum. She was born and raised here and wisely left to sail around the world with the Merchant Navy when she was eighteen. She and my godmother have been drunk/stranded/arrested in most international ports. I'm doing my best to continue their legacy but so far all I've managed is a parking ticket in Hartlepool.

Mum met dad on shore leave and they were soon engaged. The blushing bride-to-be celebrated her engagement by buggering off back to sea. I'm not replete with manners but even I thought this was cheeky.

She always defended it airily: 'Oh, he had a cat for company and I brought back knick-knacks.'

This may explain dad's fondness for novelty figurines; for a year they were his substitute for a real life woman. Let's not dwell on that scenario, just don't leave him alone with your Wedgewood.

These two created a mixed-race genetic tombola, which my brother definitely won. He's a symphony of rich brown colours, while I am a ringtone of yellows and greys. He looks like something you'd carve out of mahogany, I'm the proud owner of an overbite and jaundice and would only be hot stuff in Springfield.

Mum once cracked the quip, 'Natalie got the brains and Michael got the looks,' but we refused to chuckle at something that made him feel thick and me feel ugly. Plus, we queried the bountiful reserves of 'brains' and 'looks' that Lord and Lady Plentiful thought they were dishing out. Michael and I have nothing in common but DNA and our love for each other. We'd rescue each other from a burning building, but if we then ended up in hospital beds next to each other the chat would run dry.

'Hot in there, wasn't it?'

'You are not wrong.'

Yet we always united against mum and dad when necessary. The joy of a four-person family is that every argument can split neatly into two against two, which feels like a nice sporting fight.

Since Michael left, all our fights had been wonky and less satisfying. We either split two against one and the outcome was obvious or we descended into three-way yelling. I was thinking of recruiting a ringer, an ex-politician with debating skills and time on his hands who would always take my side. But I didn't think I could afford a good one and I didn't want a bad one sleazing over mum and nicking our cash.

Whingeing aside, I was genuinely very grateful to have a home to go to. It was very kind of my parents to have me back, I was aware of how much trouble I'd be in without the luxury of this safety net. I was very lucky. I reminded myself of this regularly; especially on my seventh day back home when we discovered that dad had never heard of Facial Soap so had spent a refreshing week using mine on his body willy-nilly. (If only it was just on the nilly . . .)

Chapter 2

OL' CREAKY AND THE BETRAYER

The final step in dismantling my adult life was to bring all of my belongings back home. Unfortunately home was already full of my parents' stuff. I was basically inserting my life into someone else's, like reluctant Russian dolls. So my life had to be packed away into the garage. But mum couldn't just dump it in there – no, that would be 'messy' – so she arranged everything into a bizarre bedsit layout. I hoped this wasn't a hint, I didn't want to live in the garage.

The arrangement looked unnervingly like some sort of Art. I had to browse for my books and clothes through ladders and twine. If Bear Grylls has a library, I imagine it's like this. Poor sod, no wonder he spends so much time in the woods.

Mum interrupted my moaning about Bear Grylls to say, in an unnaturally chirpy voice, that we just needed to compromise and we would get along fine. I couldn't really see where she was compromising, whereas I was having to do things like Washing Up As I Went Along, meaning I settled down to eat knowing what every meal looked like in rinsed-out remnant form. Yummy. I always thought this would be the weak point of X-ray vision: 'Here's sexy Jake, dipping for a kiss, and we know what his bladder looks like.' Where's the mystique?

Still . . . I hadn't lived at home for years; perhaps mum was 'compromising'. For all I knew Monday was Gun Club night and every Tuesday she hosted mixed-doubles nudey wrestling. Perhaps she was graciously suspending these activities while I was there, but I was unconvinced until I found concrete evidence, like a bullet-riddled jockstrap in the magazine rack.

I perched on one of the sturdier piles of life-detritus and phoned Craine.

'Yesterday's Aubergine Mousse,' he greeted me fondly. We'd never really settled on pet names for each other so we used arbitrary words and let tone do the work.

'The Bitumin-Dipped Weasel,' I reciprocated. 'I'm in the garage,' I said sadly.

'OK. Feel around the walls, you'll reach a door eventually.'

'I'm not locked in. Mum stuck all my stuff in here.'

'What, everything?'

'Yeah.'

'So you get out of the shower, wrap a towel round yourself and head to the garage for pants and socks?'

'Fine . . . Nearly everything. I'm allowed one box at a time in my room. I'm dressing by Lucky Dip, I look mentally ill.'

'I heard a thing on Radio 4 or one of those, where when things are bad you write down all the positives of your situation.'

'Why?'

'To remind you of them. And stop you going on at me, you moany cow.'

I sloped up to my bedroom, in clothes that already smelt 'garagey' and made my list. It read: 'Carpet, Stocked fridge, Good mattress'. I had clearly over-estimated myself, it would seem that I am a creature of very basic needs. I was tempted to nudge the list up to a more respectable length by adding, 'Get to know mum and dad better', but I wasn't sure if that definitely counted as a good thing. The day before, I'd learnt that dad liked to indulge in after-school snacks after work. I found him nibbling through a plate of cheese and cheese and onion crisps.

(I know it's confusing written down. It made more sense on the plate, but only a bit.)

Snack time was quite endearing. Less welcome was the revelation that dad and I STILL bickered constantly, this wasn't just a mid-nineties phase. On my first night home, we watched TV in frosty silence for forty minutes, after a squabble about a hole in my tights dragged on through dinner and was such an enemy of the general will to live I was surprised the food on our plates didn't collapse and rot. My final word on that matter: I was right. Tights don't become useless once they get holes at the toes, they evolve into leggings. It's the Circle of Life.

Those peaceful forty minutes came to an end at about the forty-minute mark, when dad started talking. He was reading aloud from the newspaper, as I lay on the sofa with a crisp sandwich. The decision to move home had been a panicked last-minute one and so I suddenly had to kick a 10–20 a day habit. I had to do it instantly as my parents thought that I had stopped smoking six years ago, because that's what I told them. I was aware that the nicotine withdrawal was not going to help familial relations. The only way to stop myself from screaming and sucking on the car exhaust was constant snacking. My hands were on an endless merry-go-round of poking things at my face.

So I twitched and nibbled, dad read to us and mum watched her usual autopsy/crime drama, *CSI: Someplace*. Nothing said 'home' to me like a rib-spreader advancing on mottled blue flesh, so it was an idyllic family scene except we hadn't asked dad to read aloud: quite the opposite. Mum kept shouting 'Shut UP!' and cranking the TV volume up to ear-bleeding levels. The living room vibrated with the sound of a woman being raped to bits. It was a blunt way of saying 'I'd rather listen to brutality than your idea of chat.' Mum and dad watched so much of this gruesome stuff, you could merrily butcher someone in our back garden, knowing that if they stumbled upon the scene their only concern would be whether they'd seen this one before.

Dad was reading out an article about a woman who went back home to live with her parents and how it destroyed her self-esteem and made her feel suicidal. This was dad's idea of a Welcome Home. I was surprised he didn't just leave me out some towels and a razor blade. I informed him that, unlike her, I didn't feel like a failure.

'Really?' he said, in tones of great surprise.

'Yes, actually,' I replied. Thanks to four years as a gigging stand-up comic I was no longer troubled by much in the way of ego and the little I had was seemingly indestructible, an emotional cockroach surviving in the most hostile environs, such as that conversation.

Dad turned the page. And began talking again.

'Oh. I see your um, whatsit, that chap' (this vagueness despite the fact that the name was right in front of him and he had brought the subject up in the first place), 'your Colin Firth' (we don't own him, we just like him) 'is in a new thing called *The King's "Speech"*' (this last word said like it's a made-up word). 'He's the um, the one that came after Henry.' ('Edward?' we suggested. Simply because the royals don't have much imagination with their kids' names and because we seemed to have been dragged into a desperate, confused game of charades.)

'Yes,' said dad and he subsided for a bit.

We thought he was done; we dared to hope so. But no, dad is a long-reigning champion of the never-ending, droning sentence that makes people want to punch themselves in the face. To general despair and eye rolling, he began again:

'Looks like he's going to get a thingy . . . a gold er . . . well, probably gold-plated . . . gong?' 'Oscar, I believe it's called, I believe . . .'

I took one for the team and created a diversion so that mum could skip out and pop her head in the oven. I told him that I needed to be in London tomorrow so I'd walk to the train station with him. In return he regaled mum and I with the tale of how yesterday he had got a train at 11:06 that was in fact, actually, the delayed 10:45. Fancy that!

*   *   *

And that was the first night of my Month At Home (as I had formally named it. Just so we all knew it was temporary and would soon be over. If you want, feel the weight of the right-hand side of this book and scoff at my misplaced hope). I went to bed soon after to sniff my handbag for old cigarette smells. Then crept back down for one last glass of wine, to ease myself through this tricky transitional period. There's little sadder than tiptoeing past your sleeping parents at midnight, avoiding the third and ninth steps – Ol' Creaky and the Betrayer – to get another glass of cheap red wine.

Dad had evacuated all the good wine from the house as soon as he heard I was coming back. He had no shame in saying, 'You can't have a glass of wine, there's nothing cheap enough for you.' Every time I wanted to open a new bottle he would taste it first as if he was in a fancy restaurant, swilling the wine around his mouth, smacking his lips, before he'd pronounce this 2010 vintage 'rough enough for you'. Other times he'd conclude, 'Oh no, this is too nice' and screw the lid back on.

When my parents drank they were 'enjoying a nice glass of something,' when I drank I was apparently a shambolic tramp, trousers held up with discarded dental floss, doing wet burps and defending her life choices. Admittedly, it was hard to entirely refute that image when I found myself necking sherry in bed: stupid rummaging for wine in the dark.

Chapter 3

LADY WATFORD

Watford is my hometown; I was born and raised there. It's bred no loyalty in me, I've simply had twenty-eight years to eye it up and hate it. Test me on my dislike – I promise you, I will have prompt and vehement answers.

My parents and I have never seen eye to eye on Watford. They say it's nice, I say they're confusing 'nice' with 'horrible', probably, I console them, they've got a bit confused by Nice biscuits, which is an irresponsibly confusing brand name.

'No,' they snap, ungratefully shaking off their blankets, 'we are not confused, it is NICE.'

'Yes, yes,' I coo, tucking them in harder.

Watford is one of those places where if anyone is ever, inexplicably, listing its charms, they will invariably say 'good transport links'. This means, 'don't worry, you can leave it quickly'. A town that uses the M25 as a permanent emergency exit is not going to reach Venice/Disneyland status any time soon. If a friend said he had a new girlfriend who was brilliant because 'we've got no mutual friends so it'll be easy to dump her without awkwardness,' you would not leap to peruse your hat collection.

I will concede, in the Pro column, it is near where Jane Austen grew up, plus the nearby M25 and canal make it a good base from which to see out a zombie apocalypse. Other than that, I'm all done, thanks. Watford is a place where a man will call another man a 'legend' for giving him correct change . . . from the till, in the shop where the Legend works. Thankfully Man A rarely wields civic authority, otherwise his low criteria for legends would have us prancing through the streets daily, waving effigies of That Bloke Who Gave Ian Correct Change.

The prospect of moving back was daunting; when I left I was adamant I was gone for good. Growing up, Watford felt so far away from The Fun. The mysterious unspecified Fun I suspected everyone was secretly having. Aged fifteen, my Saturdays followed a religiously rigid schedule of travelling alone to Camden, London. Home of arty, alternative types like me who were misunderstood everywhere else. My only companion, an inch-wide red streak in my hair. I only had that thanks to WEEKS of silent weeping over breakfast. And sure, maybe the packet said 'Warm Chestnut Brown', but I'd left it in for an hour and it was definitely red.

Every week I'd reach Camden to realise:

1. I'd spent all my money on my train ticket and I was hungry, having shunned a packed lunch.
2. Camden scared me, the people looked weird. I'm all for a bit kooky but of rein it in chaps!
3. My proudest possession, my Spliffy jacket,[3] suddenly felt silly somehow.
4. That man was whispering 'skunk' at me but I didn't smell, did I? Did I?

I'd hide in McDonalds, eke out a Happy Meal, unable to share its joy, then scurry back to Watford, full of my stories of the Big City. 'Yeah, well Camden,' I'd sigh on Monday at school, 'it's just got so commercial?'

Even at twenty-eight, with the Spliffy jacket in the loft, I still

---

3 'No Mum, the man on the back is just holding a funny-shaped cigarette . . .' The only time Teen Nat and Mischief made contact. Just a gentle brush, but worth recording for posterity.

wasn't reconciled to the geography that Fate had dumped on me. I was the plucky brain-box who strode off to the City of London (twelve miles away) to conquer the world (do stand-up comedy in small rooms above pubs). Now I was back, because I'd fucked it all up. It felt so humiliating. I had to assume it was character building. Either that or Life was a masochistic bitch, brainstorming ideas with a drunk.

Over the years I had become pretty comfortable with failure, and after four years as a stand-up comic I was pretty much on spooning terms with the concept. Not that my career was going that badly, more that you hone your set through a hundred tiny failures, of moments when you pause for a laugh that never comes or comes but isn't big enough and you realise that bit needs to be shorter, that bit needs to come earlier and that bit isn't funny and never will be. Failure starts to feel like a helpful straight-talking buddy, maybe she's a little blunt sometimes, can hurt your feelings a little, but she's just trying to help.

However I couldn't see this situation in quite such matey terms. I'd worked so hard to build my independent adult life on my precarious career. It had been a laborious slog, constructing it one tiny piece at a time, and now The Real World had stamped all over my Lego spaceship.

When I left home it felt like a fresh start, I left behind my friendless former self and was free to reinvent myself: "S'up guys, they call me The Luurts. Guys . . .?"

In Watford I felt haunted by Younger Me; the sort of lonely girl who'd spend Friday night wearing *Just Seventeen*'s recipe for a raw egg hair mask. Regrettably *Just Seventeen* did not stress the importance of rinsing this mask out with cold water. I used hot water and cooked an omelette into my scalp. It looked like I had flung sanity to the wind and fashioned a hat of puke. Eggy-headed teen Nat dogged my footsteps. Of course she wasn't bothering me alone, former school 'friends' helped.

Some years earlier, Michael was back for an annual visit and we were dancing in a nightclub, as best we could, given the stickiness of the floor. If you ever feel unloved, walk through a nightclub in Watford. The floor will hug your every step, grasping at your feet with a needy, alcoholic clinginess and you'll feel adored.

Now, contain your surprise but I am a brilliant dancer. Well, not me exactly, Drunk Me. Drunk Me is brilliant, I hope you all get a chance to meet her. I'm sure you will; she's around a lot. She funks out and quips like her life is a well-scripted sitcom. As Drunk Nat grooved sassily and Michael nodded encouragingly, a girl approached, an old foe from school. She'd been one of the rich cool girls, but a Watford version; if I were a bitch I'd call her Daddy's Lidl Princess. So I shall.

Daddy's Lidl Princess had always liked to point out my flaws, as if they weren't immediately bloody obvious. It was like we were on a shopping channel for social outcasts: 'Let me just measure that . . . yes, the trousers end a full two inches above the ankle. Perfect nerd measurements, a modern classic here, these will flap quite audibly as she runs to double Latin.'

She hove into view – it pained me to note that she'd put on a little weight. She hauled her dimpled bulk towards me, waited for her hula hoops of flesh to settle back into spam-like stillness, snorted, 'Where did YOU learn to dance? The library?!' Then dragged her meaty carcass off with perfect comic timing.

The thing with 'slams' is that they don't need to be clever or even make much sense, they just have to be quick and nasty. That's why I glaze over when people tell me about the great comic they saw who 'slammed' a heckler. It's easy to make a drunk look stupid, they do most of the work for you. As this drunk learnt, frozen mid-*Macarena*.

This time around, I was trying to keep a low profile while I skulked at home for an . . . indeterminate amount of time. Skulking was proving tricky, however, as mum is a local celebrity; she has taught at the local school for 140 years, so countless generations have passed through her dubious care. In Next, teenaged boys greet her with scared grimaces; I assume because she once taught them, or perhaps she gets tanked up and fights strangers in the evening. (Who knows? Everyone's entitled to a little privacy.) In the supermarket, children's eyes widen at the sight of her buying ham like a normal human. Tugging their mothers' bootleg jeans, they whisper, 'Missis Luurtsema is out of school!', as if surprised she wasn't packed away at 4pm along with the crayons.

I wish. Instead, she would come home and yell at me for my inability to follow her (stupid) favourite dishwasher-stacking system. Or drag me into the forceful current of her Plans for the Day. Whenever I'm home, I bob in mum's wake while she strides around flapping her multiple To Do lists. From day one, I was spending my afternoons following her around the shops, enticed out with, 'Come out – treat yourself! You've worked hard today, I'll buy you one of those soups you like.'

I learnt to dread The Bits. If I helped mum and dad with The Big Shop, I knew what I was letting myself in for. I cleared out my diary; I brought a book. But whenever mum assured me that we were just 'popping in for bits' I would be outraged to find myself standing in the biscuit aisle an hour later, feeling like the victim of a glorified kidnap. Staged by the only people likely to pay a ransom. Obviously, Craine would in theory, but I'd be dead by the time he worked out his online banking.

It's not that mum was a dithery shopper. If anything, she was too decisive and I'd get railroaded into Yakults. I don't like doing shots of booze, no matter how cool it looks in films, it makes me feel queasy. So there's no chance I'm going to begin the day by flinging back a neckful of sugary gloop, thank you.

The main reason these shopping trips got so lengthy was the amount of time mum spent deliberating over a parking space. Is there enough room for me to get out? She'd peer around and agonise, as if I'm the size of a hippo and always exit a car by flinging the door open and waiting for a crunching noise to tell me what's out there.

Usually such a decisive woman, parking is her weak spot and I couldn't stand it. I'd hop out and do a cheeky Charleston to demonstrate the ample room, but she was never convinced and we'd nudge in and out of the space while she calculated its pros and cons. I'd get irritable and start asking exactly how long was she planning on staying? Was the Asda car park our new holiday home? If not, did the spot have to be perfect? Really, only the car has to like it and it seemed content enough.

She'd ignore me to pursue her musings: 'Is it me? Does it really tick all the boxes? Has it got the Wow Factor?'

Mum whinges about the time I 'waste' on lie-ins, but arguably I recoup these lost hours by parking decisively and leaving the scene swiftly, while she measures up her parking space for curtains and invites friends around for a second opinion.

Another anxiety was about people opening their car doors onto hers. I was adamant that she'd be liberated from this paranoia if I just went at her Renault with a hammer. Then she could drive a battered crapwagon feeling serene that the worst had already happened. Mum had a better solution: Mother and Child parking bays. Roomy enough for her liking and with the added perk of a potential row with someone who objected to her abusing the system.

Her argument was, 'Well, they didn't have them when you were small and I needed them, so I'll use them now.' I assured her that nappies had come along in leaps and bounds too; I could shimmy into a Pampers if that would make her feel better. She'd fiddle with the radio and ignore this.

Really deep down, she did know that she was in the wrong and this is her least favourite place to be, except perhaps the spidery bit of the garage. So she would park and get out, desperate to be challenged so she could grab me and declare, like Oscar Wilde in a noisy room (she will never just say something if it can be announced), 'THIS is my child!!'

I had no interest in being used as a prop in her shameful antics so as soon as the handbrake was on I'd slither out of the car and scuttle off. She'd pursue me, trying to stay close enough to the car that if some poor sod glanced at it she could interpret it as criticism and retort with the killer line, waving my struggling body aloft.

'Well,' she'd defend herself, in wounded tones, 'he was judging me.'

'Too bloody right he was,' I'd snap, wriggling free and fixing my collar, 'you'd just chased me across a car park. That's not normal, even for Asda. You looked like a short-sighted Child Catcher.'

The second reason shopping trips took so long was the number of times we had to have these conversations:

'Oat and raisin cookies or white chocolate ones?'

'I don't really like cookies, they're just big, damp biscuits.'

'You have to have them, they're on offer.'

'It doesn't mean you have to . . .'

'Oat and raisin or white chocolate?'

'Fine. Oats, please.'

'I'll get you both. Now could you eat your way through four packets?'

'No! I'm munching through two under duress, can we not add to the pile?'

'FINE. Oh no, no, you're very welcome.' (Followed by some resentful muttering about not knowing why she bothers.) Mum has never understood that shopping should be consensual, not a fight where the loser has to face a week of food they don't like.

Operation Interminable Shopping Trip didn't speed up once we were out of the car and through the first two or three arguments. At this point, Lady Watford would bump into various members of her vast social circle and stop to chat. Her mates would usually have a teenaged daughter hovering awkwardly by their side. Not my mum of course, she had a daughter who was nearly thirty lingering withered by her side.

I'd venture a bit of chat with the other daughter. ('How's work?' 'I sort of arrange buns in a shop on Saturdays.' 'Right, of course. Soooo . . . That Justin Bieber, eh?')

We reached a new low when my opposite number was a

five-year-old girl. Our mums nattered while we loitered awkwardly, staring at our shoes. I tried to extend the hand of friendship by staring at her shoes, but she didn't like that and started to cry. I blamed myself but really, she brought nothing to the table. Time to accept personal responsibility, you tiny dullard.

Mum's friends would always ask about my work. 'It must be so glamorous being a comedian,' they'd assure me. I'd rack my brains and fiddle with the mushrooms. I'm not very good at boasting, plus between you and me, my store of things to boast about is pretty meagre. I'm browsing amongst 'The Time I Stood Next to Neil Gaiman' and 'Sometimes at Gigs I Get Free Sandwiches'. Comedy is 50 per cent exhilaration because 'that new bit worked', 20 per cent gloom and 30 per cent 'why oh why isn't the M4 moving? I'm so very tired.'

One day I just wasn't ready. I was exhausted, I was driving so much for gigs at this time that the day before I had passed a garage selling petrol at a relatively cheap 128.7p a litre and had swerved into the forecourt before I realised that I was not actually *in* my car. Luckily I didn't come to this realisation mid-suck on a petrol pump, gloating over Nectar points.

So I was yawning in the fruit and veg section, eyeing up tomatoes on the vine and feeling grateful that we hadn't brought dad: 'Still on the vine? Pick 'em off, that's your job!' I was all set to crawl into the softer veg for a nap when mum's friend sideswiped me with a polite enquiry about my work.

And so I said this: 'Well, it is nice to work from home, except so does my boyfriend and we usually live together and sometimes he'll have a quick wee and not flush, which I find so thoughtless and disgusting that I'm determined he should know how I feel, so I do likewise. Which angers him to identical retaliation, possibly because he now can't see the original wee that provoked me. To be fair, to a forgetful man who drinks a lot of tea and doesn't cherish tender memories of every toilet trip, it probably does look like this is all my fault. And so this quiet war can escalate until you've got an unholy George's Marvellous Medicine in there that can only be flushed with a coat hanger tied to the end of a mop. And that . . . is . . . ah, is pretty much what it's like to be a comedian,' I explained to her dry-retching shoulders.

I knew this story was disgusting and boring, but I COULDN'T STOP MYSELF TALKING. I was a hedgehog charging down a Pringles tube thinking, 'It'll be all right in a minute!' I was just babbling with big staring eyes. With an admirable sense of self-preservation, mum had dumped us both and gone to stand among the melons until I stopped talking.

Thankfully, this was a rare blip. Most of the time, the public attention didn't faze me. I've always felt famous, thanks to my face. It's not an immediately pleasing face, it always looks annoyed: the petulant mouth and sullen Slavic mien of a woman brooding, 'Yes, I will fetch your stool sample, but don't expect me to like it.' And yet it's one of the most generic faces in the history of people thinking they saw their cousin's ex-girlfriend in Boots. Total strangers wave at me quite happily, certain they know me. I'm used to it, so I wave back.

I imagine that this is what it's like being really distinctive-looking, like 6'10" or blessed with humorously large breasts, people see you as a public property to be openly enjoyed. Except the skill I bring to the world is a completely unoriginal face. This is the copy, cut and paste of faces. I'd be an ideal spy.

Often when I turn up to gigs I see peoples' faces light up: they recognise me! It must be because I was on *Mock The Week*? No wait, perhaps I'm 'That Girl off That Show!' Not likely. I did my first gig in May 2007 and went full-time eight months later so I could immerse myself fully in the heady world of part-time cleaning and waitressing. (If it wasn't already obvious, I'm a bit impulsive and don't think ahead.)

I've signed a lot of autographs for people who don't really know what signature they're expecting to see when I hand it back. I used to insist I wasn't anyone and they probably had me confused with a former work colleague, but people would look so disappointed. Now, I oblige them, sign things, even pose for photographs and they all agree how nice I am, so humble, despite all that . . . fame I presumably have, with the . . . thing. Then I hope they don't see me hop on the bus.

It's a useful skill, hopping discretely onto buses. With some minor tweaks, it had evolved into the unobtrusive sideways scuttle I now needed to sneak into mum's car.

'What, me? Living at home?! Noooo . . . I'm just looking for my . . . moped, to scoot back to London. Have you seen it? It's got N-Dubz on the back of it, probably. Just some showbiz mates I brought to . . . Asda, Watford . . . I know, raaaaaandom!'

I was determined to hide out in Watford for a couple of weeks at most and be back in a flat of my own before anyone noticed I was nearing thirty and had that distinctive mum-washed smell to my clothes once more. The smell that announces to the world, 'I live with Mummy and Pop Pops! And I smell delicious.'

I also swore to myself that I would stop slagging off Watford, it was just ungrateful. The hunchback of Notre Dame didn't stagger into the cathedral wailing, 'Sanctuary! Sanctuary! . . . Oh really, you haven't spruced this place up at all? Not even some cushions? Jeez . . .'

Chapter 4

THE ODD SOCK BOX

My parents' house was the one I did most of my growing up in. It is the sort of unimaginative box a child might draw, but nice enough, with all the requisites like a kitchen, living room, dining room ('do NOT scratch the table') and a bedroom each.

It has a big garden, which my parents love, although dad is engaged in a lengthy war with it. Several bits have defeated him and so every year another section is given a whimsical name like 'The Wilderness' or 'Jungle Fever', so he doesn't have to venture there anymore, he can simply gesture towards the thorny recesses and say, 'It's supposed to look like that.'

There was no such surrender inside the house. The surfaces in mum and dad's home *sparkled*, while the poor floors gave off a more subdued air, like chastised baddies in a U-rated kids' film; they hadn't been hurt but boy, did they feel small.

My parents persecuted dust so thoroughly, I felt sorry for it. One morning I discovered a little piece of dust behind the bathroom door. I didn't recognise it at first, it looked so out-of-place. I'm no expert but I was pretty sure I was in the company of lint suspended in a fragile cage of pubic hair. I didn't know how it had evaded mum and dad but there it sat, a survivor of a particularly brutal war. I saluted its pluck. I considered scooping it up and setting it free in the back garden but feared the neighbours would see and tell on me.

I said to mum once, 'Truthfully, hand on heart, if society didn't judge you, wouldn't you just laminate the house and everything in it and hose us down like elephants?' She wouldn't answer, but she got a dreamy look in her eye.

Worktops were treated with abject reverence – they got hysterical when I defiled them with a stray noodle flipped from a pan. I was too messy for that house, we were all painfully aware of this. But, just for this Month At Home, I had to step up to my parents' rules. Kitchen surfaces, bathroom surfaces, tables, dining and occasional: a spill must not be left for a second, they assured me, or it would stain irreparably.

I didn't believe this for a second. What idiot would make a bathroom worktop incapable of dealing with water?

'Lovely toilet.'

'Thanks! It's made of meringue!'

I was permitted to put nothing upon any surface without a coaster or at least the respectful placing of a napkin (even if it was single-ply, which was surely so flimsy its purpose was merely ceremonial). As neither parent is religious, perhaps polished granite fills the God-shaped hole.

My parents' house is also FULL of cats. There are only two, but by sheer force of personality and bad manners, they seem to be everywhere. If you have parents who dote unreasonably on their pets, count yourself lucky, all this indulgence could have been lavished upon a final sibling who, it's safe to assume, would've been a twat. If my parents' cats had thumbs they'd be dangerous serial killers or toxic J-list celebrities.

Once I'd moved back home, I became an involuntary part of the cats' daily routines. Every morning, at about five, they liked to thunder upstairs, chasing each other through the bedrooms on a route that took in my desk, my windowsill ('No, it wasn't my favourite childhood piggybank, just my only one') and finally my head. It was like *Jumanji* but horrible, because it was happening to me. There are a lot of films I love to watch but if the same events ever happened to me I'd swallow my tongue and end it all quickly.

It was a daily horror to wake up with a paw in my ear and no idea why. I wasn't even allowed to close my door because the cats would hurl themselves at it repeatedly until a stroppy voice from my parents' room demanded I 'stop being selfish'. Their thinking was that if they had to suffer, so did I. I considered this pretty ignoble. No heart-stirring war epic ever featured a wounded soldier shooting his friend in the leg and saying, 'See? It really fucking hurts!'

A meandering lethargy always overwhelmed me in my parents' house, because there were so many things I wasn't allowed to touch that I'd end up drifting around like it was a sub-standard museum. My parents weren't totally neurotic; from their point of view these were reasonable precautions. I am prepared to admit that over the years I have started a couple of fires due to my short attention span and ruined countless bits of furniture. To ever feel relaxed in the dining room I'd need to defeat gravity and float blamelessly above the big, shiny table.

My latest embargo had come only months earlier. Mum had come thundering upstairs, waving something. She looked like a confused cheerleader in her senior years. I wisely kept that thought to myself. The thing she was brandishing turned out to be a piece of cream-coloured sofa. I didn't really understand. I hadn't realised the sofa came apart, it looked faintly obscene, like she was waving one of dad's ribs.

'You're banned!' she cried triumphantly. 'Banned! From the pale-coloured sofa!'

She waggled the bit of sofa at me, which I recognised as the armrest. It seemed bigger out of context, but that was by the by.

'See?' she said, gesturing delicately along a seam, like I was being scolded by a shopping channel presenter. 'It's all filthy from where you sit there and do this (and she made a creepy claw motion like a tyrannosaurus rex impersonating Fagin) with your greasy hands.'

Now, I'm not a vain woman. Looks-wise I neither scare children nor inspire poetry. That's fine. But I firmly refuted this greasy-fingered, furniture-caressing grotbag image she was trying to thrust upon me.

My opinion was disregarded, however, as mum carried her amputee sofa bit back downstairs, continuing to yell as she went. Craine had already been slapped with a lifelong ban for an incident with a tomato and now I'd joined him in soft furnishings exile. If she kept banishing loved ones with this biblical zeal the dark-coloured sofa was going to get uncomfortably crowded, while she reigned alone on the pale one, ignoring our attempts to flick soup at it.

My parents cleaned the way drunks drank. They cleaned regularly, for special occasions, before parties, after parties, before visits, after visits, they even cleaned my room around me while I dozed at 8am. I don't mean to sound ungrateful but when you wake up to see your parents silently folding your clothes around you, it feels like you're in a coma and being tended to.

Mum strove for order to such an extent that she had a little box of odd socks, like mementoes of a foot she once loved. The first time I found this box I accosted her with it. I demanded full disclosure. Did she have a secret love child and was he a foot? Or a nudist who couldn't quite commit? She wasn't as amused by this as I was and tutted that, of course, obviously, this was a place to store odd socks that had temporarily lost their other half.

I think most people would have just chucked them in the sock drawer, then continued with their life, hoping, reasonably enough, that the other sock would be along soon enough, given the fairly limited travel options open to a sock: foot, laundry basket, machine, foot again. But not mum, she had created a Singles Club for them. We refer to it as the Odd Sock Box, and mum's the only one who thinks the adjective refers to the socks.

*   *   *

It was easy to mock my parents' attitudes, and fun too, which is why I did it so much. But I had experienced the other end of the spectrum; my boyfriend Craine and I didn't enjoy that much either. Craine is the kindest, most gracious and witty tramp you'll ever meet. To him the world is his serviette; I've caught him wiping his hands on his trousers, his hair, the wall, even me once when he thought I was dozing. He tried to pass it off as a hug but I had pizza down my arms. He's just one step away from blowing his nose in the curtains.

Everything Craine does is messy. You can trace his path around the house by the trail of destruction. He opens cereal packets like a bear – ripping them open down the middle then pawing out the innards. After his first visit, several years earlier, mum and dad mused over breakfast: 'I'd love to see him get out of the shower.' Before I feared we were heading for the sort of trouble that only Jeremy Kyle could 'fix', dad followed this up with 'Does he just grab handfuls of water and leap out?' 'Or,' countered mum, continuing a discussion that had clearly been rumbling on for hours, 'does he shake like a dog? I just don't know how he gets water everywhere. I found some inside a cupboard.'

I considered myself to be the reasonable middle ground between mum and dad's fastidiousness and Craine's belief that tidying was just a matter of HIDING mess, leading to dirty mugs squirrelled away in drawers, to be discovered weeks later sporting their own green knitwear. But insultingly, my parents considered me and Craine equally squalid, so when I moved back with them I was determined to prove them wrong, I was going to be clean.

It was a challenge, their house was untenably pristine and decorated throughout in colours called Soft Stone, Gentle Fawn and Almost Oyster (keep trying, big guy!). I needed a base foundation of dirt to work with, something to absorb the smaller stains and spills, help everyone chillax a little. I believe strongly in the ebb and flow of dirt – things get dirty, you clean them, they are clean – pause for celebration – then you set about dirtying them. Not mum, she will not tolerate the ebb and flow. She is King Cnut enthroned upon a Hoover. She and dad are hard to please.

Within the first week back I had Cheerios for breakfast, mum took one look at it and sighed, 'WHY do you always fill your bowl up so high? You know your dad and I hate that.'

The implications of that were mind-boggling – they had actually had a conversation about this. How did such a thing begin?! Were they watching TV one night and one of them said, 'Ooo, ooo, I've just thought of another thing our first-born does wrong,' and the other one hauled the *Book of Nat Fail* out and said, 'Go on . . .'

Not to bring up a tedious argument about the distribution of parental love that has rumbled on pointlessly for decades . . . BUT . . . my brother once vomited on his own face during a drunken sleep and they didn't even wake him up, they just cleaned him and joked about it in the morning. Pretty laid-back cool dudes, no? But me and my generous cereal portions provoked such disgust, I swear they were thinking, 'Could I assemble a violent mob at this time on a Tuesday?'

What if I had tipped those Cheerios on my head and feigned sleep: surely a similar situation? I toyed with the idea but rejected it as I didn't fancy rotting milk in my hair all day. Instead I stomped off to London to do more house hunting; a task that had already become a Sisyphean ball-ache.

Craine and I had recruited a flatmate by that point, as Misery loves company. No one ever asks how Company feels about this but the look on our future flatmate's face said: 'Not thrilled'. Our third party's name was Tiernan Douieb, but most estate agents went for Tinman Dooby on the forms. Tinman is a very funny comic and a good friend. Somehow, even after the year that was to follow, he remains both those things.

My relationship with Craine had taken an unexpected turn. We used to wake up every day together, write side-by-side in happy harmony, then head off to our respective gigs and reconvene in the early hours of the morning. I'm not saying it was the perfect life, but it felt suspiciously like it. Occasionally we'd wonder where we'd squeeze children into this set-up, but I hoped by then we'd discover that my womb was full of Lego or something and Craine could grow them for me in half an eggshell.

Our tiny idyll had collapsed, and been replaced with something not fit for purpose. We were waking up in our childhood bedrooms and spending the day in our parents' way. ('You're just going to sit there all day, tippy tappying on your PC?' 'YES. This is what my job looks like.') We spent the evenings creeping through a sleeping house and the only time we saw each other was when we were house hunting. It's impossible to keep the romance bubbling when you're house hunting, even a smile feels like a stretch and snogging is a bit inappropriate, unless it's a really nice house.

That day we saw two flats so bleak I felt tearful. Bits of it were rotting; I presumed it was self-harming and quite right too. I just could not imagine us living a happy life there – in every room I saw montages of our future misery. I foresaw myself sobbing in the bath as Tiernan bundled a dead dog under the sink, and Craine watched *Hollyoaks* while scratching his face into tagliatelle.

Sometimes being shown flats this bad felt like being threatened, like someone was waving a knife in our faces rather than a windowless bedroom:

'You want this to be your life, hur, do ya bitch?'

'No, no, please God no!'

We all agreed, if a flat looked dingy on this sunny day, in winter the walls must actually sweat shit.

At this early stage of house hunting Craine was 'helping' in his inimitable way by emailing us details of beautiful flats far out of our budget.

'Isn't this nice?'

'Yes, Craine, thank you for clarifying, it would be nice to be wealthy. Glad you've finally settled that fiendish debate.'

I retaliated by sending him pictures of women far more attractive than me and destined never to be his, due to geography, death or high standards. He declared that he was going to haggle down properties by fifty quid a week, which was bold chat for a man incapable of walking past a homeless person without handing over his shoes and wallet. We agreed, if he started haggling we'd end up paying more, with some clause that we had to turn the bathroom into a critically acclaimed deli.

The three of us hovered around a bit after the viewings. Tiernan was also living with his parents, so we were all keen to not go home. I suggested that we join the similarly circumstanced teens loitering outside Chicken Cottage, but the boys weren't game. So we sloped off back to our parental homes. Tiernan had accidentally eaten his dad's packed lunch yesterday and there'd been sulking and terse notes left on the fridge ever since. His misery delighted me, I felt less tragic squabbling with mine over their manifesto that There Is Only One Way To Stack A Dishwasher.

I returned home, poured a restorative glass of Fanta and was immediately chastised for filling it too high. I counter-accused them of being nit-picking bastards and stomped upstairs shouting, 'Oh Natalie, stop breathing so loudly! Do you have to circulate your blood so noisily? Your self-esteem's all over the floor and I'm trying to Hoover . . .'

A triumphant exit, reasonable and mature, though slightly ruined by spilling Fanta on the floor. I scrubbed at it with bubble bath and just managed to remove it when I heard mum coming up the stairs. I leapt into a naturalistic pose – sitting on a chair, back to the door, breathing deeply with rage (I had to incorporate panting). Mum stood behind me and rubbed my shoulders a little.

For a woman this inflexible this was the closest we would ever get to an apology. So I stayed silent, showing that I accepted it. Harmony was restored. On the understanding that tomorrow's breakfast was only eight hours away and it was unlikely that familial harmony would survive the Cheerio test, but at least we could sleep in truce conditions.

Chapter 5

BALLS

'Good morning' is a phrase I consider as wildly optimistic as bidding someone a 'Merry blood-clot'. Perhaps there are some nice mornings, some dew-dipped quiet triumphs of life, perhaps there are some dishy English Defence League members, doesn't mean I'm going to loiter round Luton in a St George bikini.

I used to love my mornings, I would spend them sleeping; there's more than one way to appreciate something, it's not all Oohing and Aahing and flinging your curtains open. I'm a stand-up comic so I work nights and this is great. I like my nocturnal life, it's quieter and there are fewer queues for things. But in the family home everyone sprang out of bed at 7am and if you didn't, they'd assume you died in the night and start eBaying your stuff.

When I was a kid mum would wake me by ripping the duvet off me and throwing it onto the floor. I'd shamelessly fling myself after it and crawl back in. Every morning was like some horrific birth as I was wrenched into screaming consciousness by a deranged midwife with unrealistic targets. She used to dress and undress me with the same brutal haste. I have big ears, it's a wonder they're still attached.

Living back at home confirmed that she still liked to wake me up this way. After a tug of war with my duvet that I only won because she had to go to work, I ended up back in bed, shaking and traumatised, my hair sticking to my sherry-sticky mouth. (Some of you are probably touching yourself right now, don't feel bad, this is a very sensual book.)

On the plus side, I remembered, when the hiccupping stopped, I could now choose which side of the bed I exited from! This was never an option in any of my flats; they were always so small the bed had to be shoved against the wall and every morning I'd clamber over Craine, who'd wake up with my elbow in his throat and give me a croaky scolding.

The whole bed thing may well have been the day's highlight, I reflected, as I padded off to the bathroom. I'd forgotten that, like minor celebrities, the cats were convinced whenever a door was shut on them it was to deny them access to the Best Party Ever. So they'd fling their bodies desperately against it until you relented and let them in. At which point you'd have to deal with a small cat sat in the sink, sneering at your naked body while you tried to bathe.

You may be thinking, 'Nat, a bath, in the morning?! You decadent swine.' The Luurtsemas have never had a shower, so it was bathe or stink (and I wasn't given free rein on that one).

When I first encountered a shower at a friend's house I hated it, it was like being attacked by hot rain, a frantic noisy experience that culminated in me stumbling out of the bathroom clutching a broken bit of it, saying, 'It . . . just came off in my hand!'

'Your violently flailing hand?'

'Yup, that one.'

The phrase 'power shower' was a double threat to me, like 'a sustained beating'. Over the years I've established an uneasy truce with them but I'm still not one for a romantic shower with a close friend/life partner. I panic. It all gets a bit *Apocalypse Now* and shoulders get bitten.

The bath wasn't a perfect system though; my parents worried that it was a wasteful way to wash so we weren't allowed deep bubble baths, just small miserly ones that barely reached the hips and felt like a pair of moist low-slung trousers. You'd sit there, arms folded, a patient look on your face, while your legs wrinkled. Afterwards you'd never achieve that ideal 'clean' look, more the look of someone who fell asleep with their top half in a time machine while their nethers withered.

My brother used to eat a fried breakfast in this position, ketchup perched on the loo seat, cup of tea in the soap dish and he never experienced a moment's indigestion: a testament to his colon but not to the bathing experience.

I was dipping into a cheekily deep bath when dad rapped on the door:

'Don't touch my balls!'

'You what?'

'You 'eard. My balls. Don't touch.'

(A couple of contemplative splashes,) 'They're called bath bombs, Dad?'

I was delighted he was getting in touch with his feminine side but he was doing it armed with his Homebase vocabulary. To dad, aftershave, soap, bubble bath and shampoo all huddled together under the term 'smellies'. When he requested 'smellies' for Christmas everyone had to take a plunge into the unknown. Basically he'd requested A Thing That Smells. It was a dangerous game; he was risking gift-wrapped dogshit.

I got out of the bath and towelled myself dry under the scornful gaze of Maggie the cat. She can really make a person feel bad about their body. I bet she's the reason mum's always at Weight Watchers. I sashayed to my room on tiptoes with everything clenched.

My days were a lot lonelier than they used to be. Dad and mum were at work for hours while I sat at home writing. I really missed Craine. Mum and dad liked this new set-up because it meant that 'the cats have company all day and night!' Yes, I agreed. If by company you mean me shut in my bedroom ignoring their Come Hither mews under the door. Then yeah, they were getting loads of that.

I disliked this arrangement, it gave me a reputation for sloth that I didn't deserve but couldn't shake off. I might have spent the day at home but I spent my nights out working. There were just no witnesses to this, apart from various service station night managers, with whom I was now on nodding terms. Well, I nodded at them, they did an uncertain bob back and never initiated it, but damn it those long journeys home were lonely.

Once in my room I could unclench and return to my daily preoccupation: scouring the internet for a flat. We were orienteering that graph where the X axis was Money Spent and the Y axis was Niceness Of Home. If we just pushed X upwards, just a tiii-iny bit, the houses got much nicer. But it was always hard to work out how much rent we could all afford, as there was no reason or reliability to our earnings. Tom, Tiernan and I all earned enough money from gigs and writing to live comfortably IN THEORY. However, comedy demands that the flow of money goes both ways, so even as money comes in you have to fling it right back out again, paying for travel, accommodation and an annual trip to the Edinburgh Fringe where everyone sort of throws several thousand pounds in the air, has regrettable drunk sex and hopes that this is somehow 'good for their career'. (SPOILER ALERT. It rarely is.)

This endless flow of money to and fro means that the idea of a comic's income is pretty fallacious. You might as well stand on a beach, watch the tide ebb and flow and declare that you own all the water. All you can do is enjoy the soothing sound of money moving around and try to nab a stray tenner from the surf for groceries.

Of course I tell mum none of this or she wouldn't sleep at night, so I say things like, 'look at that Ricky Gervais! He's doing all right, isn't he? And he can't even drive . . .'

Still, disregarding all that for a moment (because how else would I sleep at night?), I sneaked our budget a whisper upwards on Gumtree. Ooo. Suddenly I had entered the territory of wooden floors and fireplaces – a dangerous but seductive combo, like shellsuits on bonfire night.

* * *

In my experience, the things that should shove rent up or down are the staff at your local Tesco/train station/all-night newsagents, because you'll see them so often they'll make such a difference to your life. My old newsagent used to greet me with, 'Hello, Trouble!' and I'd giggle. I'm not Trouble, I'm not remotely troublesome and I'm not really a giggler either, but around him I could be both those things and it was exhilarating! Like being on a Log Flume! So people tell me. I sensed 'Hello Trouble' was out-of-character for him too, but he was in a frisky mood one day, tried it, didn't get pepper-sprayed and thereafter for a minute a day, we got to feel like sassier versions of ourselves. THAT is what you're looking for when house hunting.

Inspired by mum and her endless bloody lists, I drew up a list of what we did and didn't want from a flat. The Don't list said 'Nowhere to live' and the Do list said 'Somewhere to live'. I doodled the word 'Hygiene' but knew I'd cross it out for the right place.

I was taking control of this house hunt. Ordinarily I'd just follow like a sheep but I couldn't do that anymore, not as a recovering Silly Person. I used to be chronically useless. When I was twenty-five I still didn't really 'get' buses. I got on them but then . . . chaos and confusion. Friends would have to phone me and guide me to their house like air traffic control. However, when I met Craine he was so dangerously inept I had to up my game or we were going to end up inside-out and dead in a ditch.

Mid-squint at a photo online that I hoped was a cupboard but was probably a bedroom, I heard mum bang home for her lunch. I remembered, with a stab of fear, that I'd left a dirty mug in that most contentious of places: right by the dishwasher, but not in it. This was like waving a red rag at a bull who'd spent all morning neatly folding his red rag collection. Despite what my parents thought, I never left anything there in the spirit of delegation. It wasn't a hint to someone else to manoeuvre it that final difficult six inches into the dishwasher, I would honestly just forget. I wish they'd accept 'I am an idiot' as a reasonable defence, but no. Sure enough, I skidded downstairs to find mum eyeballing my mug like Robinson Crusoe staring at the footprint. On a bit of sand he'd only just raked.

Chapter 6

JESUS LIVES! (RUN LIKE HELL)

As you can see, my parents aren't cool. I'm not one of those dicks who flaunt groovy 'rents: 'My mum's really chilled, you can say whatever you want in front of her.' To them I say, 'Wonderful. I'll just pop upstairs and yell "pissflaps" at her then.' People who boast of laid-back parents invariably introduce you to an uptight harridan who doesn't smile with her eyes. Don't try peering around her for the easy-going sweetie you were promised, she will fix you with an icy stare that does nothing to encourage those 'pissflaps' plans.

As a teenager my mum always said, 'I'm your mother, not your friend.' Given that I didn't have any friends until I was seventeen, this felt like a rather cruel remark. All I heard was 'NOT EVEN YOUR MOTHER WILL BEFRIEND YOU'. I appreciate now what she meant: she wasn't here to be popular, the importance of loving discipline etc. I knew a lot of girls whose mums were so determined to be the envy of the school gates that they went clubbing together. Mum had strong views on such behaviour, I think it was the emotional neediness and overpriced booze that repelled her most.

But she was kidding herself. I wasn't cool, I never went club-bing, her presence in this imaginary scenario was a moot point. She might as well have said, 'When you walk on Mars, I won't interfere, I'll stay in the shuttle with a copy of *OK*.'

Mum is the dominant personality in our family. Not that we're wussy, more that she'd probably be the dominant personality in al-Qaeda. She stomps along that fine line where strident and intimidating meet and start slapping. Her name is Gaynor, sometimes people shorten this to Gay and no one has ever teased her about this. Her name could be Cockface Shithead and people would call her Mrs Shy Theed with a straight face. She's got a lot of fight. Too much if I'm honest, like those occasions when the security guard is reaching for his walkie-talkie.

This excess of fight is probably left over from her childhood, which from my pampered viewpoint looks a bit dreadful. Years ago, her childhood home on the South Oxhey council estate was up for sale and she, my auntie Janet and I all went on a viewing. They hadn't been back since their twenties when they had cut all contact with their mum, so they were itching to reminisce.

It was a small house, and I think they were hoping to impress me with 'Look! Three sisters, mum and dad all slept up here! Oh the olden days, you don't know you're born, blah, blah.' But I was too accustomed by London-living to be much impressed. I regaled them with tales of my friend who had to sit side-saddle on the toilet because it was so close to the wall and kept his microwave in his wardrobe – dogs always bothered him because his trousers smelt delicious.

Despite my best efforts with these brilliant anecdotes, the rest of the evening dragged. That viewing was a bleak forty minutes and I speak as someone who really knows her bleak; I once worked in a re-insurance company; that's a company that sells insurance to other insurance companies. Even typing that makes me feel tired all over.

I mooched glumly round their old home for about ten minutes before I thought it was time they took requests. I demanded they dish up some pleasant memories, something free of the words 'dislocated', 'smashed' or 'priest'. Or, I suggested, they should feel free to invent a happier childhood to make this evening more enjoyable for me. Or, they countered, I could go wait for them in the car.

I chose to ignore this, so after a period of deep thought (while the confused estate agent tried to show us round a house that mum and Janet knew like the back of their hands. Poor sod, I was taking a grim satisfaction in his misery) they showed me a false bottom in the wardrobe where their dad used to hide alcohol. He was a teetotaller, so this was just booze he kindly saved for guests. Which I thought was bloody nice of a non-drinker, like me having stores of butt plugs, in case guests felt the urge. But one detail niggled.

'Who was trying to steal it?' I asked, not unreasonably. 'The booze, who was he hiding it from, in the bottom of the wardrobe?'

'Well, no one,' they answered in snitty tones and did the 'why did we bring her?' eye roll at each other.

'I drove,' I reminded them. 'So this booze; if he wasn't hiding it, why didn't he just put the bottles in the kitchen, in a triangle formation, like everyone else?'

They fell silent, so I educated them. 'You know . . . the triangle of alcohol. I think of them as The Team. As in, 'Is yelling cock jokes at drunks a worthwhile existence? Looks like a question for The Team!'

Apparently, nostalgia crumples in the face of a little light questioning and I 'ruin everything', they explained through the car window.

This trudge down Memory Lane was enough to paint a grim picture of mum's early years, so I understood why she grew up a little 'feisty'. (I love how certain behaviour from a man would be considered criminal, but in a woman it can be brushed aside as 'feistiness'. I don't make the rules, I just enjoy them.) Still, understanding her didn't make it any more comfortable to witness things like this:

Mum: I think your oak needs a tree surgeon. It's dropping branches into our garden.

Neighbour: Sorry about that, I'll sort it out.

Mum: S'alright. (Pause) I mean, I could hack at the branches my side and then chuck 'em back at you. I won't, but I could. I'd be perfectly within my rights.

And suddenly the conversation veers off down a pointlessly argumentative avenue, thanks to mum's declaration of the things she could do. I could fling dog shit at passers-by. I don't though, neither do I inform them that I could, as I think that ruins the cordial atmosphere I've created by NOT flinging dog shit around. When I first moved back home, a woman came round one morning to ask if we knew whose van was parked down the road, because round there people are obsessed with the question of whose cars are parked where. In London, provided no one's car is on my face, I'm easy. Mum's response was a ringing, 'I'm innocent!' If our lives were ever made into a film, the director's main challenge would be to trim down the drama.

Mum and dad are well suited in this respect, their relationship is built on their mutual love of arguing and Being Right about everything. Mum came home on my fifth day back with them and I heard them begin to bicker. She hadn't even put her bag down and they were straight into the argument they'd launched that morning. They squabble like monkeys grooming each other, it's just a way of saying 'Hi' and 'I care enough about you to say no, you put the plug in a stupid place, it's not that I'm bad at finding plugs.' When one starts a dispute and the other one doesn't bother to tell them they're a waste of skin and teeth because 'that's the box for underechargeable batteries' the originator deflates and looks unloved.

Mum put her bag down and the original disagreement segued seamlessly into a heated debate about the wind: whether it was blowy or just a temporary gust. It was obvious that this one had legs: mum was eating yoghurt throughout. They're a professional outfit, when they bring snacks to a squabble, it can run and run. The last big argument they had with me was a fully catered event, it was clear they weren't going to let anything interrupt their treatise on Why You Must Make Lists, Natalie.

Dad's a strong competitor, but my money was on mum. She can

argue until her last breath, she has a very strong sense of justice. How nice you think, tipping your hat to a pillar of the community. No, no, you misunderstand; by 'strong', I mean 'melodramatic and inappropriate'. Her ideal holiday would be as a steerage passenger on the Titanic.

I watched that film with her, and her whole body tensed when the heavy-handed class injustice subplot swung into play. Her lips whitened, her chin went up.

'Just let me at 'em,' she was clearly stewing, 'unbelievable customer services, I'll speak to their manager.'

She'll even get her dander up over a missing button on a shirt. 'Give me that,' she'll say, in menacingly quiet tones, 'I'll have a little word with a shop that takes advantage of you.'

If you want to mimic this, as my brother and I used to on rainy afternoons, remember to make 'you' sound synonymous with 'brain-damaged worm'.

I think this is why she liked to paint me as a complete idiot, it cast her so easily in the role of protector and the story remained neat, the strong taking care of the weak. The day I make a success[4] of myself, I'll probably have to hack off my ears so she doesn't feel redundant.

'But Mum, who'll keep my sunglasses from slipping off my head?!'

She'll sigh, feign weariness and follow me around holding them in place, glaring at anyone who dares stare at the Earless Parade.

This description might make her seem a little controlling. If so, I congratulate myself on an accurate portrait. When I was learning to drive she perched reluctantly in the passenger seat, but refused to relinquish any more power. She angled all the mirrors to face her, leaving me driving blind. She may not have had the steering wheel but she had the all-important visuals. To this day I instinctively brace for impact when I hear: 'I'll *tell* you when it's safe to go.'

---

4 I favour an elastic definition of this word, depending on how my life turns out.

I came home one day to find her obsessively researching sewer systems, because a neighbour had come round to talk about the drains (I believe they call this La Vida Loca). He had dared to say 'perhaps I should chat to your husband about it?' Mum had interpreted this as pure hate-dipped misogyny and instantly dedicated herself to studying drains, so she could interject in their manly chat with obscure terminology and show them who was the real shit-pipe expert. Yeah, in their faces! (Metaphorically, let's hope.)

I supported her in theory, I am a staunch feminist but there are some things I'm willing to let slide. If men yearn to chat drains with other men, let them I say. For me it's a grey area, along with spiders, The Bins and getting out of bed to see what that noise was. So I cheered her on, but really hoped the drain was blocked with discarded gay porn and mum was muscling her way into an awkward conversation that our neighbour had tried to avoid. Even then I'd like to think mum would throw herself gamely into proceedings.

'And this is . . . *Throb* magazine? Right, so it's formed a sodden plug at the mouth of the pipe? Uh huh, I see . . . yikes, that's big.'

She has only one weak spot: my brother and I. Her pride in us is fervent and blinkered, she'll boast of our questionable achievements to anyone who'll listen. Anyone except us obviously, we get compliments like 'Why are you *still* spotty?' I only know she's proud of us because strangers tell me they're sick of the sound of my name. She starves us of praise deliberately, because she worries that we'll get big headed.

Chance'd be a fine thing. But I have a theory. Apparently the African bull frog is a docile cutie until it tastes meat. If it lives life ignorant of meat it will always be a placid joy of a frog. But the moment it plucks a meatball from the froggy Tree of Knowledge it becomes an insatiable thug.[5] I think mum fears our self-esteem

5 This may not be true. It's one of those facts I like too much to risk finding out it's untrue. *Paradise Lost*, frog-style.

would react the same once it tasted a scrap of flattery and we'd become monstrous beasts staggering the streets roaring, 'Tell me my hair looks nice!' Gangs of men on the front row in comedy clubs are often seized by the opposite urge; desperate for the comedian to tell them their shirt is shit. They get rowdy if this urge is unfulfilled. I like to think it's a very mild sexual fetish and they go home to masturbate over thoughts of a stranger disparaging their socks:

'Go on . . . mock the colour, you know how I like it. Yeah, it's pink, stereotypically unmanly right? Aaahh . . .'

Once I was stranded in Watford, I knew mum wanted to parade me around the school where she worked and yet this had to be done in a way that kept me away from the froggy Tree of Knowledge. Her solution was to adopt the attitude of an electric car owner. Oh yes, it looks silly, it's not for everyone, she rolled her eyes, arm-in-arm with me, but it's quite fun, plus having it showed everyone what an open-minded person she was. This approach led easily into stories about the recent stupid things I'd done, then into a jazzy megamix of the classics, like how I didn't realise the M25 went both ways (pardon me for keeping my eyes fixed on my bit of the road, not looking all over the bloody place).

Having shown me to her workplace, mum then showed her workplace to me. I had to walk around it twice: once admired, then admiring. There's really nothing like a Catholic Primary School at Easter time. Pictures of Jesus loomed from the walls, his face a mad nest of wool, glue and pasta shells, above the declaration 'Jesus Lives!' The resurrection is a tricky bit of theology and it seemed like most pupils had gone for a zombie interpretation of events. George A. Romero's latest: *Jesus Lives!* ('Run like hell').

'The thing with Jesus', I confided in a stray four-year-old, 'is only a head shot will take him out. That was the Romans' mistake.' He ran off sobbing, to spread the Good Word.

Mum's school had been recently renovated and she showed me every classroom individually, despite most of them being identical. This tested my new house-hunting vocabulary to its limits. I started drying up after Classroom Three: 'mmm, reassuringly square,' I offered, then, 'oh, this is a spacious one, goes all the way to the walls doesn't it?'

I don't know why people forget the basic rules of what's interesting when they're showing someone around their work, is it because it's so familiar to them? I'd trail off during a guided tour of my toes. I bet that's why the president doesn't do the White House tours, pretty soon they'd end up squatting by a cupboard while he rambled 'and there's always biscuits in here. Even if I eat them all. When I come back . . . biscuits again.'

I once visited my friend Tom Deacon when he was presenting a BBC show. I anticipated full-frontal glamour with Tinie Tempah perched cherry-like on top and braced myself to feel violently jealous. Yet within seconds Tom was pointing at a kettle, announcing 'and this is where I get my tea', while I did an 'Oh, riiight' face. My jealousy crumbled and I felt only pity: my kettle was nicer. Showbiz can be so cruel.

I hid my boredom during mum's Tour Of Tedium because I didn't fancy a public telling-off while wedged tightly in a child-sized chair beneath the slobbering face of Undead Christ. It is hard to anticipate mum's moods, I usually look out for birds fleeing the trees and indigenous people making themselves scarce.

This is mum and it's how she's always been; she and my brother both have geological personalities – mountains erode quicker than they rethink their opinions. Dad and I flip-flop a little more. Someone has to or we'd still be embroiled in the Christmas 1999 argument, Walk Vs Nap: the Grudge Match. This is why any tiny changes in the situation at home threw me a bit, I was expecting to return to the Marie Celeste, with cobwebby parents waving me off to university.

But things had changed. They had adopted a new system by which to live their child-free lives. The natural order in the house had undergone a reshuffle and I had slid dramatically down the pecking order. It was brutal, I was now clinging on beneath the cats and their mate's dog ('he's so good-natured'). Terrible view from down there. I was determined to fight my way back to the top spot. Top three anyway, I just wanted to overtake that bloody dog. But it wasn't going to be easy.

Chapter 7

A NEW WORLD ORDER

My parents' garden is a grotesque dystopia that would make Beatrix Potter puke.

'Beware,' mother hedgehogs whispered to their children, 'the small man who will kill you with kindness.' This was a fairytale land where wildlife frolicked in bounty, but it had been doing so for ten years and the frolicking had descended into corpulent staggering.

There were woodpigeons in that garden the size of chickens, drunk on my parents' loving care. Squirrels staggered wheezily through the trees, occasionally proving too heavy for a branch, sending their lardy arses thumping onto the lawn, like it was raining heart disease. The Weather Girls seemed reluctant to reform and serenade this, no matter how many times I called.

As soon as a light autumn drizzle approached, my parents would gibber with anxiety for any wild animals who weren't getting seven square meals a day. They'd make their infamous lard balls, which were melted lard, nuts, seeds and bacon scraps, placed in jelly moulds, frozen and strung up from a nearby tree, to drip enticingly. They looked like greasy bath bombs, though if you were foolish enough to pop one in the tub you'd never be able to slither out again. These culinary garden treats took longer to prepare than our human dinners and I would occasionally nibble one in protest.

One morning, watching a magpie tend the grass-burn on its belly, I decided that I was glad my parents loved us less than wild-life; their affection was clearly a carcinogenic deathtrap. Keen to help, I pondered how to communicate bulimia tips to the birds via simple mime. Nothing sprang to mind that I'd want the neighbours to see, so I just littered some women's magazines around the lawn, I was sure they'd get the idea.

Animals rouse strange instincts in my parents; tender devotion expressed via calories. It's a mercy these instincts are siphoned off onto wildlife because I don't want them. Were it not for birds and badgers taking one for the team, I'd be typing this with pencils sellotaped to my large greasy fingers while mum carefully adjusted my gravy IV drip. My functioning fingers are a testament to good, moderate amounts of love.

I remember one night, years ago, my brother and I were having our tea in front of *ThunderCats*, when mum came home from a waitressing shift bearing a pot of beef bourguignon. Without breaking pace, she marched it through the house to the bottom of the garden and emptied it under a tree 'for the foxes'. Michael was so outraged he flung his Findus crispy pancake at her head.

Dad is the only other person who would condone this behaviour. When our elderly cat was in her final days, he wrapped her in a blanket and walked her slowly around the garden so that she could smell the flowers and get a bit of fresh air. I watched him waddle away, bending at the knees to create a suspension system that ensured a smooth journey for her. He's a very good man.

He hadn't changed while I had been away, when I was back home we went to an over-ambitious barbecue where the host spread-eagled half a lamb rather gracelessly on a barbecue. It looked weirdly slutty. If Damien Hirst and Hannibal Lector ever collaborated . . .

At the end of the night, when fifty people had picked the flesh off its bones and I'd seen vegetarianism in a new appealing light, dad asked if we could have the carcass please.

'This'll feed twenty foxes!' he said gleefully.

'That's all very well,' I said, 'but we don't have twenty foxes, at most five or six wander through our garden.' And so, mum twisted in her seat to hiss at me, it was all my fault when we ended up driving through country lanes at two in the morning looking for a ditch in which to dump our dead body and let it fulfil its potential as a buffet.

I made the best of a bad situation and sung *The Sopranos'* theme tune throughout, 'for atmosphere', but they hadn't seen the show and my efforts were unappreciated. I switched to 'The Circle Of Life' and they got on board with that.

I think dad finds animals more restful company than human beings, they're simpler and less chatty. Even as I watched him glide round the garden with a swaddled cat, I knew that if he'd tried that with a sickly family member, awkward straddling aside, he'd have faced a barrage of, 'Oh, not this bit of the garden, it's all spidery . . . That bush is looking tatty, innit? Not been tempted to trim it, like, ever?'

Within seconds he'd have upended us in the compost to get our own bloody fresh air. Dad preferred simplicity; he's an easily annoyed man. But to his credit, he's also an easily amused man. Things that delight him include:

1. People falling over.
2. Handsome trees, despite the lukewarm response from loved ones: 'Brilliant birch.' 'I'll take your word for it.'
3. Competently executed DIY.
4. Grotesquely overweight people. (I wouldn't mind it if he did it subtly, but he'll walk past someone lardy and, while his legs continue, his head will remain fixed and staring. It then becomes a race to remove him from their earshot before he starts airing his opinions. There's no

malice in it, no judgment, just the simple observations of a man born without a tact gland. When he's being driven anywhere he will say: 'McDonalds. B+Q. Cinema. Small dog.' He says what he sees, a disciple of Roy Walker.)

He can be an embarrassing companion when you're Out and About. Shepherding him through public places is reminiscent of when I was twelve and my pet rabbit became obese. To this day I don't understand how as she was the only thing in our garden on a balanced diet and she got loads of exercise from dry-humping the other rabbit at speeds that made her bum blur. The vet instructed us to walk her. To help, mum bought a little harness with carrots on, which she worried was insensitive because you wouldn't pack a kid off to Fat Camp in a burger t-shirt, but the rabbit harness market is a niche one apparently and there wasn't much choice. Shuffling down the street with a fat bunny on a daintily embroidered lead is a lot like venturing out with dad.

He was getting worse as he got older; I think with every year that goes by he gives less of a fuck about a stranger's quizzical stares. He is going to be a nightmare in his twilight years. (It's funny how that phrase has taken on new meaning in these vampire-obsessed times. I'm sure I'll be less amused when I have an octogenarian sucking at my neck.) I offered to take him and mum out for dinner one night as a Thank You For Rescuing Me From The Gutter, but mum got a better offer at the last minute; this left dad and I eating together in Pizza Express, looking like a blind date where one of us regretted not reading the small print.

Dad ordered a Leggara pizza, those ones with a hole in the middle filled with salad (as if that's a decent substitution: 'So I've taken your car but left you a veruca sock'). He spent the meal obsessed with his missing inner circle of pizza.

'I paid for it, I want it, where is it?' he demanded, shoving his salad out of the way so he could stare at his exposed bit of plate.

I defended it as a low-fat option, but saying it out loud did highlight some of the flaws in the scheme: 'We'll sell you less food for the same price, Chubber!'

He was convinced that Pizza Express were selling the chopped out middles as kid-size portions and kept scowling at children nearby, eyeballing their dinner to check they weren't eating what was rightfully his. Parents didn't know how to react, no one likes a strange man lavishing so much attention on their child, but even the most neurotic parent knows paedophiles don't glare at their kids whilst perving at their plate.

He really was getting grumpier by the day while I was living with them. I could've blamed myself, but self-doubt is an ugly thing so I pushed the responsibility onwards, like all emotionally healthy people should.

As a peace offering I started offering dad lifts in my car but stopped doing this very quickly. He would use this time we had together sealed inside a metal prison to deliver lectures on Why You Will Never Understand Home Contents Insurance (my response of yes, but I will ALWAYS identify the correct use of an apostrophe, was not given the weight it deserved). If a person gives you a lift, I would think the one duty of the passenger is to sit there and play nice, but no, dad liked my generosity to evolve into fury.

He also liked to treat me to a torrent of criticism about my driving. I am a brilliant driver, because over the years I've done some gigs that were so rubbish I drove away from them thinking 'well, at least I got to practise my driving! Now where's that all-night Offy?' And dad was trying to insinuate that I was a bad driver?! Dad, who only drives at one speed: thirty-five miles per hour. He uses this down country lanes, on motorways and round corners. Years ago he drove my little brother and I somewhere and on our return we announced to mum that 'Daddy has lots of friends, *everyone* was beeping Hello at him.'

This is irrelevant to dad. Please, for a moment, think about everything you've done today, every little thing. Now, imagine that you are adamant that everything you've done is the best, the ONLY way to do it: from the way you buttered bread to the path you took around the sofa. Congratulations! You are inside Gustaaf Luurtsema's brain. Crawl out the ear when you're done.

Whenever the men in my life piss me off I walk three feet behind them, call them 'Sir' and flinch when they talk to me. Sometimes the historical gender power-imbalance seems so worth it when it yields this sort of richly rewarding fun. It's cruel but effective as, given the choice, most men will say 'Fine, you're right, that _was_ Bill Murray in _Morrisons'_ rather than look like a wife-beater. Stuck in my car I didn't have the leg-room or the audience for my usual tactics and was forced to sit it out.

He was blethering on about how resting my hand lightly on the gear stick while I drove 'wore out the gears'. NO. I refused to believe that. How heavy did he think my hand was? Surely it weighed no more than a thick-cut slice of bacon? Plus, I pointed out, slapping the gear stick for emphasis, surely dads aren't meant to foster a Fat Hand complex in their daughters? I'm not saying treat me like a princess (I am realistic) but don't be rude about my extremities.

He tutted impatiently at my introduction of Emotion into his Mechanical 'Facts'. (I knew that would annoy him, which was precisely why I did it.) He then alleged that when I stopped at the traffic lights (fighting the urge to sail sedately through red and really give him something to bitch about) I needed to go down through the gears, fourth to third to second, otherwise I would 'wear out the brakes'.

'No!' I yelped. 'THAT is how you wear out gears, not the weight of a fat hand.' Drivers around us turned their radios up.

He made a dismissive noise and said 'ask your friends, they'll tell you I'm right' and I informed him that this subject would NEVER come up as my friends and I have good conversations, not the lumpy grey affairs he subjected me to.

Look, I said, here's a much more interesting conversation we could be having: 'Um, okay . . . what was your first impression of mum all those years ago?'

He said, 'That she rested her hand on the gear stick too much, THUS wearing out the gears.' He's good. He's very good.

You might wonder why anyone puts up with this and I think it's because he's very small. Small people get away with everything under the assumption that they're cute. This seems very unfair to me; my mum, my brother and I are huge, our limbs just don't stop. Sometimes we console ourselves with words like 'willowy' and 'statuesque'. More often we need words like 'sorry' and 'dustpan and brush?'

Dad once dug out some clothes he wore in his early twenties and I couldn't wriggle into them. He scoffed at my shoulder width, I countered with some louder opinions on small people and their bitchy ways and we parted on frosty terms. That was back in the days when I had my own home to march off to in a sulk, before stomping six feet into the next room was the only dramatic exit available to me, unless I wanted to go sit in the garage with my furniture.

Dad's mum, our Oma,[6] was tiny and got away with a lot of shit. The last time we saw her she was in a hospice and, on hearing she'd taken a turn for the worse, we'd raced from Watford to Holland and burst into her room. Probably terrifying her in the process but if the Luurtsemas have rushed to get somewhere we bloody well want you to know about it.

We barged into Oma's room and she lifted her tiny head to exclaim: 'Ooo, Gaynor has got so . . .' (she mimed an air accordion until she found the word) '. . . fat.' Then with perfect comic timing she laid her head back and closed her eyes, tuckered out from all the pleasantries. I looked at her thinking a) This is where

---

6 That's Dutch for grandmother. Though she was actually Indonesian. But then moved to the Netherlands. God this is complicated, I'm beginning to see Nick Griffin's point of view. Let's just all stay where we're born and marry the neighbours. In fact, no one to stray more than ten miles from their point of conception. Bad luck babies made by boat-based bonking!

dad gets it from, b) She wouldn't get away with this if she wasn't 4'10" and c) I'm going to have to cover sniggering with sobbing, mum's got my passport.

We love our Dutch family, mainly for this sort of behaviour, but we don't see them very often, sadly only funerals demand we all drop everything and congregate. I've got cousins I've never spoken with at a normal volume; whenever I see them we're whispering over a sandwich buffet. These sort of interactions don't furnish a person with the day-to-day vocabulary necessary for fluency, all the Dutch I've got is sympathetic platitudes, which will not help me locate the butcher's in the Hague while telling everyone about my hobbies.

I'm currently nibbling on a chocolate 'N' that dad bought me in Holland. He went over there for another funeral last week and returned laden with goods. I'm worried he shopped throughout the whole trip and squeaked into the service with a trolley. I never trust him to behave when mum and I aren't around to kick him. The chocolate initial is a nice Dutch tradition, it says 'Here is a gift and I know what letter your name begins with,' which is really comforting if you've got an absent-minded parent.

Dad was a confusing man to live with, and I was becoming aware of this in a way that had escaped my notice the first time I'd lived with them. In my defence, back then I was a teenager and full of feelings that were more acute than anything anyone else had ever experienced. You might've thought the same when you were a teenager and that is sweet but wrong, my emotions were way more emotional than yours. Fact.

My teenage years were such a mess that my parents burnt all the evidence. There are no photos of me between thirteen and eighteen, because I was so ill and nuts (more of which later). I should Photoshop a couple really, so I don't look like a spy who's been parachuted into a family without a backstory. That would explain a lot. But I have childhood memories that shoot holes in the theory. My earliest memory is of being five and confronted with a nightmarish wrinkly bloated worm-monster that everyone seemed bizarrely pleased with: my new brother, allegedly. I was sceptical ('Yeeahh, I'm fine for one of them thanks. Send it back where it came from, see if there's a Sylvanian Family Treehouse up there, now *that* I want . . .').

Whenever I felt impatient at dad a quick peek around one of his sheds usually softened my heart. (Yeah, you heard, sheds plural. Suck up your envy, kids. He's got several, pullulating round the garden like wooden mid-life crises.) His sheds are his personality turned inside-out and damp-proofed. Everything in them is neat and orderly and run according to an inexplicable logic.

One lonely day, while mum and dad were at work, I paid a visit to his newest shed. He was particularly proud of this one, he built it all by himself. When he finished he extended a rare invite to visitors, so me, mum and their two best friends, Hilary and Peter, dressed up and squeezed into it for a launch party. There was champagne and fun and disregard for personal space. Then I cut my leg on a hacksaw and mum got cold and we realised people could see us from the street and we were five adults crammed in a shed singing 'Shed, Shoulders, Knees and Toes'.

I hadn't been allowed in since and I discovered that he'd been busy out there, building a little crazy paving path up to a patio just big enough for a solitary deckchair. He'd also installed a motion-sensitive light. A security feature he'd never bothered to install on the house. I thought the family home was nice enough, but if ten feet away a burglar is trying to rob a shed in the mistaken belief that THIS is where the flatscreen is . . . it's time to redecorate.

I peeked inside and realised if anything ever happened to dad, I could never go in this shed; it would be too heartbreaking. He had little hooks to hang his tools on (tools I suspected were mainly used to build storage solutions for themselves . . . it's a self-perpetuating shed, an outdoorsy Mobius Strip). He had also retrieved anything we'd ever binned, 'just in case' and squirrelled them away in here.

We're not a religious family (which is odd, given how much we love rules and shiny things, we'd make perfect Catholics) but I think dad found spiritual solace in recycling. He pooh-poohed it for years as hippy crap, but then realised it upheld all the tenants he lived by: thrift, neat little boxes and shouting at people who got it wrong. Now he was Mr Earth and woe betide you if you scraped a baked bean into the bin. We could've made a jumper out of that!

Soon after moving back I realised that dad didn't even trust me to use a bin correctly. He took the bin from my bedroom and clearly approached it like an editor with a client's crappy first draft: 'Riiight, I see what she was trying to do here but . . .' Silly me, of course that snotty tissue was just at the beginning of a long and useful lifetime of service.

I bet dad secretly longs for global ruin. In a post-apocalyptic world where official currency has collapsed and the barter system holds sway, his sheds of nails and wire will become a New World Order NatWest. 'Swap a hammer for your house, Mr Abramovich?' 'Til then he'll sit on his patioette, admire the hedge and dream of a day when Europe is buried in fizzing ash, scaly babies wave their tentacles at the moons in a despairing SOS and finally the Luurtsemas are RICH!

The apple didn't fall too far from the tree, I should admit I own a tin of Buttons I Like The Look Of, as well as scraps of fabric, some the size of a stamp, because 'you never know'. I'm not sure quite what one never knows, unless it's that if one day a small insect comes to stay and we need to make him a bed, these scraps of fabric will ensure the Luurtsemas won't be embarassed. I fear in years to come genetics will rear its ugly head and at forty I'll be sifting through my neighbour's bin, pausing only to eye up an oak and yell 'Cor, thassa biggun!' at anyone unlucky enough to waddle past.

There's no way I'd be able to get away with this behaviour the way dad does, I'm not small and I don't look remotely like Mr Bean, from any continent. It's a tricky skill, teetering along the fine line of offensive and endearing. I was starting to appreciate dad's skills, he was a Baryshnikov of social embarrassment and all we could do was fling roses or pretend we didn't know him.

Chapter 8

THE SEVEN-WEEK ITCH

I found a grey hair. I was contemplating it grimly one afternoon while downstairs mum yelled (more to herself than in search of a response): 'I never know how you manage to get avocado so many places in the sink. Is it natural talent or have you been practising?'

I had rinsed a plate, in what I considered a competent fashion. I didn't want to give it too much thought because if she got me thinking this forensically about my every action I'd be paralysed with self-analysis and unable to blow my nose without fear. She'd love this version of me.

There was a heavy blanket at the bottom of my bed, draped on for show (I told dad we shouldn't let mum see the Ikea catalogue, she gets ideas). When I slept I moved and it would fall off the end of the bed and she'd wake me in the morning complaining at my destructive ways. I'm sorry I can't live like a catalogue, I'm not 2D!

She's the only mother who'd be a little bit pleased if her daughter died in her sleep because at least the bed would be unrumpled.

The grey hair, Ol' Silvery Jim, was another firm reminder that I was TOO OLD to not be rinsing lightly soiled plates exactly how I wished. We were still house hunting with dogged obsession. Every day I would go and look at some shit flats and then return home. It wasn't a daily routine I'd recommend. Then, just as the seventh week (of my Month At Home) hove into view, we actually found a flat! Was it nice? No! Of course it wasn't but it was absolutely OK, really very all right.

Mum got overexcited and started saying her goodbyes. She patted my grey hair and said, 'I will miss you when you go, but . . .' and we both nodded.

No need to say it, I would miss them too, but . . . Example seventy-three: I yearned for a day when someone wouldn't watch me chop some mushrooms and pop them on a Margherita pizza then yelp, 'What are you DOING?' as if I'd rubbed it under both armpits rather than jazz it up with a bit of basic veg. When I said this was an entirely normal thing to do, dad snorted derisively, christening my pizza with a mouthful of beer and taking it up to unacceptably jazzy levels.

We put a deposit down on the flat, our nostrils twitching at the faint scent of independence but then the landlord asked what we did for a living. Given that he had acted like 'self-employed' was a coy way of saying 'crack whore', we didn't relish telling him we all told jokes for money. This revelation made his eyes bulge like a squeezed hamster.

He demanded to see not only our bank statements but those of our parents. Now Ma and Pa Luurtsema don't hang on tightly to their dignity (in many cases I wish dad would tighten his grip), but this felt a bit rude. Thankfully, once we'd persuaded three sets of parents to photocopy three months of bank statements, the landlord decided that he'd rather just return our deposits and forget he'd ever met us. Idiot. He was acting like we wanted to strip and stroke his prettiest son, not rent his skanky two-bed in Wood Green.

Once this flurry of near-success had settled back into failure, I resumed my earlier work. I wanted to pluck out Ol' Silvery Jim; I felt a person shouldn't have grey hairs AND hotpants and I was not ready to give up my 'Peter Pan in provincial panto' look. It's a signature aesthetic that I've really made my own, largely because nobody else wants it.

Mum warned me not to do this. She swore that if you plucked out a grey hair seven came to its funeral. I liked the idea of a circle of seven mourning hairs, but surely this truism is flawed. If they were going to a funeral they'd be black. What sort of attention-seeking tart mourns in silver?

I was tempted to pull out Silvery Jim AND twenty hairs around him, to whip up a culture of fear and quell any ideas of holding funerals: 'Forget paying your respects! ANY one of you could be the next to go, there's no time for ceremony! Ruuuun!'

Hopefully any other greys would scatter into Witness Relocation schemes. I could tolerate grey hairs anywhere else but my head. Let's face it, if a sexual partner halts play to point out a grey hair they've found nestling in your crevices, they're probably not The One.

If I'm honest, I was focusing on Silvery Jim to distract myself from larger issues. I'd been home nearly two months and when-ever anyone asked me or my parents how things were going, we'd begin with a chant of 'of course I love her/them very much,' in the tone of voice usually heard around the words 'BLAAH BLAAH BLAAH'. This done, we could then launch into the fun bit, which was slagging each other off, without fear of anyone pulling a disapproving face, because Love Is . . . bitching about each other but sort of not meaning it, not really.

Mum knows most of Watford so she had hundreds of people to whinge at. By contrast, I was an unpopular child who went to a school full of army, navy and RAF kids, so even when I did make a friend she'd invariably live in The Congo and I'd spend my summer holidays writing her needily long letters, wondering if it was racist to assume The Congo didn't have a Topshop. So I didn't have anyone to complain to, as I complained one night in a Facebook status. Instantly forty or fifty people responded with sympathy and I knew I had found my answer. Thank you Tim Berners-Lee!

That night I started writing about my cruddy life online – in what I thought of as 'fond vignettes of family life', what a more legally minded person might have called 'gross invasions of privacy'. I prefer vignettes: it's French, a bit fancy.

This sneaky bitching was textbook passivity from me, I don't tend to argue with people because I'm placid. 'Like a cow', mum says. Which I resent, but don't say so.

I'm not a saint; I do have a list. Just a little list of people I hate. Most of them probably don't know they're on there – I was raised to be polite. And I have no plans to act on the list, crossing names off once I've had my revenge. The list is a long-term plan. When I die, I will have a funeral, where I'll be cremated to the *Jurassic Park* soundtrack so it's excitingly dramatic and then a close friend with a loud voice will read out The List.

'Fancy that,' people will say to my secret nemeses, through a mouthful of buffet dim sum, 'Nat hated you. Should you really be eating the ham?'

Within minutes of posting my grumblings online a girl emailed me to commiserate, saying she was in the same position and it made her laugh. Another emailed and another and another; I replied to them all because, as Ol' Silvery Jim would attest, I didn't have much else to do that day. It was incredible, it seemed like half the country was putting dinner on a tray and having it in their room. I read some articles about it and found that we had a name; we were called the Boomerang Generation. For the first time since I moved back I didn't feel like such a loser, I was part of a gang! A gang of losers.

Dad was tickled with the name Boomerang: 'Because you come back right?'

'Yes Dad.'

'But the novelty wears off really quickly and then everyone's sick of you and wishes they could get rid of you but they can't because you ALWAYS come back!'

(Thank you, Mr Suppressed Irritation . . .)

'And you don't really do anything useful and . . .'

(Okay, I'm putting my headphones back in now.)

It was heartening that some of my new pen pals had proper jobs, ones that began in the morning and involved Microsoft Outlook and even THEY were back with their parents. Heartening, but it hardly seemed fair, this recession seemed to be biting all over. I couldn't object if it bit me, I have chosen a bloody stupid career path. Well, I say career path, it's more like staggering through a copse hoping to find a dead rat to gnaw and a bush to lie under.

I had a long conversation with one girl and we engaged in long chatty emails for a few weeks. How nice, I thought, there are upsides to this. I'm making friends! I was wondering how to ask if she fancied a drink, without accidentally ending up on a date, when she upped the ante and sent me a Facebook Friend Request.

I clicked on her profile and suddenly a few details shuffled sideways and assembled into a worrying new shape. Her admirable knowledge of books, her well-rounded interests and impressive awareness of different academic fields; I had seen these as the attributes of a top-quality friend/accidental lesbian life-partner, which they are. But they are also the attributes of a schoolgirl.

She was living with her parents because she was a schoolgirl. So, not to nitpick, but her situation was not exactly the same as mine. She had not made a failed stab at independence, followed by an inglorious return home, where she had accidentally groomed a schoolgirl. 'Oddball perv living with parents, talked online with SCHOOLCHILDREN.' I really must wean my parents off the *Daily Mail*, it's making me think in outraged headlines. 'Requests FOREIGN fruit.'

I'm uncomfortably aware that if I had been arrested for a crime at that point, all of this would have looked bad. My blog would be a prosecutor's dream. Look what the press did to Jo Yeates' landlord and he just had weird hair. Of course he did it, everyone agreed at the time, look how weird his hair is. Okay, he didn't do it, but the point stands. Imagine if *he'd* lived with his mum; he'd be eyeing up the John Grishams in a prison library right now.

Of course Christopher Jefferies was worse than me because he was a teacher; that was pretty damning evidence, who voluntarily spends all their time with children? Sickos! It's sad that we seem to mistrust anyone who doesn't puke when a kid hoves into view. Is there an increase in paedophiles or in obnoxious kids? Youngsters so twatty even their parents assume no one could like them for their personality. If you think all your offspring have to offer is sex, I suggest teaching them some manners or an instrument.

Thanks to my jailbaity little friend, I felt I had reached a new low, even for this plodding adolescence-encore. So I decided to do something bold, to shake things up a bit. I bought some orange eye shadow, as I had never done that before. I splodged a bit on and remembered that I'd never done this before because it's so obviously a bad idea. Tearful Albino Rat has yet to have its twirl in the fashion spotlight. Oh well, nice try, I told myself, sponging down my eyes.

This eye shadow thing hadn't given me the kick I was looking for. When I was younger and found myself in similar gloomy funks I would pep myself up by getting something pierced. I'd feel I'd achieved something as I gazed at a piece of my flesh, rudely violated by metal. It hurt, but I had done it, I had chosen this.

'Well,' I would conclude, staring at it, 'there's that then.' I didn't say it was a sense of *huge* achievement.

On grey days, with nothing good on telly, I'd get another earring popped in, but some days were so dull they demanded more drastic action. By twenty-one I had six studs in each ear, one in my eyebrow, one in my nipple, one in my belly button and one in my clitoral hood (imagine how boring THAT day was). I used to love the whole experience. I relished the fear as I slunk into Obese Tattooed Steve's tattoo parlour. (I loved the use of the word 'parlour', as if that would inject doilies and gentility into the situation.)

I loved the terror, the pain, the sense of triumph afterwards and even the grim satisfaction of watching the wound scab and heal. I'd feel like I'd conquered something – something self-inflicted, sure, but my feelings were as genuine as if an enemy had challenged me to a fight, between their needle and my nipple (possibly the most useless weapon to choose) and I had emerged wounded yet undefeated. I'd stride away, chin held high to hold back the tears I was too proud to shed in front of Obese Tattooed Steve. Of course, striding was out of the question after the clitoral hood piercing but I shuffled, crab-like, with as much dignity as was available.

I only have a few of these piercings left. The earrings were so painful that I had to sleep very still on my back, the slightest move of my head provoking stabbing pains. As a result, even though I removed them all years ago, I still sleep like a corpse. People lucky enough to share my bed assure me that this is creepy and prompts the occasional finger under my nose to check I'm alive. My eyebrow and bellybutton piercings grew out of me, my body stubbornly rejecting these alien objects no matter how much I tried to push them back in hissing 'this was forty quid you twat! Stop pushing forty quid out of me!'

One particularly slow day in the library (there was a Dominican monk I used to eye-flirt with, when he didn't turn up the day dragged), I mused sadly on all my hard work being slowly evicted from my body. I guess there's the same futility in eating expensive food. You only really get to rent it for a day.

The nipple piercing lasted longer than the others, my body didn't reject it for some reason. It may well be that armoured nipples are the next evolutionary step and I was The Future. Sure, this sounds unlikely but imagine how stupid the first thumb looked on the first monkey-man unfortunate enough to grow it. Or the first person to say, 'Pop a lid on that, I'm going to drink my coffee on the go!'

'Really, a hot staining liquid, in transit?'

'Truuust me.'

Sadly, even if it was the next step for mankind, my nipple piercing was still doomed to die young. On a night out I staged a classic Nat stratagem – 'Let's pop back home, grab more booze and go out partying all night like rock stars!'

This was always a ruse to get back to someone's house, where I could slump on a nearby bed and refuse to move. It was never a popular decision but such are the penalties of selfishness and laziness. Everyone was shouting at me to leave now and dance on a table. No, I informed them through a dribble-soaked pillow, I was going to sleep now so Ha. To illustrate my point I started getting undressed (not my usual debating tactic, but I thought pyjamas would show how serious I was). I whipped my top off, swift as a busy stripper. Sadly the piercing was tangled in the top, and . . . my memories become hazy at this point . . . But there was a lot of blood and suddenly everyone was happy to accept my first answer and leave me behind.

The clitoral piercing lasted even longer, as it was actually the most practical one: invisible, unobtrusive yet there to make any bus journey so much fun I'd frequently miss my stop. I still smile fondly at certain buses. (Hey 109, call me. Any time. I know you're twenty-four hour.) Despite mum's furious mutterings, my most personal piercing never did set off an airport security scan. Though she would routinely get pulled aside. While I jangled past unmolested, her furious whispering looked like the prayers of a zealot and would earn her a patting-down so thorough I really thought the security woman should buy her dinner.

Sadly this piercing was another doomed relationship between flesh and metal. I was walking out of an internet cafe one day and heard a delicate tinkling note. I looked down to find my most intimate piece of body jewellery winking coyly back at me. I hesitated, unsure of the etiquette in this scenario (oh Debrett's, where are you when I need you?), before concluding that it would not be The Done Thing to retrieve it. I abandoned my last investment in Obese Tattooed Steve's parlour and strode home metal-free for the first time in years.

Finding myself stuck in homelessness and inertia, I felt this familiar itch for excitement and control. The eye shadow had let me down and I felt my best work with Obese Tattooed Steve was behind me. I mean, it was in the past, I hadn't got my bottom pierced (although dimples would be nice, winsome no?). It was time for something new and drastic.

I decided I was going to cut all my hair off and be that sassy, kooky short-haired imp, the building-block of indie American films. I've always felt deep down that I'm meant to be a tousle-headed scamp. Sadly, no one ever passed the message on to my ears, which are large and wonky, or my head, which is laughably small. It's like a fleshy periscope I've shoved up through my shoulders; I only look normal in caricatures.

But vanity be damned! I went to the cheapest hairdressers I could find and announced 'All off please!' while an aspirational soft-rock soundtrack played in my head. I was a little worried when my hairdresser called her colleagues around to admire the first half of my head: 'Look how straight that is!' she marvelled. Call me picky but I don't like it when people get giddy at achieving basic-level competence in their profession. High-five after open-heart surgery, do it over my stitched-up ribs if you want; but not after a routine bit of business at the oral hygienist.

Thankfully I left the hairdressers with both my ears and eyebrows. I tousled my hair and skipped gaily home, pausing the gaiety only to spit out bits of hair. Cut hair is like sand in its amazing ability to burrow into the most unwelcome of places. The terrorist who can combine a biochemical attack with these materials will be laughing. Maniacally I imagine, in some sort of compound. But this could not cramp my joy. I called mum, graciously inviting her to join my fun. Why not, I had plenty, I decided to spread it around.

Mum ruined everything with a response of undiluted fury. She's always said that the women in our family are not beauties but we are tall, with good hair and a level head in a crisis. She says our hair is our Only Glory. She claims now that she said Crowning Glory and anyway, 'what's the difference?' Oh nothing, I sigh, just the difference between a pretty girl with nice hair and a wig on a pig. According to the Only Glory theory, I'd just knocked a third off my meagre appeal. Mum interrupted my counter-argument (about things like The Allure Of Wit . . . it was pretty weak) and asked this dangerously benign question:

'What did you do with the hair?'

'Just swept it up.' (I really said that, I was panicking and Grammar, sensing trouble, had picked up her cullottes and legged it. Useless bitch.)

'Oh Natalie . . .'

'What. What now?!?'

'You should've given your hair to a charity.'

'To mop up oil?'

'What are you talking about? Shut up. One that uses human hair to make wigs for children with cancer.'

'Well . . . yes, of course, I would've done that, if I knew it was a thing that people did.'

'Those poor kids.'

'I didn't know it was a THING!'

'I knew.'

'Yes, evidently . . . so why didn't you tell me?'

''Snot the sort of thing you go around telling everyone. It's not a happy topic of conversation.'

(Sigh.)

(Sigh.) 'So, do you want to talk to the cat?'

At the end of conversations like this I knew I hated one of us but I wasn't sure who.

Chapter 9

THE CABBAGE MOUNTAIN
SHUNS A CARROT

It's an old family joke that I can't cook. Like most family jokes, it's not true but no one lets this detail hold them back from the ROFLs. On Craine's first visit to the Luurtsema home, mum quipped about my horrible cooking to him. He laughed dutifully, with confusion in his eyes. The confusion of someone who has lived with me for two years, been well fed throughout and never cooked a single meal.

Actually that's not fair, he once cooked me a romantic meal of sea bass. Sadly, early in the cooking process, in between 'dropping it in the sink' and 'poking it with a spoon', he found the fish's rectum and associated tubing. 'Romance' was suspended for the more immediate gratification of chasing me round the flat, squealing 'aaaaaaannnuuuuuuss!!' and trying to flick my face with it. After that I couldn't approach dinner without retching and we agreed to abort Mission: Romance. Especially as he threw the anus at me and we never found it. The thought of that discarded bumhole haunted me throughout our tenancy of the flat.

If I were a braver woman I'd point out that dad does most of the cooking, mum's only ever mastered Putting Something From A Bag Onto A Plate. Basically, she fans out lettuce. She can also carve a tomato into a fairly convincing rose but it won't fill you up till dinner. Her speciality dish is Mango Chicken, ceremonially wheeled out for birthdays and dinner parties. The ingredients of mango chicken are some chicken and some mango chutney. The real skill of this dish lies not in the cooking (obviously) but in the acting required of family members – it's a real ensemble piece.

I will let guests mingle for four to five minutes then obediently sniff the air.

'Mum,' I'll demand, flailing with confusion, 'What are you cooking?'

'Mango chicken,' she'll beam.

'Mango . . . Chicken . . . ' dad and I will echo, rolling these unfamiliar words around on our tongue. 'Well, sounds exciting!' we conclude, flinging caution to the winds as we embark on this culinary voyage into the unknown.

But I was still considered the worst cook in the house, and yes, I believe cats and plants were included in the census. Which was pretty rich, given that a typical evening now involved me staggering home after a gig and being 'greeted' with things like microwaveable salmon en croute and the words 'eat this quickly, it went off last Thursday'. My parents treated Best Before dates like a challenge. They unearthed foodstuffs from the freezer so old I swear the house was built around them.

So when mum said, 'Why don't you cook us shepherd's pie tonight?' I began to list the reasons why not. But she ignored me and declared that it 'would be nice'. I've said it before; 'nice' is a much-misused word. The thing is, I have tried to cook for them several times and it's always ended in fights. I can't stand it when they criticise my cooking, I'm middle-class now, and my sort KNOW how to cook!

After university made me posh, I discarded my Watford roots quicker than a dandelion clock. I got an unattractive fringe, I worked in digital media, I may have been a yuppie; I never got tested. I do remember mysteriously not finding *Nathan Barley* funny as I watched it in my Shoreditch loft apartment, assembling a vintage outfit for that evening's warehouse party. With hindsight, my back goes hot with shame.

I bought a Jamie Oliver book and embraced its wisdom. I tried to spread the good news and phoned home to inform my parents that vegetables didn't need to be boiled until they collapsed, nor diced so small they could dance on the head of a pin, but to no avail. The snobbery went both ways; I cooked a meal for them once, dad choked, pulled something out of his mouth like I'd sneaked a turd in, and cried 'WHAT is THIS?!'

'Cabbage,' I replied.

'Oh god Natalie, cabbage?!?!'

We both knew he'd wanted me to say something mad like fennel, but I wasn't playing. In my defence it really was cabbage.

But mum was adamant that I should cook dinner and in my role of glorified squatter I felt it was my duty to be obliging. So we convened in Asda again. That place seemed to draw us like a magnet. It's so big we may simply have been victims of gravitational pull.

I mooched around the aisles behind mum; six feet behind like a wrinkly teen. Cooking for them would be fine, but I had to do it exactly how they wanted and their methods are questionable. The space race occurred at a pivotal point in their childhoods and I assume this is why they eat like astronauts. They like flavour in a sachet sprinkled over a meal. A meal which is the same thing as the flavour in the sachet, so there is a chance it probably already tastes of itself, without help. My parents do not take that risk. It amuses me when celebrity chefs talk about the 'combination' of flavours in a dish – the Luurtsemas don't do that, we agree on one flavour, like 'creamy' or 'meat', then pursue it relentlessly.

Mum put a shepherd's pie flavour sachet in the trolley.

'Do we need this?' I asked.

She sighed, and looked pained: 'We always use it.' She is a whiz at ending 'discussions' in the first sentence, side-stepping that tedious airing and sharing of opinions.

Still, I rudely persevered: 'Do you? Do you have a chew and think "Bugger me, there's barely ANY modified starch in this, where's the Es? My gums aren't itching at all!"?'

I ditched mum and her stupid sachets and sought solace in the clothes section. I spotted a dress I liked but when I reached for it, it twitched and ran away. For a second Asda trembled on the verge of *Fantasia*, then I realised the hanger was caught on a woman's coat. I hovered behind her, I wanted to ask her for it, but she had an army of small children with her and she was busy yelling at all of them.

I dithered, poised to leap in as soon as she drew breath but she was so good at hating her children that she'd mastered a trumpet player's circular breathing. She had so many children and clearly disliked them all. You'd think after you hated the first two you'd shrug and buy a dog, but I was clearly in the presence of fertility over logic. Her vehement loathing of her kids, and the need to tell them about it, was keeping her very busy but I couldn't just unhook the dress off her. I was sure she didn't want it, but still possession is nine tenths of the law. The squatter's favourite fact, though I wonder if they'd mention it if they were kidnapped?

Mid-yell, my quarry suddenly swung around and I found I had been tailing her a little too enthusiastically as we were now nose to nose. She smelt nicer than she sounded, flowery, with a hint of vanilla. I think even she felt she'd been too verbal at her kids as she immediately leapt into a defensive position. Perhaps I looked like I was judging her. I was judging her, obviously, but I thought I'd managed to keep my face neutral. She asked me what I wanted and I should've said 'the dress' but her question contained the word 'fuck' and no appreciable drop in volume so I took it as rhetorical and scuttled off.

I raced back to mum, who was still perusing sachets. We returned home in moody silence (it was mainly hers but it's hard to be convivial on your own). Back home I started peeling the potatoes, badly, apparently. Mum shoved me out of the way and began whittling them into wet Twiglets.

'In London,' I said, 'in London they leave skin on mashed pota-toes, it's *rustic*.'

'Well, we're not rustic, we live in the suburbs,' mum retorted.

Damn. Sensing my weakness, she pressed home her advantage, because apparently I'd put the peas, carrots, meat and potatoes into ALL the wrong pans. Silly me! Did I not see that the third-smallest pan was CLEARLY the pea pan? What is wrong with me?! Am I broken in the brain or something?

Once we'd transferred everything into new pans, she retired upstairs, covered in potato and triumph. Dad got home and was outraged! I'd only forgotten to dust the modified starch sachet over the meat hadn't I?! I was too tired to argue, so I dumped the dusty crap in there and watched the pan's contents pucker then congeal into meaty custard. At which point dad spotted I'd put the peas, carrots, meat and potatoes into ALL the wrong pans! So we transferred everything back into the original pans, I washed up eight pointlessly soiled pans and stomped off to my room to share my rage with the internet and think about cigarettes.

After a while they both came and banged on my door, yelling, 'Who are you talking to?' Sweet victory. They might have domin-ion in that house, but the internet was my kingdom.

'The world,' I informed them. 'I am telling on you to the world.'

There was some muttering by my door (I assumed dad was having another bash at explaining the internet to mum. Good luck), then they walked away. I had a rare taste of Victory. I savoured it before it got drowned in ethyl methyl phenylglycidate.

We ate dinner in a thoughtful silence, broken only by dad pointing out vegetables I hadn't chopped as small as he'd have liked and me elaborately scraping chemical gunk off the root of my mouth. As always, I was aware that neither of us was behaving with much grace but I'm still convinced I was right. It's a horrible family trait, our desperate ravenous need to Be Right.

I felt a lot of self-doubt in my parents' house, due to my parents fondly predicting 'you're going to cock this up' whenever I began menial tasks. They trusted me on the big things. If anything, they had too much faith in my mental capabilities. If I decided on a whim that I'd like to be a doctor they'd nod, 'Yeah, I can see you in a white coat.' But if, after a long day of brain surgery, I tried to WASH said coat, they'd start saying their goodbyes to loved ones and begging me to postpone my plans so they could enjoy one last sunset. Ever since I set fire to half the kitchen with a Weetabix,[7] I was not trusted with any domestic activities. They made me paint my toenails in the garden.

After that stressful evening I avoided the kitchen for several days. But by the end of the week I had to venture in as my friend had asked me to bring a salad to his birthday barbecue and I was determined to do it from scratch. Mum and dad were out of the house so there was no hovering with bandages or doom-laden commentary and I was enjoying myself, I even said 'bosh' a couple of times. I was certain that I was actually quite a good cook if I was just left alone to do it.

This giddy confidence didn't last, as I made a mess of things almost immediately; in fact, the rapidity of my mistake was the only impressive part of the operation. I misread the quantity for the first ingredient when shopping and assembling the meal and consequently found myself looking at the business-end of three large shredded cabbages. I expected a monstrous hamster to shuffle dozily out of it. I decided the only logical next step was to pursue these ratios throughout, or else Nat's Coleslaw would become The Cabbage Mountain Shuns A Carrot and no one was going to coo over that on the buffet in south London. I reflected that this sort of thing never happened to me in my own flat, it was like I dropped IQ points with every mile north on the M1.

Dad came home as I was stuffing the salad monstrosity into a third bowl. Mum turned up a little later, as I clambered down from seasoning the summit. She offered to fetch the wheelbarrow

7 I absent-mindedly popped the cereal biscuit in the microwave, but the fire was localised and dealt with, *thank you*.

but I ignored her. They stood in the doorway smirking as I tried to work out how to transport six pounds of cabbage. In the end, I strapped it around my body like a veggie bomber.

The observant of you will probably spot that I had a bit of time on my hands at this point – there's no need to make coleslaw from scratch if you're NOT trying to kill time. If I was Andy Dufresne in *The Shawshank Redemption* I wouldn't have bothered scratching at the walls, I'd have got some cabbage off Red, rolled up my sleeves and whiled away the years in a frenzy of shredding.

I had all this spare time because after two and a half months at home I had stopped bitching about all the horrible flats on the market and started pining for the glory days of there being any flats to look at. I started to get nostalgic whenever I smelt damp and attempted to recreate the feel of house hunting by lingering near the compost heap and ripping up the tenners I used to spend on travel.

'The market's gone quiet,' estate agents shrugged at me.

'Well wake it up then!' I wanted to scream at them. 'I've just been given a demonstration in How Much Nicer It Is When Cupboard Doors Are Closed Gently, I can't take much more of this!'

I saddled up my coleslaw and waddled into London for the barbecue and then onwards to meet Tiernan 'to talk about things'.

My coleslaw was not a success, I think people were scared off by its size. Possibly they feared that digging into it would cause an avalanche and no one wants to die under cabbage. It also looked a bit suspicious, dwarfing everyone's daintier homemade treats, looking like something I'd found in an alley by a kebab shop. Still, Tiernan kindly feigned enthusiasm when I dragged it to meet him.

'Look at that!' he cried.

Very clever, the tone suggested excitement but the actual words committed to nothing.

This meeting was very theoretical: there was nothing we could achieve, beyond bitching about the injustice of life and nibbling at the hefty leftovers of my coleslaw. So we started debating such crucial issues as what sort of pet we should have when (if) we ever found a home. Tiernan was in favour of no sort of pet, a complete absence of pet. I wanted a large cat or a small dog, the size was important as I firmly believe a pet should be nothing you can tread on and kill by mistake, but nothing you couldn't beat to death in a fight if you had to. Not that I want to, just if I had to.

I was spending far too much time daydreaming of the domestic bliss that would one day be mine and I had perhaps got carried away. Tiernan was adamant that I'd hate the hassle and responsibility involved and I heard myself say, 'Yeah, I've only just freed myself from the commitment of contact lenses.' I acknowledged that if a disc of moist plastic demanded more of me than I could give, a sentient organism might be beyond me.

I do hope children are less hassle than contact lenses. (Monthly, not disposable, I'm realistic.) I might just delay motherhood until new advances in science mean all children need is an overnight float in saline solution or a mound of shredded veg. Either way, I can only imagine what a mess I'd make of child-raising with their grandparents loitering around muttering, 'Really, Basil? She's really going to call it that? And what is it, girl or boy? I can't tell under all that cabbage . . . Oh god help us all, she's trying to make a sandwich, I'll warn the coastguards.'

Chapter 10

THE CHOSEN PEOPLE'S CHOSEN PEOPLE

Three months in, I was on a downward slide and determined to seize back my adulthood. I sat mum and dad down for a frank chat about rent. I wanted to pay them a reasonable amount to reflect my gratitude, but of course, I made it very clear, nowhere near the going rate. Nowhere near, due to the reduced quality of living I experienced living with people so evangelical about the Best Way To Arrange The Soups In The Cupboard. ('See how we can see all the labels at a glance, isn't that better?')

I loved my parents to an illogical degree, but they were the worst flatmates I've ever had, including the couple who skipped out on a three hundred pound gas bill because 'they didn't remember using that much' (who *remembers* gas?) and the man who simply didn't understand conversation. He would deliver long monologues on subjects from the inadequacies of the 134 bus route to the idiocy of the council tax quarterly payment system. If you offered your opinion, he would wait, dead-eyed and listless, until you stopped your mouth-noise, then he'd resume, with no acknowledgment of anything you'd said.

Pretty soon, the moment my flatmate and I heard him come home we'd drop everything and scrabble to the safety of our bedrooms, at desperate speeds. I nearly broke my nose on the door frame once. To spare his feelings, we tiptoed, like cartoon burglars. I caught the neighbours over the road training binoculars on us once; I think out-of-context this all looked a bit weird.

Nevertheless, I wanted to be an adult about this and pay my parents rent. The décor was pristine and my bedroom was south-facing, that had to be worth a few hundred a month, even with mum and dad's personalities dragging the value down. Mum was adamant, she didn't want a penny, this was my home and it always would be. Dad glared at her and said how about he just ran up a little tally every month of what he felt I owed them? I said I didn't know what sort of business model this was, where you 'guesstimated' what you thought someone should give you and wrote it down on a little secret piece of paper. However, it turned out to be fiendishly clever, as every time I dropped a glass or ate all the salami he would give me a meaningful glare, grab a pen and glide upstairs to 'add to the tally'.

Not paying rent was brilliant, I'm not going to lie. I was spending hundreds of pounds a month honouring poorly paying gigs in London that had been a five-minute bus ride away when I'd booked them and the Bank of Nat needed all the bail-outs it could get. After one London gig I was drifting back to the tube station in a happy daze, delighted with my night. I often feel like stand-up is like algebra, there's an almost mathematical art in presenting the audience with all the necessary information in the most sparse and elegant way possible, setting them up for a punchline to come out of nowhere. When I feel myself using too many words in a set-up I can feel the mood of a room turn tetchy under a barrage of needless information, there's an unspoken feeling of 'this had better be good now we've come all this way'. It's a lot like when a friend marches you around town for twenty minutes to find 'this amazing Lebanese place'. It is rarely amazing enough to justify wet socks.

The gig that night had been zero waffle and maximum LOLs and I was delighted. Until I found that in my joyful stupor I had wandered back to our old flat. I stood outside, watching the new tenants cooking dinner, longing to turf them out and get my lovely old life back. I remembered this couple; they were the first people to view the flat and the boy was so tall he had stooped uncomfortably in the kitchen, declaring it 'perfect'. I fought the urge to say 'mate, you can't fit your own head in your own home. "Perfect", really?'

That should've rung some alarm bells that the rental market was not in a peachy condition. His expectations of life had taken such a mauling that now a place could be 'perfect' even if it refused to accommodate his body in its traditional shape. I stood outside, watching them for a socially unacceptable length of time. At least I didn't compound my crime by surrendering to the urge to wail at the windows, 'Give me my life back!! I've made a terrible mistake!'

Eventually I stopped loitering and went home. I had to be up early the next day as the rent-free sponger soothes her guilt by giving lifts, running errands and picking up groceries. I soon felt like their old-fashioned housewife. I made the mistake of voicing this and was deluged in sarcasm. After a while they started queuing up for it: 'Wait, wait, my go, I've got a good one!' It seemed I fell a little short of the ideal housewife, apparently.

While at home, mum suggested I work some shifts with her and dad. They work evenings and weekends as a waitress and barman. The rest of the time she's a teaching assistant and he's a . . . wait, give me a minute . . . it's something in accounting. The only information he ever gave me about his job was that he sold bombs. I scampered into school full of my news and caused quite the stir at Show and Tell. A phone call home established that he'd actually said 'bonds' but my ears were pounding with my love of drama and I'd misheard.

My brother and I used to go waiting/waitressing with our parents all the time; my wages put me through university and laser eye surgery – without catering I would have a greatly inferior head by now.

My parents have a gruelling work ethic, something between an ant and China. As a comic I spend a lot of my year creating an hour-long show to take to the Edinburgh Festival, at great expense, and when mum heard about this she suggested I get a temp job as I was only working a couple of hours a day. ('Explain the situation, I'm sure they'd let you do it in your lunch hour.') I struggled to explain that it was a lot more work than it sounded, but I was just babbling words like 'creative' and 'focus' while she stared at me through narrowed eyes as if I was far away.

These words made sense in London, said around London types whose only objection to the manbag was 'but why can't it be a Polly Pocket lunchbox?' When I unpacked them in Watford they seemed to have died in transit. They hung in the air and I got that 'morning train home from Glastonbury' feeling: 'I don't know WHAT I'm wearing or why. Sorry . . . I, I really smell.'

Returning to waitressing felt entirely appropriate as every day I was regressing further back to teenaged me. As I was getting ready for my first shift I got a text from a friend who had married recently, bought a house and was now expecting her first child. This was sobering news. Not that I fancied any of those things, but it made me acutely aware that my life seemed to be sliding backwards while other people marched onwards. Typical that I had to revisit adolescence as I hated mine more than anyone else I knew. So of course I should be the one cursed with having to do it again.

Determined not to mope, I sent a congratulations text, tied on my apron and reminded myself that at least I had breasts and hope – two things I'd found so elusive when I did adolescence the first time around. Plus I'd always liked waitressing; it's a straightforward job and often makes people very happy. Despite this enthusiasm I'm not a good waitress. What I don't drop, I eat. Sometimes I do an unhygienic combination of the two. Years of this have given me an immune system you could trot into a biochemical apocalypse and dressage out the other side.

We've always worked for Jewish caterers, having carved a profitable niche as gentiles you could let loose in a kosher kitchen without fear we'd muddle up the system. We should really have business cards: 'The Chosen People's Chosen People', showing us posing hilariously yet respectfully with gefilte fish. Mum loved a kosher kitchen, she felt safe and calm amidst all the rules. I've never seen her look more radiant than when perusing a strict dairy drawer. Ostensibly Church of England, she's happy to overlook the whole Jesus thing for a clearly labelled spoon compartment.

This niche has left me well versed in Judaism but only from a party-planner's perspective, like a really superficial Jew.

'Where you off to?' I'd ask a Jewish friend. 'Oh that synagogue? Don't go there, such tatty décor, the cloakroom's a disgrace. There's one just around the corner that's had a refurb. It's lovely, go there. Tell the rabbi I said don't touch the balloons! He'll know what you mean, it's a private joke.'

So while I don't know much about the theology of a bris, I can cater the perfect menu for one. (Basically anything but mini wraps.)

My least favourite jobs were for Orthodox Jewish clients on the Sabbath, a day when they weren't allowed to do any work, from carrying something to turning on a light switch. You don't know a glum adolescence until you've spent another Friday night following a stranger from room to room, manning the light switches while he looked for his glasses. And of course, if he was over forty they were invariably on his head.

The sound of my underwhelming teenaged years is 'Oh, young lady?' called from a darkened corridor. That and a thirteen-year-old at a Bar Mitzvah jangling his dad's car keys at me saying, 'Look, I can go and get my ID out of my car but I'm parked miles away, let's not waste each other's time. Now, twelve pints of the amber nectar *please*.'

Ah, the power of working on the bar. I remember a garden party attended exclusively by douchebags who all talked to me like I was a babbling idiot who'd been raised by pigs. I mixed them Pimms the colour of coffee and when the hostess puked in the pool I knew my work was done.

Sometimes on the Sabbath, calamity would strike and I'd have to try and fix an oven or fiddle around in a fuse box while our clients hovered anxiously behind me flapping their hands, offering detailed instructions but zero tangible help.

At times like this it felt like God was being a bit mean with his believers: 'Now don't eat this stuff, except on Tuesday afternoons when you have to eat LOADS of it and now get the whole family around for dinner buuuuuut, you're not allowed to touch any appliances!'

'You what? C'mon God, this is impossible.'

'Ah ah ah, no cheating!'

Religion seemed like a life lived by *Just A Minute* rules. But I never said that, I thought it might impact negatively on my tips.

In later years our clientele grew and shifted away from our frum clients to more easy-going types and I could scale back on my light-switch commitments. Small solace when, at the age of twenty-eight and living with my parents, I was back in the pinny at engagement parties of girls my age. I'd scan their family photos and peek around the urn, hoping I didn't know them.

'Nat! So what are you up to at the moment?'

'I'm . . . oh . . . I'm . . . Argh! Would you look at that, I've smashed a glass into my head! Must go, let's chat soon.'

While I was at home, mum very sweetly wangled me a job waitressing at a party for a famous TV comedian, 'because you'll like that! Because you're a comedian too!' She sprung this news on me as I drove there and I hid all my dread behind a big thank you smile. When we got there I peeked around the kitchen door and I realised the room was swarming with work colleagues.

Not for the first time, I cursed my decision to move out of my old flat. Was a small flat really such a bad thing? There was less to clean, I could make a sandwich, have a wee and turn the telly on, all without moving my feet. And I don't think I ever really explored the idea of cosiness fully: 'Let's pretend we're The Borrowers!' etc. But apparently Past Me had decided it was unbearable, flinging Present Me right in the shit, offering mini burgers to my own PR team, fretting about Future Me's burgeoning schizophrenia. From now on, I swore, I would make no more decisions. I would bob flaccidly through life, letting it push me hither and thither while I stayed limp, which is the best policy in a collision anyway.

Mum had given me this job because she thought I'd enjoy it, so I couldn't skulk any longer. Time to look cheerful, like a daughter from an advert. I grabbed a tray and slapped on a joyful expression.

I strode out, teeth gritted and napkins folded. People behaved as usual, pointing at something the size of a baby's thumbnail, querying its contents, despite the fact that my opening gambit had been: 'Mini Yorkshire pudding with caramelised red onions?' Did they think this was my idea of a hello? Had the cool kids tired of 'Whassup' so soon and replaced it with 'Mini Yorkshire pudding with caramelised red onions, Blud'? It was frustrating as I already felt the name was inelegantly detailed, but the chef had rejected my more poetic alternatives. I still say 'Mouthpleaser' would be more fun to offer around a room: 'Tonguefoolery, Madam?'

So when idiots ask what's in our mini Yorkshire puddings with caramelised red onions I fight the urge to reply 'Offal and sand. The name? Oh that's just what we *call* it, not what's in it. The chef's a kook! You don't have to be mad to work here, but . . .'

If I'm ever offered anything I never question the waitress – I greet everything with 'brilliant, thanks!' and stuff it in my mouth. Eighty per cent of the time this is the right thing to do. The rest of the time . . . my skin heals quickly.

As I chaperoned my tiny food around I found I had been worrying for nothing; no one looked at me once. I handed out savoury snacks to my wider social circle completely unrecognised. It's amazing more criminals don't use waitressing uniforms. Or maybe they do and we've never noticed. A woman I had known for six years clicked her fingers at me then happily troughed her way through the contents of my tray. I stared bemused at the top of her head (she's short, we weren't playing an ad hoc game of Twister).

She was utterly oblivious to my face loitering above her, even though she usually greeted it with 'Hello Lady Face!' and festooned it with a kiss: sloppy insincerity that made me cringe and then feel bad for being so cold. So gobble gobble, Lady Face, eat up all my guilt, yum yum. She finally finished and I said thank you as I thought someone should and it didn't look like she was going to.

Years of waitressing have made me acutely aware of the importance of manners. I've met a lot of lovely people, clients who remember your name and say thank you. And I've met some utter dicks. Just as you learn more from bad gigs, I think I've learnt more from the utter dicks, I'd watch them and think, 'note to self, NEVER be like this person'. I was standing behind a buffet one day and a young boy sneezed on me. Just openly fucking sneezed on me, holding his hands aloft as if to move them out of the way, because surely there was no role that they could play in this scenario?! I can't stand people who don't instinctively put their hands up to block a sneeze. Those people are worse than rats; they spread disease and are unpleasant to look at. At least rats scuttle, these people walk around brazenly as if they're welcome in the world.

Snotbag's mother squealed, 'Ugh! Did you sneeze on the food?'

'No, no,' her friend reassured her, 'He did it on the . . . ah . . .' and gestured at me.

I stared at her in silence, absorbing my status as the creature too lowly to justify a noun. Fair enough, I thought later, as I wiped my snotty arm over the sandwiches, what is the word for 'someone so inferior that she doubles as a public hanky'? I guess I should be thankful they didn't use my fingers as toothpicks.

If I'm ever rich, I'll be polite and I'll enjoy my money. I will quaff cream, bathe in olive oil and give to charity by skipping through their offices flinging fifties, yodelling 'Call me Willy Wonga!' I will not act like having a new kitchen installed is an ordeal. Some people whinge so much about it I assume they're having it inserted into them.

I used to love the fatalists who greeted every event in their pampered lives with a wince. The world had so far seen fit to bestow them with health, family and pots of cash, but they still acted like Destiny's squashed victim. They'd peer anxiously into the oven before parties and say mournfully, 'Well, it smells all right at least' as if the chef is going to shrug and hit himself in the face with a spoon.

We'd bring the food out and these gloomy twats would yell at each other through us: 'No, TRY IT, Sandra, it's . . . it's actually quite nice!'

Is it?! Bloody hell, I'll tell the chef, he will NOT believe this. Fancy that, Sandra, you paid a catering company to cook food for your guests, was there not a glimmer of hope that we might offer up something edible? If you're that pessimistic, just save your money and serve crisps. No one hates crisps.

Adding up my years of waitressing depresses me. I doubt there's a child in north London whose Bar or Bat Mitzvah I haven't schlepped mouthpleasers around. I have waitressed at hundreds of weddings, funerals and engagement parties and, though the wages have seen me through sixth form, university and some comedy promoters' inability to pay at speeds faster than 'glacial', I can't help feeling I've been robbed of the most memorable days of my life.

Not robbed, more like inundated with the most memorable days of other peoples' lives. I'm jam-packed with unwanted memories of other peoples' stupid fucking happy days. If someone wed me our special day would be the thousandth wedding I'd helped to organise. 'Dearly beloved'? Yawn. 'Luckiest man in the . . .' Yeah yeah, big whoop. 'Loving angels instead?' 'Course you are, Robbie. Years later, trawling through the memories, how will I separate mine from those of strangers'? It's hopeless. I'm not sure I even enjoyed my Bat Mitzvah, from what I remember there was a coffin and a sleazy usher.

I decided if Craine was ever masochistic enough to wed me I would try to be a nice bride. So many brides were mean to us, embittered by a year of starvation and the unhappy knowledge that they'd never fit into that dress again. One sip of champagne and they started giving at the seams. They should've just chubbed up, been a happy hefty bride and enjoyed decades of smugness whenever they tried the dress on. Unless they couldn't shift the wedding weight. Admittedly, it's not a perfect plan.

I don't remember many weddings, but a couple stick with me. My favourite is still the krazy couple who insisted on only Vodka Red Bull for their reception drinks, because 'we don't do things by the book, sorry! LOL.' I really admired their bold strivings for uniqueness. They were two of the dullest people I'd ever met, so I appreciated it was an uphill struggle.

Thanks to them I spent a hot July afternoon fighting wasps off their sugary idea of refreshments while telling their relatives, 'Noooo . . . sorry, I don't have any water. How about some Red Bull? No, no orange juice I'm afraid, but can I interest you in a really weak Vodka Red Bull?' One plucky old pensioner went away sucking an ice cube in a napkin. Thank god for world wars: useful prep for this shitstorm of a nuptials.

For the first dance the bride and groom shuffled around a bit to 'A Whiter Shade Of Pale' and I mentally shortened the odds on them seeing their first anniversary. It was lovely to see a private, unrehearsed moment between them where neither of them was yelling footnotes at their audience, spelling out their uncontrollable zaniness and desire to defy convention. Sure, defy conventions if you want, I don't mind, but do you have to defy ALL of them? Even those rather useful conventions like 'give your gran a chair, she's swooning against the Marilyn Manson statue' and 'sometimes on a hot day people need to drink some water, however boring you think that is'.

My softening towards them stopped the moment 'A Whiter Shade Of Pale' stopped with a synthesised scratching noise, they both turned to the audience, yelled 'AS IF!!' and started pogoing to 'Smack My Bitch Up'. By now guests and staff were so desensitised to their wacky shit that we all stood there, dead-eyed. The overwhelming mood of the room was 'Uh really?' and I noted with some satisfaction that this song was longer than the bride and groom had anticipated. They pogoed for five long minutes, sweating pure sugar, while their guests chatted among themselves and handed around ice cubes in napkins. A cheery blitz spirit prevailed. In fact, the happy couple's twatty behaviour was a real boon to the party; it gave all their guests a common enemy and fostered an atmosphere of real conviviality.

Come to think of it, when I married Craine I'd act like a complete tool so all my guests could bond over rolled eyes and catty mutterings. I'd take one for the team so everyone had a nice time and I'd send them all away with a note revealing my tactics so nobody thought badly of me and they all felt guilty for behaving so predictably. I'd make Derren Brown an usher and we'd violate the minds of my nearest and dearest. Now that would be a fun wedding, there's a chance I'd remember that one.

And we'd have wedding photos no one minded flicking through: 'Oh, is that you pretending to slit Craine's throat with the flower-girl's fingernail?'

'Ha, yeeaah. "Tiny little jabs in a concentrated area! Aim for a vein!" Derren was yelling from the pulpit . . . Seriously, *such* a nice guy.'

I spent the rest of my shift pondering my wedding plans, then went home and phoned Craine to tell him the good news: our nuptials would be awesome! And I'd got the florists down to a shortlist of four. He was a little lukewarm, frankly. His clothes had gone missing in the move and we'd only found them that week, in mum and dad's garage. It would appear that I had packed them with the kitchenware (I had drunk the cooking wine[8] to save room and had made some unconventional decisions beyond that point. Such as pouring rice in all the boxes to act as bubble-wrap.)

So Craine was forced to wear whatever he could find at home – an assortment of outfits from his teenaged years. Slumped in

---

8 Yup, cooking wine. You may know it as 'wine I left uncorked on the radiator so now it tastes like witch's piss'. But I like to keep a veneer of sophistication on my scummy life.

Bath in a neon tracksuit that had got mysteriously tight since he was seventeen ('but just on the stomach, isn't that weird?' 'Inexplicable, My Melted Windmill'), Craine wasn't feeling too romantic and wasn't about to get down on one knee. Probably for the best; I think his trousers would've given up under the pressure. It was hard to make life plans together when every day saw us slide further and further into childhood. At this rate we'd be clad in nappies debating the merits of tracker mortgages.

Chapter 11

FAFFING

'I've wasted years of my life here,' mum confided one afternoon. Usually that phrase is the starting pistol for a traumatic year of divorce and having to do MDMA in a nightclub toilet with your mum, but on this occasion she was sitting in the car on the driveway and she had a good point.

Dad and I are faffers. It's only when we're leaving a house and there are people waiting for us that we attain complete clarity on The Things We Need To Do and a list of tasks unfurls before us. Only when we are wearing our coat and shoes and gloves do we realise that, of course, that orchid in the bathroom needs dead-heading ASAP! And we stumble upstairs to deal with it while mum rests her head gently on the dashboard and weeps for her wasted years.

I remember a scene in *Working Girl* where Melanie Griffith leaves her apartment, cramming toast in her mouth. She looked so cool, how could anyone leave the house so decisively? I marvelled. I wanted to be just like her, but my version involved cramming toast in my mouth then heading upstairs to dead-head that sickly orchid, adding the sin of trailing toast crumbs to my charge sheet.

By my mid-teens mum had finally Had Enough and yelled at us all about our inability to leave the house within twenty minutes. We were mid-faff at the time and got scolded in the hallway in all our coats, hats and gloves, clutching toast and rotting orchids. I hate being told off, I blush all over. By the end of her tirade I had blushed myself to dangerous levels of heat within my insulating layers and tottered to the car quite light-headed, vowing that if I was ever stranded on top of a snowy mountain like in that film,[9] I would stave off hypothermia by thinking of all my most shameful moments.

After this, my dad, brother and I were determined to prove mum wrong and for years we would leave the house at reckless speeds whenever we heard the jangle of car keys. Every outing began with an unseemly rugby-style scrum at the door as everyone fought to get to the car first. We'd reach the car within seconds, panting, clutching handfuls of each other's hair and dabbing at bleeding lips with them. Then we'd drive off in triumph. And drive back almost immediately as everyone realised they'd left wallets/trousers/ovens on in their scramble to be right.

We would do anything to be right. We'd gladly all perish in a burning inferno so long as when we were bobbing limply in agnostic limbo, one of us could turn smugly to the others and say 'I TOLD you that wasn't the best type of smoke detector to get. But no one ever listens to me do they, oh noooo, what would I know about anything?'

Once it was just mum and dad at home, I guess a scrum-for-one was a lonely experience, involving punching yourself in the face, so dad had started playing a new game. Now mum sat in the car, one eyebrow quivering gently, a wispy barometer of the storm within, as dad locked the front door caaaaaarefully, straightened his jacket and headed towards her. Then stooped to examine a pebble on the floor, was that one of his? Or perhaps a stray pebble? A wild one, if you will. He smiled to himself. No, waaaait, he knew where it came from! And so he picked it up and returned it to a flowerpot with the reverent care of a diamond-setter. Now he was ready to get in the car. But just a minute! Was that moss on the front lawn? Best go take a look. Ah no, it's just grass! It's

9 That film. You know. Oh you do, that film! The one with the man in . . .

funny, grass and moss do look very similar from a distance, he explained to mum, mouthing it with exaggerated care, smiling broadly at her while she filled the car with Abba to drown out the screaming in her head.

Watching dad faff, I felt like I was in the presence of a master artist. I also felt extremely impatient and like I wanted to slap him. Like all great artists, he inspires a complex range of emotions. My overwhelming one was pity for mum, I realised now what she had been suffering alone. No wonder she yelled at me so much, faithless deserter that I was. They had gone really weird since my brother and I left home. Dad had, unarguably, led the charge into the Loony Outback, but she'd followed.

I knew mum had worried about Empty Nest Syndrome when my brother and I had left. Dad was engrossed in a shed catalogue and she'd hissed over his head, 'What am I going to talk to HIM about?!' I sensed she wouldn't welcome the reply 'Sheds?' so I just shrugged helplessly and dragged my suitcase to the car.

While I'd been gone they'd taken up hobbies, which I whole-heartedly approved of, though it had horrible consequences, leading to video footage of them skiing, which was painfully slow even in fast forward. Somehow when mum and dad sheathe themselves in TK Maxx skiwear they gain superpowers! They can defy gravity and slide down a mountain so slowly it's like they're on the bloody moon. I consoled them that, in terms of time spent getting up the mountain versus time spent sliding down it, they were getting more value for money than anyone else. Sure, they were missing out on the extras like adrenalin or the thrill of speed, but they had longer to look at the scenery and discuss their travel insurance mid-zigzag.

My parents had discovered loads of things to do once their children were no longer the thankless shitty centre of their world. Which was wonderful, but as I was back for this Month At Home[10] I expected a return to the bad old days. It was a bit of a struggle,

10 Sorry, did you not know? April 2010 lasted for about twenty-five weeks. Yes it did.

they seemed to find each other fascinating nowadays, and I had to spend the first few weeks back home elbowing my way back in. Very sweetly they considered their boring anecdotes much more enthralling than mine. They were wrong but they outnumbered me, so I had to fight my corner.

I think I'm fascinating. Which is lucky, given how much time I have to spend with myself. If I'm honest, when I die and my life flashes before my eyes, I'm expecting it to take days, as most events will demand inclusion, some may be repeated because they're so engrossing. You could NOT edit down the good stuff any tighter. I've ridden an elephant and met TV's Billie Piper, where do you trim the fat off this?!

Sadly my parents didn't see it this way. Often I'd be halfway through an anecdote and see their eyes slide away from me and to the telly. Even when it wasn't on. That was just hurtful. I was telling dad about how I met Billie Piper ('met' is a grotesque exaggeration but that's part of my storytelling skill) and he stared at the blank TV screen and sighed wistfully.

'Yes,' I said pointedly, manoeuvring myself in front of it, 'she's on the telly isn't she? Which makes this an interesting anecdote.' Pearls before swine.

Living with my parents could be so difficult as a sane, rational person. One morning, a few weeks into my interminable Month At Home, I woke to an empty house with the radio playing. I hate that and they knew it; it always felt like they'd left in a hurry, clutching their passports and yelling, 'Leave Nat, there isn't time to wake her, the wolves are circling!'

Once I'd settled my mind with a peek at the news, both mum and dad called me from their respective works to say they had seen our neighbour-over-the-road's cat sitting on the drive 'looking confused' and I had to check on it.

'Well,' I said. 'We're all a bit flummoxed by the mid-terms.' This genial quip wasn't well received because, 'Actually, Natalie, there's a busy road there.'

I thought this was some complicated joke but, as I waited for the punchline, I realised, with a sagging feeling, that it wasn't coming and I was going to have to pull a coat over my pyjamas and check on a cat. How the bloody hell does a cat look confused anyway? I'm not being racist but it doesn't have the eyebrows for it.

Mum had DRIVEN past it – she had to judge its emotional state in a quick glance at 30mph. Funnily enough, dad walked past and chose the exact same word to describe this emotionally ravaged feline, he didn't plump for wistful, hungry or contemplative. They both concluded their split-second assessment with 'confused'. They were good at this. Whatever 'this' was: rapid animal assessment. A niche skill, they could do triage in an animal war, but wouldn't find much work outside Narnia.

It was hard to know what this situation required, so I took the *Financial Times*, an abacus and Craine, who had chosen a poor day for a visit. He had already endured a 7am visit from mum tiptoeing through my bedroom humming 'I'm not here, ignore me,' while she dug some socks out of my drawer and he shielded his nipples. In recent years my bedroom had become a communal storage area and our semi-naked presence in it didn't seem to make any difference. It was like living in a handbag.

Craine brought nothing of use to the enterprise, but I wanted to share the suffering. I explained that we had to go see how a cat felt and he looked blank and said 'furry?'

'No,' I explained, stuffing him back into his coat: 'emotionally'.

He got more angry as the stupidity of this sunk in and as we stood on a traffic island in the middle of the road he started gesticulating furiously and a bus had to swerve. It was dangerous but I sympathised, this was one of the more pointless things mum had made me do, and it was an inglorious long list.

We searched the front garden, hoping that the neighbours weren't in as our good deed might have seemed more criminal than kind. We couldn't find the cat, I think Craine scared her off by repeatedly yelling, 'What are we doing?! WHY is this happening?!'

He is a man that wails, 'Why is this happening?!' a lot. He is Life's beleaguered plaything, a poor little will o' the wisp, tossed and battered by events, all he can do is whine as he spins. But, you know, in a sexy way.

I decided it was time to go once a small gaggle of passers-by had gathered to stare at Craine in his pyjamas in a bush. It was visually arresting, a man grappling with gardenias whispering, 'What the crispy fuck has gone wrong with my morning?' It was time to sell tickets or take him home.

Craine argued that I could've just said no to my parents' instructions, but it never occurred to me – owning a spine is more trouble than it is worth for a house guest who won't leave. Consequently, I always did what they told me to, it was easier and minimised the risk of shouting. I rarely achieved success, but I would try, then give up and lie.

So we went home and I called mum and dad to assure them that I had encountered perfect feline clarity. If anything, I embroidered, warming to my theme around a mouthful of Coco Pops, 'She's really got her finger on the pulse hasn't she? She could teach those bozos in Westminster a thing or two!'

'He.'

'What?'

'He's a he.'

'Ah, that explains a lot. Well, still great to meet him.'

Back on the driveway I reminded mum of these incidents while she dusted the dashboard with a tissue. Funnily enough she had only hazy memories of those incidents when she hadn't bathed herself in glory, but could remember in forensic detail all the times she was right about something, like that time we witnessed a car crash where a man tried to drive off without swapping insurance details, so she stood in front of his car. That was bloody impressive, we both agreed, nibbling some mints we'd found in the glove box.

Remember the man you ran over in the Harlequin car park? We cackled gleefully. You can't save spaces, everyone knows that.

Not even if you fling your arms and legs into an X shape. It just gives mum a more precise target to reverse into. Plus the situation becomes so farcical that security won't believe your story and we'll leg it while you're trying to prove you're not on drugs.

I quite liked this time we got to spend together while dad navigated six feet in eight minutes. If he was a more thoughtful man I'd think that's why he did it, but he's not That Guy. I think mum treasured this time too, although to a lesser extent as she then leant her head on the horn.

I seemed to be spending a lot of time doing things I didn't enjoy during this period of my life. Partly this was due to mum and dad's feline-centric whims and partly due to the grinding tedium of finding somewhere to live. Our fourth month of house hunting was approaching, nerves were fraying and I had felt the need to institute a new rule. I insisted that from now on we house hunted in twos as this reduced the chance of estate agents greeting us as a gang, with 'Hey guys', which in turn reduced the risk of me pinning them to the floor with my knees and pushing complementary pens up their nose until their eyes went inky. This house hunt may have corroded my usual bovine placidness.

'Hey guys' said in a mindlessly brisk 'n' breezy tone of voice, uttered by a man in shoes so pointy they'd arrive a couple of minutes before his face, really bothered me. I understood that they met a lot of people every day, but so did I, and I managed to avoid treating venue staff and audience members like faceless borgs. 'Hey guys' made me feel like a pissed-up victim of an 18–30's experience, indulging in some 'classic' generic fun. This greeting felt like it should be followed by 'Okaaay, I'm just going to squirt some cream on your genitals and I want everyone to introduce themselves to the person to their left and lick them clean. Okey dokey, when I say "Where's my?" You say, "Soul!" Where's my . . .?'

So it was safer to house hunt in pairs. It minimised the risk of my violence. Plus, we then amused ourselves by talking about the missing flatmate.

'And your friend could have this room?'

'No no,' we'd smile blandly, 'He'll HAVE to have the one at the back because it's darker.'

'Yeah, he needs it dark,' we'd agree nervously, not looking at each other. 'Oh god,' I'd remark, tapping a kitchen tile. 'Is this . . . is this a turquoise blue to you? He is not going to like that at ALL,' and we'd wince at some painful tile-related memories.

We began house hunting pleasantly and maturely but that was four months ago. At this point, we were miserable. And if we were going to be miserable, so was everyone else. A miserable stand-up can be a terrible thing; we drag our moodiness around the country then shine lights at it and amplify it through a microphone. It might feel like the gig is fun because we've still got our punchlines, if anything our grumpiness breeds more jokes, but there's no twinkle in the eye, and you'll find us sobbing in the car park. I asked the audience at one gig if anyone else was over twenty-five and still living with their parents.

A man of thirty-two was. 'Ha! I win!' I thought to myself. I thought this very loudly, out of my mouth. He looked unamused. I asked why he was living with his parents. Going through a divorce apparently. Thankfully I kept my honest response to myself. Yelling 'TWO–NIL TO ME!' at a man going through a tricky patch was not the way to win over a crowd. Though I doubt this whingebag had to spend his mornings hunting for a cat to 'see how it felt'. In fairness, however, he could clearly leave a house more decisively than me, judging by his speedy exit in the interval. Two–all; Advantage Luurtsema.

The car door opened, letting in cold air while dad carefully retied his scarf before getting in the car. Mum and I bristled with fury watching him tend to his own body warmth, while disrupting ours.

'Okay,' he sighed, tired from all his twatting about, 'where are we off to then? Will I need money? I haven't got any on me.'

Mum and I assured him in testy tones that as we weren't off to some magical non-capitalist vision of the future YES he probably would need money. He sighed as if WE were at fault and strolled back to the house.

I once saw two ducks engaged in an elaborate mating ritual where the male spent a lot of time splashing his lady love with water, pushing her around and generally being a dick. In her situation I'd have bailed after five minutes, saying, 'You know what, mate? I'm busy, I've got a lot on: I don't really need this.' But she stuck with it, possibly having few better options in the Watford canal. It occurred to me that I was witnessing the human equivalent on this driveway. It's one way of showing love, to dedicate quite so much time to annoying your special one. But that didn't make it all right, mum and I decided, as dad sashayed elaborately towards the car and we drove off without him. 'Ave a bit of that, duckwit.

Chapter 12

TWIHARD TIMES

So, four months into this big paused period of my life and the fun had thoroughly ebbed. I tried to tempt it back with a cravat, with little success. In my parents' house I had an irritating lack of privacy; no one was particularly fascinated by me and yet they had a strange habit of commentating on my every move:

'Getting some crisps?'

'Yes.'

'Off back upstairs?'

'Yes.'

'Taking your bag up?'

'What do you want? Why are you subtitling me?!'

After months of this I felt like a disgruntled pug being dragged around Crufts. I yearned for a localised super-injunction, something legal that would enable me to walk across a room and pick up a pen without a droning commentary that made me hate myself for being so boring. I became self-conscious, feeling obligated to tap-dance into the room, star-jump to a cupboard, get inside my packet of crisps and ride them upstairs like a sack race. Only to earn the remark, 'Getting some crisps then?'

I spent increasing amounts of time in my room where I could move around without comment. I felt a strong urge to hide and retreat into fantasy. Not striding around in dominatrix gear, getting fresh with the postman; this would've pushed dad over the edge. He already had a pathological fear of catching me in a state of undress, so every morning he'd wake up, fling himself into the bath and scramble into his clothes, disappearing downstairs until I presented myself fully clothed. I guess he feared I'd picked up fancy London ways and now began the day by running naked from room to room, screaming 'Gok Wan, Gok Waaaaaan!'

So no, not that sort of fantasy, I was immersing myself in something much more dweeby: *Twilight*. In my quasi-teenaged state, I had succumbed and read all the vampire chastity porn books in a week – those things really do fill that gaping hole in your life that should be filled with joie de vivre, no wonder teenagers love them. I got a little carried away and was toying with impersonating a haggard seventeen-year-old. This way I could live at home for five more years and just front it out. 'Me? Thirty-three? Don't be silly, you can smell the UCAS on me!' It seemed to be working for Edward Cullen.

With this new tactic in place I continued ignoring the painful reality of my life. Follow me everyone, this is the path to mental serenity! As an added bonus, spending all this time reading in my room reduced the risk of messing up the rest of the house. But consequently mum would come home to a darkened house after work. Her response was characteristically calm; flouncing about yelling, 'Just once, just once, I'd like to come home and not have to turn lights on!' For a woman with two jobs for twenty years she made a bloody big fuss about flicking some switches. Is she hard-working to her knuckles then cursed with lazy fingers?

Anyway, I refused to apologise, just because I wasn't titting around the house flipping light switches like a C-lister in late November. You know if I had done, she'd have stormed home enquiring WHY it was necessary that the Luurtsema home be seen from space?!

I found a lot of comfort in solid teen fiction, it really was my friend through these difficult times, but I couldn't shake the fear that I was mentally regressing. A few months in my childhood bedroom and my mental age was sliding backwards so fast its nineties fringe was flapping in my eyes. I couldn't even blame the fact that I was surrounded by *Smash Hits*' stickers and cuddly toys, because my childhood bedroom wasn't like that, it looked like that of a frumpy ninety-year-old.

My parents insisted that I had a grown-up bedroom when they redecorated years ago. They had been badly burnt by my brother's whims. He wanted a *Thomas the Tank Engine* bedroom; they had no money so had to work hard to assemble it piecemeal, a kooky Fat Controller bin one week, an overtime shift and a train-shaped mirror another week. Three years later, they had completed his dream bedroom. But during that time puberty had dawned and Michael was having very different sorts of dreams. Certainly nothing you'd want to decorate with: 'Could I order the clock in the shape of two gigantic breasts? It does moan the hours right? Thanks. And any idea about the delivery date of that Brazilian wax rug? Surely you can just pop it in an envelope?'

So my bedroom has always been muted flowery things and plain furniture. Plus, after six years' absence, it had become a handy dumping-ground for all the miscellaneous shit that didn't belong anywhere else. I was reading teen fiction surrounded by gift soap, camping equipment and a couple of dumb-bells. The feng shui was all over the shop.

Among the miscellany lurked bits of teenaged Nat. I had a couple of posters, now tucked neatly under my desk. I used to have a Blur poster on my bedroom ceiling so Damon's face was the last thing I saw every night. Until the Blu-Tack perished, the poster fell on top of me and I woke up thrashing beneath them, realising that wish fulfilment was a slippery thing. I never trusted those child-molesting popsters again and they were relegated to the wall behind the door.

I moved on and developed some devoted childhood crushes but, being a prim child, I wouldn't let myself fancy any pop stars once they got married. With hindsight, I think I took their wedding vows more seriously than they did. (Yes, I am talking to you, Mark Owen.)

Mum has always had a touching faith in my ability to have any man I want. She said to me years ago, 'I'd be happy if you brought Gary Barlow home, perhaps Mark' (oh, if she only knew), 'Jason and Howard at a push if they had a wash, but I do not trust Robbie Williams, I couldn't in all honesty welcome him into the family.'

I assured her that I found this very touching but that really, the men of the world were not obediently laying their genitals out in velvet-lined cases, waiting for me to browse the treats on offer and draw up a shortlist. She sighed. 'Had to say genitals, didn't you . . .' No doubt thinking, 'and that'll be why you'll end up with Howard.'

The other poster was one that came free with *Smash Hits*, and it was just covered in lots of pictures of the era's pop stars. I've never really cared for music, but as a socially castaway tween I knew this wasn't acceptable and clearly thought a picture of lots of generic pop stars would get the message across to any visitors: 'Look, I like music okay? All of it, equally . . . him, him and her and them. OK?'

I'm still a little ambivalent about music, and hate the fact that people's first response to this is to play me their favourite songs. WHAT do you think this will achieve?

'Oooooh!' I'll cry, 'Nearly thirty years of indifference have now been swept away by the bland lyrics and repetitive beats of your favourite song. It's a miracle!'

No, that's not going to happen, I'm going to sigh, shuffle my feet and offer up comments like, 'Still going, this song, isn't it? Yup. Long one . . . looooong song.' And then you'll be offended and it'll somehow be my fault.

It didn't help that mum and dad inexplicably listened to a Golden Oldies station when I was growing up so the musical references of my youth are that of a pensioner. At family weddings I always end up dancing with the grandparents to 'our' favourite tunes: 'Oh, remember jiving to this at the Ol' Penny Ha'porth with the GIs?'

'No, Doris, I really don't!'

This social maiming didn't make school any easier, and this just made me resent music more.

'What's your favourite TLC song?'

'Did they do "Tie A Yellow Ribbon Round The Old Oak Tree"? It's a jazzy number. About the . . . war that I assume is happening at the moment, despite *Newsround* never mentioning it. Must be just a littl'un.'

Unfurling my *Smash Hits* poster I found TLC and All Saints pouting crossly at me, in their sturdy combat trousers. They looked so quaintly demure with just their bellybuttons peeking out, nary a nipple, whip or chain to be seen. They could do a car boot sale in those outfits. And they weren't licking *anything*! They might as well have been simpering in a wimple they looked so adorably chaste.

Sat in my childhood bedroom, clutching a children's book, I realised I'd reached the age where all pop culture from my teen years was Correct and Excellent and any new developments annoyed me. What a time for that revelation. I filed it away with the Discovery Of Ol' Silvery Jim in the column of things I wished I'd experienced in my own adult, independent property. Oh well, could be worse, if my brother was in my position he'd be facing his mortality in a train-shaped mirror.

I was becoming increasingly intolerant of current pop stars. I'm sure I'm just a repressed old lady but Rihanna baffled me with her panting insistence on telling us how she'll go at it all night long and how convinced she is that she needs a man to 'really work her body' like it's a temperamental old banger going up a hill.

She will keep on going at the sex for hours, you can hurt her if you want, she'd like that, if you wanted her to like that. She is adamant, she will work EXTREMELY HARD at the sex. See that? Bite it! Come on!! Go at her like she's got no nerve endings! You'd expect someone so professionally successful to have more self-esteem.

I couldn't imagine who would be aroused by this diligent attitude to sex, except for project managers who like to keep things on-budget and on-schedule, for which you really needed that sort of 110 per cent team-player. If I was a teenaged boy surrounded by this music, I'd be very confused. It is the unappealing language of the masochist flinging herself wild-eyed and jaw-gritted into an aerobics workout.

Surely any half-sane sexual partner would be backing away from her at this point, clutching his cardigan and waffling nervously about the busy morning he has tomorrow.

'It's not that you're not mind-blowingly sexy, of course you are, you've told me, repeatedly and named an international tour along these lines . . .' (fumbling for the door knob), 'it's just I am quite tired and I don't think I'm ready to beat each other with chainsaws until we orgasm. Verse three did make it sound tempting but I'm a martyr to tennis elbow.'

A generation of pop starlets and socialites crawled, begged and licked their way across contemporary culture, presenting themselves like monkeys on heat and it just seemed weird to me. I'm baffled that at some point we all decided we'd celebrate sluttyness. Beauty, I understand, but promiscuity demands NO special skills beyond a working batch of genitalia and an easy-going nature. Being a competitive tiddlywinks player has more barriers to entry and should logically be held in higher regard, but you don't see tiddlywinkers smouldering on the side of buses with their new fragrance, Flip Me Off!

It seems such an arbitrary thing to celebrate, why not glorify other weird things, like lack of punctuality; leading to generations of boys boasting about all the dental appointments they've missed: 'I don't even KNOW what that little hand does, ya get me Bruv?'

But who am I to judge? You might ask, as I sat engrossed in fantasy, at my childhood desk. Oh fuck off, I'd reply, because I warned you I was getting childish. Still, I was happy enough there. I loved that desk, I used to study there for hours. My studiousness amazed my teachers. I went at learning like Rihanna went at penis.

'But Natalie!' they would (clearly be fighting the urge to) exclaim, 'You spoil us, this is so unnecessary! You're already the cleverest in class!'

They never actually, overtly, said it but we knew. It was all in their eyes. Then I went to university and everyone was clever and no one was surprised that I liked learning, they just had the sheer bloody cheek to expect it! So I stopped immediately. Turns out that 'love of learning' I'd been flaunting was just a petty lust to be the best. And if I couldn't be the best, what was the point?

The housing market still hadn't woken up, it seemed to have the yearly routine of a tortoise, which I'd never realised before as my house hunting had never dragged on beyond a month. I had a lot of time on my hands, which I'd imprudently filled with vampires and I thought I'd stave off weirdness by taking Craine out for fun, Watford-style. He had been hiding out at ours for the last week after his dad had hit upon a brilliant wheeze for our housing woes:

'The YMCA, Thomas! It's a wonderful scheme and I'm sure you're still young enough to qualify.'

I decided to shove a bit of the romance back into our lives and knew just the place. If you ever find yourself in my home town, possessed of an urge for japes, then strap in, you're a libertine in the suburbs and this is how we cut loose! Drive along a dual carriageway for a few miles, to a deserted patch of ground by a petrol station, you know, the sort of place where you'd execute a small-time gangster. Here you will discover a cinema, a Mexican bar and a bowling alley all huddled together like a desert mirage. There's the distinct implication of 'Here, have your Fun, but keep it out here, away from decent folk,' and it makes bowling feel confusingly dirty. I love the economy of it, like they racked their brains for the three activities to satisfy every Bacchanalian whim.

'What do people want?'

'Beans, films and heavy balls.'

'Then that's what they shall have.'

I dragged poor Craine to see the latest *Twilight* film there, cos that's the life of a man dating a twenty-eight-year-old living with her mum and dad, I never promised him glamour. I had had a bellyful of his gloomy predictions that the film would be shit, so I spent the first hour watching it with exaggerated joy, like I was watching a fireworks display. But the constant smiling gave me a headache and I had to admit defeat. It was boring. I liked the books, despite their heavy-handed moral message. If I can ignore it in Narnia, I can ignore it anywhere. But the films do drag a bit if you don't want to pounce on Robert Pattinson and subject him to a semi-consensual sex rumpus (and I don't, I'm sure he's a nice boy but his face has too many angles – not so much cute as acute). Plus I wish he'd speak up and stop bloody mumbling; at nine quid a ticket I would like to hear all the words, thank you young man! But I'll forgive him. Puberty is a difficult time, with the confusing skin and feelings, and if R-Patz eases the process for a generation of girls then all power to him and his prismy face.

I giggled my way through the film as the only audience was four other couples and every five minutes the girls would have to explain more backstory to the boys: 'No, all vampires are beautiful and have special powers.' And, 'Their eyes go red when they crave blood and amber when they're calm.' There were deep sighs from the boys as they absorbed each piece of nonsense. By the light of the credits I saw several boys staring at their girlfriends with barely concealed disgust. I think some were dumped before the house lights came up.

Not me. Thomas Craine is not a man to fight a losing battle; he had curled up like a pragmatic cat, played some games on his phone then gone to sleep. He was dealing with this period of homelessness better than Tiernan and I, thanks to this amazing ability. He just slept through the bits of life that didn't please him – it was like he could put himself in suspended animation and only revive himself for the day's highlights. He lives his life to a *Match of the Day* template: 'Cut out the dull bits; all killer, no filler.' I should have trained myself to do the same, fostered a rare narcolepsy triggered by the words 'Getting some crisps then?'

Chapter 13

THE PERFECT DAUGHTER

'You're jumping on my last nerve.'

I love that phrase. A woman who was either black or Hispanic used to say it whenever people exasperated her in a (possibly American) sitcom or a film that I think I used to watch as a child. Ah, precious memories.

Either way I have always loved it, I wrote it in a book and saved it and kept it with other favoured phrases that I could never deliver convincingly, things like 'You worry too much!' in a Noo Yoik accent. I attempted to use these phrases a few times but they required 'feistiness', which I have never achieved, although when drunk I get optimistic and think I have. I click my fingers and say cheeky things and people put me in a taxi.

Within four months of my Month At Home (sigh), mum and dad had jumped on all my nerves, leaving me a numb lump. They did things like tidying my car without telling me. How kind, you think, but you think wrongly. They 'tidied' my Sat Nav and phone charger into a kitchen drawer. I didn't notice this until I found myself stranded in between Bath and Salisbury on a gig double-up with no way of finding the next one or of calling to explain my predicament. I eventually found my way home and enquired why they felt they needed to do this; did those electrical leads plugged into my dashboard look like useless rubbish, perhaps discarded

Happy Meal toys? They actually clung onto the tidying excuse and said ludicrous things like, 'Oh well, you're welcome' and 'Perhaps you should've checked someone hadn't removed them from your car before you set off?' Of course, silly me. Should always check that some demented tit hasn't half-inched my most mundane but crucial in-car items.

In the interests of fairness I should point out that I was clearly annoying them as much as they were annoying me. But it's my book not theirs so this point of view will get far less coverage. I was amazed by how much my every action irritated them. And I could occasionally see their point. Like the week I had had thumping headaches, which I handled with my usual stoicism (whining, crying, scratching at doors). I chalked up my symptoms to all the booze, career stagnation and emotional discouragement. But then mum borrowed my car and swiftly returned spluttering and panicked, as apparently my exhaust was pumping fumes back into my car. I disappointed them for the 30,084th time by admitting I hadn't noticed, but at least I had the good sense to not tell them I'd also been smoking in the flammable guff.

Yes, I was smoking again, because actually, I don't think many people realise but quitting smoking is a bit hard and a total buzz-kill and I thought my life was bad enough without flinging more misery into the mix.

Later that week my last nerve had a chance to grow back because mum and dad had a Night Off. I was surprised gravity didn't reverse and pigeons weep blood. My parents have worked seven days a week as long as I've known them and we go way back. Luurtsemas believe that Leisure is only for the ill and benefit cheats. It's a rather shameful thing to do with one's evening; better to announce you spent it watching *Booze Britain* and touching yourself.

They didn't quite know what to do with themselves on this Night Off. They were wearing matching cowboy hats with uncertain looks on their faces, like 'this is rer-laxing, right? I'm sure this is how people on the telly do it.' Bless them, they looked mentally ill. I didn't even know they had cowboy hats.

I drove them to their friends' house and stayed to chat for a bit, reassured that it seemed to be a fancy-dress party. Or all their friends had lost their minds. Eventually some hard glares from mum reminded me they'd probably gone there for a good old bitch about me and, if I stayed, this was going to get awkward. Fair enough, so I loaded up a pocket with nibbles and headed out the door. I hoped they were going to have a nice time. When I said goodbye dad already seemed bored, he was staring at a napkin on his knee like it had started talking to him.

Their friends had made some bold snack choices and mum was nibbling on a wasabi pea with a look of terror on her face. ('Honestly, Hilary, I don't think it's food, check the packet!')

'They are food,' I assured them from my pulpit of urbane knowledge, 'they are Japanese.'

Dad nodded, 'Yes, they are. They're made with English mustard.'

I wanted to discuss this but I was parked on double yellow lines. Pick your battles . . . We arranged I would pick them up later. It was nice to be useful to them while I was home, it made me feel good, though dad with typical gratitude phrased the request like this:

'Now can you stay sober so you can pick us up later?'

'Yes, of course. I said I would.'

'That means NO drinking, not even red wine, can you do that?'

'YES.'

'Or beer, not even beer.'

'I am not an alcoholic.'

'That's what an alcoholic would say.'

'It's also what a non-alcoholic would say, because it's true. I am not a necrophile. Is that what a necrophile would say?'

'. . . Are you drunk already?'

I drove home and sat in the driveway looking at the house. When my parents go out in the evening they turn on a reading light upstairs and the toilet light downstairs. This is to deter burglars by showing them that there's definitely someone home. Though presumably someone who was having a nice read and then became stricken with Bowelaggedon and spent the rest of the evening held hostage in the toilet by their dicky guts. If someone with stomach cramps, pants round their ankles and a finger in their Anthony Trollope deters you as a burglar, I suspect your heart's not in the job any more.

But I noticed that evening that they were performing this elaborate charade despite me assuring them I'd be home all night. I was being babysat by the fake book-reading shitter, I didn't count as a full, legitimate person; I was on a par with the houseplants. I was trying to stay chipper in my quasi-homeless state but this was a discouraging revelation, especially after a recent promotion had swelled my saggy self-esteem.

There was a cat in the neighbourhood who had found the weak spot in our cat flap (i.e. that dad installed it and it lives up to its name by being a flap that any cat can use). This ingenious feline kept sneaking into the house, slapping our cats about and eating their food. Then urinating hither and thither. The last action was indefensible – I could see how the rest of it was fun, but the urine was just unseemly. So whenever mum and dad went out I was tasked with listening out for him and chasing him away. (Another skill for the CV.)

Of course, I had no intention of chasing him away because he was the only thing in this house messier than me. I had tasted one-up-from-the-lowest status and got giddy on the altitude. That cat could wee wherever he wanted, I'd yell encouragement from the (dark-coloured) sofa. A little social climbing was worth the risk of stepping in a puddle.

Entering the house I realised that not only was I not trusted to look after the house, it was not prepared to take care of me. It was sweltering hot. And there was nothing I could do about it as I have been forbidden to touch the boiler since the mid-nineties. I always want to, as part of a twenty-year argument with dad that Central

Heating Is For Wimps. I agree that maybe that is so, but I've never pretended I wasn't a wimp, so perhaps now it's time to turn the heating on and remember what our legs feel like?

When I first came home I staged a protest against the chilly conditions by working in bed, relaxing in bed, getting dressed in bed . . . Essentially I gave my everyday activities the veneer of a moral high ground. And it would appear that dad had taken the hint and retaliated with a frankly sarcastic level of heat. I popped on my Watford FC sweatbands and sat tight, hoping that they weren't trying to cook me. They were trying lots of new hobbies that year. I hoped when dad had put his foot down at swing-dancing, mum hadn't compromised with Human Flesh: One To Feed Two.

I was starting to get nervous every time my parents went out because they always returned home with new gripes. I worried they were just driving one junction down the M25 to brainstorm in the Little Chef.

'Her breathing is weird, it bothers me.'

'Can we blame her for it?'

'Well, we can but try!'

'Quick, back in the car!'

One day, while they were at work, I had been timidly foraging for biscuits and spotted some meat in the kitchen. 'Well,' I thought, 'best leave THAT well alone.' In the kitchen I am treated like an elderly nuclear warhead with worrying rust so I try to spend very little time in there and spend that time with my hands plunged deep in my pockets.

Hours later, I had written some new stand-up 'bits' and finished off a radio script, and was feeling pretty proud. Until mum and dad burst through the front door, the cats went into hysterics as if finally my regime of terror was over, and everyone looked at me like the lazy slug I clearly was.

As a kid, mum would never let me stay home from school if I felt ill, I had to SHOW ill. The body fluid was mine to choose, but I had to demonstrate a socially unacceptable volume of it. Ten years later she was pursuing the same rule, this time with my work; they never believed I was working unless they could see something. And things on my laptop didn't count as mum considers anything inside a computer to be vaguely unreal.

Mum sat down. 'Wee-eell,' she sighed.

My scalp prickled. She was going to be annoying, she was determined to be annoying, this 'Wee-eell' was just her selecting the topic on which to be annoying. She was browsing the Buffet of Twattishness, licking her lips, fork in hand.

'Wee-eell. You could've made us dinner Natalie.'

'But I didn't know what time you were coming home, or if you wanted dinner.'

'Still . . .'

'No! No "Still . . ." If you wanted me to make dinner all you had to do was call and ask.'

'Shouldn't have to ask . . .'

'Yes! Yes you fucking should! What do you EXPECT me to do, make a roast dinner on the off-chance? It's not sweets at Halloween, you can't stop by and grab a cold parsnip later! Look me in the eye and swear that if you had come home at eight o'clock and I'd presented you with a congealed roast dinner that I'd cooked at five on the off-chance you might be home for it, you wouldn't have yelled at me. Go on, do it. Now!'

She couldn't do it, she knew she was wrong and was forced to make a rare retreat from battle. I resolved to barricade the front door in future and refuse to let her in until she'd unloaded all her Annoying on the front porch.

I wanted to do the same to dad, but he liked to lay out his Annoying in front of the television. If I drove him somewhere, he'd go all monosyllabic and restrict conversation to pointing out 'fabulous' trees. But park that man in front of the television and suddenly it was like watching with audio subtitles for the blind, if they'd recruited a raving loon during the BBC strikes. He did it all: mocking hats, greeting lead characters of shows he's watched for years with 'Who's THAT guy?!' and pointing out jokes as if they'd crept in accidentally.

'I'm sure that's deliberate Dad.'

'Pshaw, Natalie, you're so NAIVE.'

'I hate you.'

But just when I was starting to think 'sixteen weeks, so that's the limit of time we can spend together. Well. Good to know . . .' Mum pulled something adorable from somewhere unexpected. (Metaphorically.)

We both love to buy party dresses at knockdown prices. I have a burgundy, full-length ball skirt, bought for eight pounds when we were rummaging through the ashes of Clements. Mum and I marvelled at the quality and agreed, 'It's SUCH a useful thing to have.' We sighed with relief; now, when I get invited to a ball I won't have a panicked race around the shops tugging at taffeta. I'll have the perfect thing at my fingertips and not only that, I'll be able to twirl around the dance floor, chanting 'Eight quuuuiiiid!' over my lucky partner's shoulder.

Reader, I've never worn it. I've never been invited to a ball. The closest I ever got was a heckle in Kent about testicles and there's no need to dwell on that. The skirt sits in my wardrobe year after year and, although it is exciting to know I have it for when I need it, I'm getting anxious that the day an invitation finally drops on the mat, dramatic irony will come a'knocking, I'll lose my hips in a lawnmower accident and the skirt will mock me still.

Mum does the same, she has a few dresses bought in the sales for an impressively small amount, just hanging in her wardrobe, waiting. That night, dad had demanded to know 'what these dresses are waiting for?!' And mum had squirmed and looked a little guilty, which she never does because she is always right, about everything.

Dad and I exchanged looks, mentally placing bets on what she'd done: Adultery? Regicide?

'They're for when I go to Natalie's premiere,' she confessed, suddenly very interested in her cardigan buttons. My throat felt too big for my neck. How incredibly touching (if a bit presumptuous). Obviously, I'd like a premiere, who wouldn't? I like a nice bit of carpet, plus there's all that attention and waving. I only get that when I forget to turn my headlights on.

It's just . . . I didn't know what she thought I'd premiere. I'm a stand-up comic, my new jokes just sort of pop out without much fanfare. In their early stages jokes tend to be a bit stumbling and mutely received, certainly nothing you'd want to dress up for. If anything, tit tape would pile on the pressure when I was trying to feel my way through a new 'bit'.

I had zero things to premiere. I had stuck with the same margarine for quite a while, maybe it was time to mix it up a bit, debut a new one? Even the laziest churnalist was unlikely to bother us for quotes: 'Is it butter? It isn't?! Well, I am incredulous . . .'

Perhaps I should've just hired us a red carpet to sashay down in our bargain dresses, one that led to a nearby bus stop or Wagamama's, so we could finally scratch the itch. Mum would probably enjoy a Wagamama's more than sitting through some comedy. She didn't really like comedy: 'Bit needy isn't it? Always trying to make people laugh.' To which I'd make a scoffing noise and roll my eyes as if she hadn't said something crushingly perceptive. Whenever I meet an arrogant comic (I know, I thought they were a myth too), I amuse myself by thinking 'four minutes with my mum and you'd be trying to find the nearest Temping Agency through your tears'.

Mum was also a little fixated on Wagamama's. Whenever you brought up the subject of eating out, she'd sigh wistfully, 'No one's ever taken me to Wagamama's . . .' She started saying this a few years ago, without ever giving us the chance to take her in a non-resentful atmosphere of 'Oh finally!' So now we will not take her. She bangs on about it so much we'd call it Nagamamas if we were a more 'Let's Play Charaaades!' sort of family, but we're not.

If you pun around my parents they react like you've curled out a fresh one on the hall rug. For a Dutchman and a dyslexic woman, language is a functional tool to be used responsibly, and

wordplay is just running with scissors. As a child I had to beg for
Alphabetti Spaghetti.

You might think it's cruel we won't take her to Wagamama's:

'Come on Nat,' you're probably tutting: 'She works hard for
you guys, why not treat her?'

To which I say, 'You naive fool!' She got so much more pleasure
out of whingeing than she'd ever get from eating noodles. And
deep down, really deep down, she knew this. This family loved
her too much to deprive her of the joy she got from sighing, 'Well,
I wouldn't know about tofu, Hilary, no one's ever taken me to
Wagamama's.'

I'm probably the same. The day that burgundy eight-quid
delight is finally upon my waist and I'm gliding off to a ball will
be such an anti-climax. In one perfectly pleasant evening I'll have
been robbed of years of joyful anticipation.

Sometimes, in the middle of the night I'll put it on and glide
around in it, or just sit and work in it so I feel like a princess
while I write jokes about poo. (Oh shut up, it's a living. Barely.) I
can't see how a jerky waltz could be more fun than stroking the
skirt's shiny folds and gloating, 'One day, my Sweet, one day we
will dance together while I yell your price above the live band and
other girls hit themselves in the face with canapés because they
spent over a hundred pounds on a skirt that doesn't swish half as
loudly as you.' And that's a great feeling: competitive, aggressive,
yet feminine.

That night I stuck the skirt on as there was nothing good on TV. I
pranced around a bit but it was too hot for silk formalwear, really,
so I stripped off down to nothing but the skirt and Watford FC
sweatbands and settled down to work. I woke up in darkness to
mum and dad standing over me, dad with eyes averted.

'Thank you ever so much for our lift,' they chorused (they had
clearly rehearsed this in the taxi). 'So nice of you to stay sober
and awake long enough to drive us back from one of our many
nights off.'

Sometimes I could see why I annoyed them so much. I covered my modesty with a cushion and attempted to apologise but my apology got shoved right back where it came from and they continued the heavy sarcasm. They probably enjoyed the character assassination more than an actual lift. Actually, that's it, they loved being in the right, I had simply gifted them more joy by cocking up yet again!

I didn't share this thought with them, I just rustled up to bed, congratulating myself on understanding them so well and finding the less obvious ways of making them happy. Between stranding them late at night, not cooking them dinner, not moving out and not taking them to Wagamamas, I really was the perfect daughter.

Chapter 14

NAT'S USUAL

Luckily I was going away the next day, so all the ill will could dissipate in my absence. I had three gigs up north and was looking forward to time away from the bickering co-dependency of home. But by the second day I was so lonely I drove to the nearest shopping centre just to be around people. I couldn't find anywhere to park and trundling my car in via the piazza, nudging shoppers aside, seemed a bit rude, even for The North (I'm joking . . .). I parked on some wasteland, ignoring my mum's voice in my head identifying this as the sort of place big men settled disputes with iron bars. I didn't care, so long as they didn't dent the Yaris.

I love my car, it's a beige Toyota Yaris Verso – the number one car of choice for the elderly and disabled. Fact. Google it, treat yourself. Now gaze upon it. The word you're reaching for is 'aerodynamic'. As in, 'this car could not be any less . . .'. I call it the Golden Sex Box.

As I abandoned my beloved car on a mysterious piece of wasteland, I couldn't quite shake the feeling I'd done one of those stupid things my parents call 'Nat's Usual'. I'd given five quid to a completely mute Indian man standing nearby who had never actually declared ownership of the concrete-chunk-studded wastel beyond waving 'back a bit' when I was parking. And surely, if this wasteland was yours, you'd make some fuss, let people know of your good fortune.

Four hours later, I staggered out of the gigantic Arndale Centre, uncertain if I was still in the same time zone, let alone near my wasteland. I considered following big men with iron bars, hoping we had the same destination, if not the same evening plans, but the risks outweighed the hope. I wandered desperately around Manchester for an hour, until it started to rain and I realised that in my rush to check out of my hotel that morning I hadn't rinsed all the shampoo out of my hair. It was raining gently and my head was starting to bubble. A downpour would turn me into an effervescing Alka Seltzer. My parents hadn't predicted this specific example of a 'Nat's Usual' but I was haunted by the thought of their sarcasm.

Just as I was beginning to mutter to myself about how this was All Their Fault, Really, I turned a corner and actually walked into my car. In my relief I didn't feel the pain on my knee, but days later mum pointed out the bruise with characteristic sympathy: 'Oh for God's sake, what have you done now?' I smiled blandly in her face and thought, 'If only you knew, you'd be so much more annoyed.'

I was so glad I didn't have to admit what I'd done, I was dreading that more than the loss of my car. I hate confirming their low expectations of me, which is why I usually lie at first, confess to something far worse, then when I reveal the truth I expect their irritation to be overwhelmed by relief. This tactic has NEVER worked, but I stick by it, I'm convinced it'll work one day, justifying years of conversations like this:

'Surprise! I'm pregnant and I have absolutely no idea who the father is!'

(PARENTAL CHOKING NOISE)

'I have a longlist, but it totally lives up to its name if yaknowhaddamean.'

(MORE CHOKING)

'Mmm, yes, life's rich tapestry and all that ... But I'm not worried about the birth as I smoke heavily, so its head should be manageably small.'

(Some gargling, the sound of two people punching the floor)

'Surprise! I was lying, hurray! No actually, all that's happened is I've spilt tea in your bed. Not the drink, the evening meal, but stiiill . . .'

I accept that my parents' low expectations aren't down to their inability to see how awesome I am, they have been established through years of poor decision-making. If you're reading this at a young age, take note.[11] My advice to you is to screw up your teens, even your twenties if you really get a taste for it, because everything afterwards will look fine in comparison. I have made a mess of my life so many times someone should follow me with a swannee whistle. Number one, we'll come to. Here's number two, to limber you up.

When I was twenty-one I started flopping about between shitty temp jobs like a suffocating fish. I didn't know what I wanted to do, although each job taught me that I didn't want *that* job, which I suppose narrowed the search down a little.

At one point I worked underground in a windowless office with eleven co-workers, in a space so small we fitted together like Tetris. One of my colleagues enjoyed this too much and I spent most lunch breaks evading his attempts to recreate the morning's position.

My job was to file parking tickets; I basically alphabetised misery. The office walls were caked in photos from outraged motorists, of their car wheels only just touching double yellow lines. Our only glimpse of the outside world was in Reception where we made a mockery of the word. We would simply receive hatred. Angry people came and yelled at us through a greasy square of bulletproof glass smeared by a thousand jabbing fingers. We had no useful advice to give; we earned our mini-mum wage through politeness in the face of this bukkake

---

11 (I'm well aware I'm preaching amidst the rubble of my adulthood so you don't need to point it out, thank you cheeky yoots.)

of rage. You'd think this situation would foster some grim camaraderie between us, you'd be a hopeless optimist; the room practically hummed with hatred.

The Law of Temping swung into action, which is that verily, if thou hatest the temp job it shall be offered to you on a permanent basis, with your hatred of it in direct proportion to the speed of the offer. My supervisor was a woman whom Life hadn't kicked in the face yet but she was sure it would.

I said that I was very sorry I couldn't take the job because 'what I really wanted', I said, cursing my vagueness, 'was a job that made me excited!'

'I understand,' she cooed, 'but that's never going to happen, is it? Is it.'

'No, Helen.'

'And this is.'

It was a dispiriting time, but I dealt with it in my usual inimitable style. I'd get home from work an hour earlier than everyone else and have a little Me Time, spending that hour holding two bags of frozen peas to my face and sobbing uncontrollably. I'd bring matters to a close when dehydration cemented my tongue to my gums, then wrap things up with some shuddering hiccups, down tools and watch three hours of *Buffy the Vampire Slayer* repeats with a face frozen into serenity. And everything was fine, because I looked fine and that is almost exactly the same thing.

This went on for about eight months until one day I bought a plane ticket to New York on a credit card that some junk mail thought I deserved. (Who was I to question its judgment?) My plan was to stay with a friend In The Big Apple for a month and hope that my shitty life improved in my absence. I was clearly not helping, so maybe if I left it to its own devices it would sort itself the fuck out.

On arrival I was immediately comforted by the discovery that my friend's life was in worse shape than mine! Sadly her suffering became mine, as she was actually, technically homeless. Mi casa-lessness es su casa-lessness! This was fine, she'd thought, as now she could stay with me in my hotel room. The hotel room I could not afford, as I'd been working on the assumption that she'd have a sofa/floor/sink for me to curl up in. Any emotional comfort this discovery brought me was dwarfed by the physical discomfort dancing in attendance.

This was bad enough, but we didn't have this crucial chat until about 3am, when we were sitting near Central Park swigging from a hilariously large bottle of cheap red (Paisano's Wine it was called. Our language skills and taste buds translated it accurately). The bottle held four litres of the bad stuff and whenever we tipped it up to swig, the momentum of four litres would overwhelm our trembling arms and send it splashing onto our heads. We wore more wine than we drank; I found some down my back the next morning.

We embraced the situation with minimal fuss and sat on a hillock choking under a deluge of acidic red and then sucking it out of our hair. This was amusing us no end and we passed a couple of happy hours with red-stained heads, faces and shoulders, looking like a pair of cheery homicide victims whose joie de vivre would *not* be quashed by a head wound.

By the time we'd seen off three litres we started sneezing vinegar. At this point one of us sighed contentedly, sensing the close of an excellent night:

'Let's go home.'

'Let's,' agreed the other.

A heavy silence fell. After a few minutes of stilted chat we'd established that we were in the company of a hefty fuck-up. At this point six men approached us from the shadows.

'Hey there,' they said.

('This is SO New York!' I gloated, the Paisano's Wine really numbing me to any troubling details of this scenario.)

'We're staying in a squat in Brooklyn,' they continued, oozing cool everywhere, while wine dribbled out of my nose. 'If you've got nowhere to stay, come stay there.'

At this point you'd be forgiven for assuming this story ends in rape and the theft of my shoes. I would've thought so too, frankly, but it was cold and, as I announced to my new best friends, I felt confident I could fight them all while my old best friend ran the wine to a safe location.

Thankfully this was unnecessary. They were the most hospitable gentlemen ever, considering the lack of running water or electricity. ('So you can sleep on my coat if you want, and we wee in this.') The next day they took me and my Mary Poppins accent to make some food-based inquiries. You could call it begging but I had such a genteel way of doing it that my benefactors invariably thanked me, as I took yet another bothersome pizza off their hands. It's good to know I have this useful skill in my arsenal, especially given the rickety nature of my life decisions. My only regret was embarking on four weeks without a wash, right after I'd showered in red wine. I looked like a strangely alert zombie for days.

I made several attempts to contact mum and dad, but no matter what sort of PR spin I gave the situation, it was always going to yield worrying postcards: 'Look at the size of this rat!' 'Can you believe I found this in a bin?!' 'Here's my new friend, Screamy Pete' (elderly punk and a lovely man, though he earnt his nickname).

Set your personal standards this low and, so long as they don't give up too soon and ship you off to military school, your parents' expectations will rarely be disappointed. Despite my lethal spilling around the pale-coloured sofa, my inability to load a dishwasher properly and the way I slammed doors 'like an animal', after my previous behaviour they found all this a relief. So I believe firmly, start your life messy, improve slowly, only achieve dignity at forty.

I'm sorry if this prompts a generation of teens to have sex up trees and wear roadkill as hats, but honestly, by twenty-seven your parents will be so quiveringly grateful you've finally put your pants on that all subsequent life choices will be greeted with bunting.

I drove home from Manchester realising I'd really missed mum and dad and I was looking forward to seeing them and regaling them with (edited highlights of) my trip. Oh wonderful, I brooded, look at me 'enjoying their company' like some sort of twat. Might as well reattach the umbilical cord now, at least it'll save me money on food. I remembered a time when it was Craine I looked forward to coming home to, that was much better, there was cigarettes and sex. But it seemed those days were gone and now I was racing home to hot chocolate from a sachet and a lengthy re-cap of what the cats had been up to.

I got home late but thankfully they were still up. I hated creeping up to bed through a sleeping house. I don't need jubilant cries of welcome every time I get home, if I was that emotionally needy I'd get a dog, but it was nice to be acknowledged. It was a fairly tepid homecoming; my tales of The North were interrupted by dad tutting, 'You make a better door than a window' and waggling the remote control at me.

I realised that this was a folksy way of saying, 'You're blocking the telly.' Frankly even if I was transparent no one would want to watch TV through me, with my opaque guts wrestling with service station food.

Not that this would've altered the tone of their evening's viewing, as they were yet again watching the corpse of a young woman being dug out of a wood. Crime plus gardening – the perfect marriage of their interests. I settled down to join the usual debate:

'I'm sure we've seen this one before.'

'We haven't!'

'We have. Look, this guy, he's about to lose his rag and punch this guy in the interview room . . . See?!'

This is a fiddly argument to have over a genre that is unapologetically formulaic. You always feel like you've seen them all before and of course you can guess what will happen next, and yes, it is oddly reassuring to watch man's inhumanity to man while you eat your dinner.

It was addling my mind to come home every night to scenes of gruesome butchery and violent depravity, I was starting to feel like Patrick Bateman in *American Psycho*, except worse cos at least he had lots of sex. My mind was slowly putrifying in a soup of body parts, rapists and handsome American men. I was sure the psychological damage would be manifesting itself for years to come, look out for me in the newspapers next year! On some sort of 'spree' or 'rampage.' Either way, I thought, nice to be out of the house, especially if it was still this house.

Once the show finished ('I told you he was the killer. We saw it a week ago.' 'Oh shuddup.') a new episode started and the debate swung into life again:

'I recognise that rapist. Or is he off *Criminal Minds*?' and I resolved to gig every night while living at home. I bet everyone would work longer hours if the alternative were to come home to this. Are hardworking successful people just the ones cursed with a horrible home life? The evidence is certainly presenting itself. Poor Stephen King, god knows what he goes home to. Meanwhile I forgot my woes in a bottle of red that dad had declared suitably substandard for me. It made me nostalgic for the paisano vintage.

Chapter 15

I'M HORNSEY, HORNSEY, HORNSEY, HORNSEY

I woke up the next morning with the sort of hangover only £3.99 wine can give you. I had a troubling memory of mum shushing me, which I took as a very bad sign, she never shushes drunks, she's got a very liberal policy on things that pissed people want to say. One of her mates has a joke about cunnilingus that I WISH mum would shush, but in ten years she never has. I was forced to assume that I was spouting remarks worse than '... the dentist said no, but you've got pubes in your teeth!' (Boozy cackles.) What could possibly have been worse than that? I fretted into my pillow. I have always operated on the theory that you can't get drunk if you drink with your parents, but the last four months were piddling all over that idea.

I'm not a good drunk – booze just inflates my self-delusion until my self-awareness suffocates beneath it. I remember saying to a friend once, 'I know some people are twatty when they're drunk but it just makes ME nicely confident!'

'Yes,' she agreed grimly, 'I can see that you think that. Now climb down from there.'

Dad on the other hand is an excellent drunk, much more fun drunk than sober. I've encouraged him to have a problem, I think he would be a joy at parties, but he's reluctant to swap a decent life for the chilly embrace of the gutter just to amuse me. Once at a party he had done his usual trick and started serving everyone drinks, so everyone thought he was the barman and wouldn't expect him to do small talk.

It always works, even at parties where you think, 'But there are seven of us crammed into a small lounge, WHY would they have hired a barman? Plus he's drunk.' Leaning against dad's 'bar', a man spilt a little white wine down his shirt. 'Don't worry,' dad consoled him, 'I know what gets that out,' and flung a glass of red over him. That party vibe swiftly soured.

Back to my night of shame, I had a vague memory of telling the room (quite literally, I remember addressing the mantelpiece with my back to mum and dad) that I was getting tactically drunk, as a prelude to my day off. A slightly spurious notion when you're self-employed, but I liked to be a nice boss to myself, to make up for sleazing on myself at last year's Christmas karaoke.

'What time?' mum had demanded, in the sort of tone usually emitted three feet above a pair of leather jodhpurs with a crop dangling beside. 'What time should I wake you up?'

I politely ignored this. I also chose to ignore her when she tried to wake me up at eight the next morning. That took a lot more effort but I had the upper hand in that she had to be at work in twenty minutes and I didn't, so I could play the long game. The long game was essentially lying still and kicking her whenever she got near enough.

I needed rest. I was a mess. My back hurt, my legs were stiff and while my hair lacked body, my body did not lack hair. I resolved that if I could get myself upright I would attempt some damage-limitation beautification. Not that there was much point, as mum and dad were proving themselves to be the world's most reliable contraceptive. They never said Craine and I couldn't have sex in their house, all they said was they wouldn't knock before entering my room. This sort of high-risk atmosphere was leading to panicky sex and people getting scratched.

So I was lying in bed, broken and wounded, when mum called

to say in her usual telephone voice (painfully loud and brisk, like I'm a Bad Dog chewing on a child), 'If you're bored . . .'

'I'll stop you there,' I said in my most repressive tones (and they're pretty fucking repressive, as you'll know if you've ever tried to invite me to a musical). I continued, 'I am not bored. I am enjoying a well-earned rest. Frankly, I'm only using the toilet as a courtesy, at this point I don't feel obligated.'

Mum: 'Well, you could always come and help us move furniture into the new classrooms at school.'

Nat: 'Today everyone who isn't me can bog off.' And in this spirit I continued to have my day of rest. Which involved zero furniture removal, funnily enough. I spent a couple of hours reading a brilliant book on etymology and learnt a lot about Pennsylvania Dutch. Look, roll your eyes all you want, I am who I am, I made my peace with it years ago, I suggest you get on board the Resignation Train. Choo choo.

Pennsylvania Dutch is an amazingly specific language: 'dachdrops' is the word for rain drops, but only those dripping from a roof; 'aagehaar' is an eyelash that grows inward and irritates your eye. I love words like this, it always annoys me when the OED lets in new words every year that mean something we already have bare words for (now there's a word that will be forgotten within a year. 'Bare' may already mean nothing to you, you may be squinting at it thinking, 'I know this word, but what's it doing here? Stupid Nat.' No, stupid OED).

Now I want a word for when you walk into a room and get the pocket of your cardigan caught on the door handle and it jerks you back, meaning you enter a room briefly, then ping backwards out of it again, which is amusing to witnesses but not the victim as, between your desperate struggles to enter the room and anxiety for the wellbeing of your cardigan, you're in no fit state to join in the merriment. That happens to me all the time and I want a concise word to save me time while I'm picking a door handle out of my frayed knitwear.

While I slumped in bed admiring words, the housing market

had woken up in a puddle of dribble, so Craine and Tiernan were back house hunting. The word 'exhaustive' wouldn't do our house hunting justice, we'd reached a point whenever we travelled in London we could point down most roads, murmuring 'Seen it, seen it, seen it' like a sort of property slut. I wish there was something useful we could've done with all the information we accumulated. All we did was bore our dwindling ranks of friends with it. Perhaps we should have set up a service to warn other house hunters of the ones it's just not worth leaving your sofa to go see? Nah, sod it. The milk of human kindness had curdled in my heart and my ribs bulged with the rancid cheese of resentment.

We had been misled by photos time and time again. It was amazing how big a poky room could look if photographed from the right angle. It became my first priority whenever I entered a new flat. 'There, I think,' I'd say, pointing at the edge of the ceiling, spotting a footprint on the coving, ignoring Tiernan's attempts to make me look at the kitchen. 'That's where they took this one from.'

Estate agents and landlords must have been bringing stepladders and ropes to do this properly, in some cases they'd clearly stood outside and poked a camera through a window. It was clever but I wished they'd just be honest.

At that point, if an estate agent had got in touch to say, 'I've got a flat, it's overpriced, shit bit of town, grotty kitchen but every room has a window,' I would've hopped on the train excitedly, so why did they insist on lying? It was just a waste of their adjectives, we'd been doing this for so many months we knew what 'reasonable'/'compact'/'good transport links' meant: a tiny rotting nook perched precariously over a motorway for a grand a month and YES, thank you, we would go look at it, braced for the high risk that some other desperate bastard would have offered on it before we got there.

On my day off I couldn't face any more of this and I was staying in bed. After I'd finished learning about words, I then found

Kanye West's new album leaked online. And sweet Jesus, that combination of mainstream rap and mild law-breaking made me feel cool, so I thought I'd have a listen. I'll admit, it was out of character but I already had my headphones in and I like Kanye – I always say the wrong thing at parties and then everyone hates me, so I warm towards a kindred spirit. I thought the album was pretty good (you can have that quote Kanye, you're welcome). As a non-music fan, I enjoyed the fact that there was so MUCH else going on: noises, sounds, yelling.

I invariably get bored of songs halfway through and think, 'yeah yeah, you've already said that'. I have been informed that this is 'a chorus', but to me it smacks of laziness. During one of Kanye's songs there was a strange rasping sound, which seemed odd but I was humble enough to acknowledge that I was not an expert. Raspy noises were the new thing in rap, it would appear.

Or not, as ten minutes later I finished listening to the album and stepped out of my bedroom, to find cat vomit everywhere, in frankly mind-boggling amounts. I expected to see one of the cats lying deflated in a corner of the room like a whizzed-out balloon. It at least answered the question, no Kanye West was not pioneering a new raspy noise in rap. Actually, if we're being honest, the Kanye West quip took about eight minutes to appear in my head. I'm pathologically terrified of vomit and so my first response was silent screaming terror and heart-flutters.

I picked my way through the vomit without looking at it or treading on it (this was tricky, but after seven years in London I've perfected the art of orienteering around pavement pizza without actually seeing it). Then I left the house. Where was I going? No idea, just anywhere AWAY from the vomit. It was purely coincidental that I was dressed – I would've left in nothing but socks and a watch if I had to. Then I made a difficult phone call:

'Hello mum. When you get home there'll be sick everywhere.'

'I see.' (Mum does a good Heavy Silence, she's known for it.)

'Right, it's not my sick. It's YOUR cat's sick. I'm blameless.

But also, I concede, useless. I'm neutral, just pretend I never came home last night.'

'Can you clean it up?'

'I can't approach it without retching and swooning.'

'Sigh.'

'I'm sorry. I did try to throw a piece of kitchen towel over it but obviously as I couldn't look at it, it was a little hard to aim. It might've landed on it, but there's no guarantee. If anything, it's probably just pointing at it. Sorry.'

I didn't feel like I'd aced that situation, but Life was playing me on my weakest point there. If the cat had asked me questions about 18th- to 21st-century novels I'd be elbows-deep in it right now, excelling. But the cat has never done that. Stupid, useless puking cat.

Stranded outside the house I thought I might as well give up on this Day Off and I called Tiernan and Craine to join their house hunting misery. They were seeing flats in Hornsey, north London. This was an area we knew little about except that it was fun to sing 'I'm Hornsey, Hornsey Hornsey Hornsey' softly in the estate agents. The flat I was heading towards had no photos but it was big and cheap and we were desperate enough to hope for the best. The best never arrived.

It was a sign of how few places were available that we invariably viewed flats in an undignified scrum with other house hunters. Technically, they were our competitors for a home, but they felt more like fellow-sufferers. Our brother-in-arms in this skirmish was a sad-eyed young man who said he'd been looking for two months so far. We nodded sympathetically.

'Four,' we said, our subtext being, 'We have suffered longer. If this flat is nice, we deserve it more.'

However, those four months had taught me that when the estate agent has to fling their body against the front door to open it, abandon hope all ye who enter here. And so we did, we left it in the stairwell where we were sure it would be nicked.

'This flat hasn't been empty for years,' boasted the estate agent.

Clearly, it was the sort of place that inspired inertia and a general unwillingness to move; the most loyal tenant being the mould spore. There was mould everywhere; it made the walls look squashy. Which gave the flat a surreal wonkiness, it was like a guided tour around the film *Labyrinth*.

There was also an unacceptable amount of pants, I couldn't imagine who would own that many. I counted the bedrooms, I counted the pants; the ratio was obscenely imbalanced. I feared I had strayed into the abode of the pant-eating men, or perhaps devout virgin Christians who wore three pairs of pants every day in case of Woman Attack. Fat chance boys, with pants that unappealing. When I know I've got someone coming round, the plumber, the BT repair man, anyone, I have a bit of a tidy up, scoop the bras out of the bookcase. I had to assume these tenants lacked that impulse, or face the horrible possibility that this flat had looked worse before a quick tidy-up.

The kitchen looked like a computer game character had tried to cook a Sunday roast but the player had only found the Kick and Punch buttons. We all peered through the doorway as if into a crime scene. Someone had to say something, something polite, godammit! We are British; it is what we do.

'Compact?' offered up Craine.

Good enough, we all nodded and ducked out. Through the kitchen window we spotted a moulding shoe sat forlornly outside. Trapped inside this shithole, we envied it.

The sad-eyed boy giggled his way around the flat with us (whenever the estate agent wasn't looking, we're not monsters) especially when we reached the bathroom. The ceiling in there was spongy with black mould, but that was okay, that was fine, the estate agent assured us; it occurred ONLY because there were three showers a day in here and inadequate ventilation to handle this. The three of us stared at him, waiting for him to put one and two together, and wondering why he thought the situation would be different for us? Did we look the sort to shower together?

At this point the five heads poked around the bathroom door all swivelled left. Something demanded attention: a smear on the shower curtain. An unambiguous smear. Someone had actually wiped their bum on the shower curtain. What sort of animal does that? I'd say, if you're so disgusted by your living conditions, how about cleaning up instead of leaping straight to a dirty protest? I bet dirty protests are statistically the most regretted protests; few situations are ever improved by faecal decor.

And if this wasn't a dirty protest, we had to assume the current tenants saw EVERYTHING as toilet paper. That explained why the shoe was outside, clearly if they brought it inside it would run the risk of wiping. The right shoe was probably gone, dragged across a tenant's arse weeks ago (amazing he'd found his arse beneath all the pants) but there was still hope for Young Lefty they'd cried in a rare salient moment and thrown him to safety out of the kitchen window. I presumed everything valuable, like laptops and pictures of loved ones, were perched safely on the roof.

We all remembered that we had Jury Duty in four minutes and had to leave NOW. We staggered out of the flat laughing at its horribleness, until I realised Sad-Eyed Boy wasn't with us. I panicked; maybe some aggressive mould had grabbed him? He was only small. I bravely launched myself back in on a rescue mission, only to find him *discussing terms* with the estate agent.

His poor flatmates: 'I've found us a flat guys!'

'Hurray!'

'Now, hands up if you're a fan of David Bowie? No? How about group showers, you like them, right Kim?'

It was upsetting to see that much desperation. I hovered to give him a stern look but he kept angling his head to evade eye contact. I circled him a bit, he rotated, the estate agent talked throughout this impromptu polka. Eventually I left him to his foolish decision and I stomped off. Not too hard, didn't want the building caving in on me like a wet meringue.

We hummed a subdued verse of 'Hornsey, Hornsey, Hornsey' then trooped off home, saying things no one nearing their thirties should say:

'Mum's got a lasagna on, so I'd better . . .'

'Yeah, I said I'd sort through some boxes in my dad's shed . . .'

'Cool, I'm going home to cry in the bath.' (That one was me, I don't have limitless reserves of Stoicism.) I wasn't sure how or why but my much-anticipated day off ended with me trudging home, chaperoned by a clinging damp smell. I then spent ten minutes hovering on the doorstep yelling through the letterbox, 'Is the sick gone? Can I come in or is there still sick? Hello?!' before mum came home and I realised I'd just been yelling at sick. My parents were right; days off were for benefit cheats. I vowed to never attempt one again.

Chapter 16

THE LUURTSEMAS Vs THE WORLD

At the end of my fifth month back home, my brother came to stay. Last time he visited he stayed with me in London, I took him to a few comedy gigs, then out for cocktails . . . pretty cool big sister stuff. This year, things would be a little different. I straightened the tins so they all faced forward and hoped he wouldn't mention it.

Michael can only come home for a fortnight a year, so while he's back he gets a desperate breathless urge to Make Memories. He's ludicrously sentimental, just like mum, she's the only person I've ever met who scours supermarket birthday cards, carefully reading the messages inside until she finds one that exactly sums up how she feels. She can genuinely read one of those trite messages doodled in a curly font and think, 'Yes. That is exactly what I feel.'

I would only feel that if one day I chanced upon a card that read:

'I like you. You're nice, overall.

Although it's unfortunate that I have to crystallise my feelings for you on this arbitrary day as, frankly, you've been a dick lately.

I know work's been hard but you've been a chore these last two months and I resent the birthday dinner we're about to have as I know, I just know, you'll insist we split the bill even though your loud mate who always calls me Natasha will probably have a twenty quid steak on a splat of lobster mousse and the only way to feel like I'm not subsidising a glutton is to have something EVEN more expensive but this is, at best, a Pyrrhic victory and could really escalate until I end up looking like the extravagant one which is so not fair.

Happy Fucking Birthday then.'

I'm not sentimental, the phrase loved ones have used is 'dead inside', which is a bit much but they may be right. Mum is endlessly disappointed by my lack of soft, squashy feelings. Years ago she marched me to the hard shoulder of the M1 to pay my respects to Princess Diana's funeral procession. This is the sort of stuff on which we have very different opinions. It led to a massive fight, conducted in respectful whispers until we lost our voices.

I wasn't being disrespectful, it just was very funny that so many parents had mawkishly brought their small children to a stranger's funeral, handed them flowers, told them to throw them at a hearse and hadn't explained the situation further. It was an unusual scenario! How were ten-year-olds meant to feel their way towards appropriate behaviour without a nudge in the right direction? So their useless blubbing parents had only themselves to blame when their children started hurling their flower missiles at the cars and saying things like, 'Five points for the bonnet! Ten points for the windscreen! Try and get it through the window!'

Thankfully for mum, Michael is on the same (tear-stained, bunny rabbit-decorated) page. With his limited time he'll try to cram as many Special Memories in as possible, which gives me the giddy feeling that time is accelerating. He once said, 'I'll never forget that time at Legoland,' before we'd found our way out of the car park.

I'm the opposite, having 'enjoyed' too much time with our parents, far from savouring it I will squander hours of it demanding they recap a *CSI* episode that I've joined four minutes from the end. I have the same attitude towards our parents that Michael does to the sun. When I visited him in Thailand I flung open the curtains, shrieking with joy to find sunshine there *every single day*, dancing and gleaming just for me and I spent my days basking in its carcinogenic warmth, while he skulked in the shade and mumbled some shit about my moles.

He reassured me that my Month At Home hadn't been the massive waste of time it seemed, as he felt I'd finally learnt how to manage mum and dad. Apparently I'd been stealthily acquiring new skills and was now some sort of Parent Whisperer. To illustrate his point, later that day I had an argument with mum and WON it. That never happens, but that day it happened.

I was giddy on victory for hours till I noticed my crowing and pointing was creating an uncool vibe in the house. Plus the argument was about washing up and was barely worthy of the word 'argument', when there are words like 'ruckus' and 'mild disagreement' lying around.

That said, the episode had ended pretty dramatically with mum hissing, 'You're really fucking me off, you know that?' and me responding, quick as a whip, '**You're** really fucking **me** off, etc. etc. (you can see where this one's going). The look on her face was a treat; it began with 'how **dare** you . . .', followed by the realisation that as I'd just echoed her, this was not a strong point on which to get outraged. I had checkmated her in a game of Diss Chess. An eye-for-an-eye-type disagreement strategy isn't always the violent cul-de-sac it's portrayed as.

Much fol de rol was made for Michael's return, more than I ever bloody got. That's fine, I was resigned to the fact that, with me, familiarity had bred contempt. And by 'familiarity' I meant 'my behaviour, personality and life decisions'. It was an umbrella term.

While he was back, we were on strict instructions to make

home seem incredible and impossible to leave. We had to achieve this mirage with only Watford and the Luurtsema family as our raw materials. You can't polish a turd but mum insisted we roll it in glitter. Hopefully one day I'll earn enough to abandon this charade and just have him kidnapped. Mum has already approved the plan: 'I don't care how miserable he is, so long as he's near.'

I was braced for our reunion, when the four Luurtsemas get together our obnoxious urge to be right about everything intensifies. I'm sure there's a science to it; the behavioural equivalent of nitrogen and glycerin but less welcome at parties. Individually we're all quite pleasant people, I've even witnessed Michael saying to someone, 'Well, you know more about that than me . . .'

He has never said that to me, and I'd honey-trapped him into some pretty me-centric conversations: 'The Weight of My Hair, How My Nose Smells, Menstruation: the Inside Scoop' and other such intriguing delights. He'd always declared himself the expert. The last time I saw him I punched his back in blind rage after he snorted: 'Right, like **that's** an expensive papoose.'

Like all good families, we had to negotiate careful paths around each others' personalities, or go armed to social gatherings. This time around, we attempted the former and spent the first few days in happy reunion, with mum parading Michael around town. Ideally she'd like people of restricted growth to prance merrily behind, waving ribbons, but they never take the hint.

Following my recent Tour of Tedium at mum's school, I felt for my brother as the latest Offspring on Display. It's like being Kate Middleton, who's always pulling fatuous 'just pleased to be here guys!' expressions. I sympathise with her; what do you do when everyone's just delighted that you exist? Of course with us it's not crowds of fervent royalists, but we've still got to decide what to do with our faces.

After four days of fuss I found Michael lying languidly on the sofa. I guessed correctly that he had been introduced to every single person in Watford and had explained his life for the twenty thousandth time. Which will take it out of a chap. Especially because whenever he tells people what he does they always ask 'and what will you do afterwards?' As if this must be a hiatus before he gets down to the serious business of living, because it sounds too pleasant to be one's daily life. I suggested he say he's having problems with his boss. This problem seemed to authenticate his life, people flitted from questioning his existence to giving employment law advice and everyone rubbed along more harmoniously.

Last year Michael cleverly dodged Watford altogether and invited us to go and see him. We packed the tea bags and set off, though truthfully, I'm ambivalent about The World; I'm sure it's nice enough but I've never been anywhere I liked more than Home.

'It's not a competition, Nat,' I hear you sigh.

Of course it is! Everything is arranged in little league tables in my head – from favourite Marks and Spencers sandwiches to Top Ten best seats on the bus. Mum is the same, but far more black and white, she has no Top Tens, just two columns in her mind: Love and Hate. So this holiday to Thailand was playing for high stakes.

Mum hated Blackpool, from the first moment she saw a woman eat chips with gravy on them ('Gravy, Natalie, actual gravy'). Mum reacted as if the woman had set a dog on fire and stamped it into a slice of Mighty White. Then she sulked and a man in a shop teased her with 'Oooo, mardy!', stereotypically camp behaviour that would ordinarily enchant her, but not that day, because She Hated Blackpool. And henceforth this sentiment ran through her like I Hate Blackpool on a stick of misprinted rock.

Now Barcelona, she'll say with childlike breathless glee 'there was nothing I didn't like about it'. She had two nice days there and now would defend it to the hilt even if it turned out to be al-Qaeda's summer hideout. Whereas poor old Blackpool could discover the cure for cancer and mum would make waspish remarks like, 'Really? In some gravy was it?' She is that mythic beast advertisers dream of – a sane adult with Strong Brand Loyalty. She drives a Renault car but someone in a Renault call centre was unhelpful recently, causing her to despise the whole company. By extension she now hates her own car and drives it with a look of long-suffering misery like she's piloting a turd.

Dad loves to travel, though not for the new experiences or broadening the mind. He'll bear these things stoically but, his face seems to say as it points towards a temple, he didn't ask for this. No, he loves the idea that no one can understand what he's saying. It's like that old question, what would you do if you were invisible for a day?

Dad would sit over his inclusive hotel breakfast and talk loudly about the state of his bowels, historically, recently and his hopes for their future. He refuses to listen when you hiss that English is a commonly spoken language or when you beg him to consider that diarrhoea noises are recognised in more places than Travellers' Cheques. He will insist he was just making polite conversation, though that's the very last thing you can call a loud monologue about your bowels. It couldn't be worse unless he gave his colon a racist nickname.

His gastric musings had immediate ammunition, even before we left British airspace, as this holiday began in traditional fashion, with us grimly eating our way through the fridge because dad refused to throw any of it away. Who's up for quiche, mousse and strangely icy lettuce? No one! But we go at it like locusts. To this day I can't get excited about a holiday unless I've had something disgusting for breakfast and as we set off dad narrates the smaller journeys happening within us.

We had a nice holiday, I'm not sure any English-speaking people in our vicinity did, but at least now they're intimately acquainted with dad's digestive processes and it's nice to have this sort of information to hand in case one is ever at a High Society do and the chat lags. However, we had all agreed to not enjoy Thailand too much, as this was contra to our plans to get Michael home. So whenever we were confronted with yet another majestic bit of Thailand, we'd have to mention Watford in glowing terms, with the clear implication that Watford was superior. It was fiendishly difficult.

It was like holidaying with your brother's wonderful mistress and trying to tempt him back to his nasty wife: 'Sure, Nastassia can pilot a plane and wrestle a shark and all this in evening dress but . . . I really love Margery's refusal to wash her face or shave . . . *anything*. Those are the sort of principles you don't see every day, am I right?'

This is how we ended up on a yacht in the middle of the Gulf of Thailand, talking about the lake in Cassiobury Park as if it was the eighth bloody wonder of the world. I distinctly remember a giant turtle gliding by as mum said '. . . and there's ducks. Sometimes.'

Michael ignored this as much as he could. He had other problems to contend with, like the fact we hadn't bothered to learn a word of Thai before turning up, so we were completely helpless. The Luurtsemas don't integrate well into foreign climes; on one holiday to Magaluf[12] Michael suggested maybe we should step outside our cautious regime of sandwiches and try the local cuisine. I ventured the thought that this might be tapas.

'What's tapas?' Michael asked dad.

Dad sniffed, 'Like Doritos but it won't stop coming.'

The Doritos confusion still mystifies me, but I love dad's idea of tapas: a relentless conveyor belt of Spanish snacks. 'Bloody hell, enough, Manuel! My wife is *covered* in crisps.' Mum's verdict on tapas: 'It's fine but someone always ends up with their elbow in a little dish of oil.'

Ideally you should try to learn a language before you travel somewhere but we argue that this robs a holiday of its mystery. We've had some lovely times getting lost due to our inability to

12 We are who we are, let's just deal with it. The family holiday before that was to Ibiza, because mum watched *Ibiza Unconvered* and thought 'it looked lovely'. We spent two weeks slipping on used condoms on the beach, saw a man puke in the sea and mum was forced to rethink her opinion. An occurrence so rare we took a photo.

read a road sign, although they've always been marred by dad's insistence on assigning blame. If we're lost it's less important to him to find our way back than to work out who originally squealed 'I smell the sea so we must be going the right way!' This is a welcome trait in a biographer but really unhelpful from a navigator. Never call him in an emergency.

'Dad, my bed's on fire!'

'Well I'm going to give that Prometheus lad a piece of my mind.'

'Chuck me a damp cloth! Some Savlon!'

'Now where's that phonebook? P, P, P, P, Peeeeeeee.'

The best thing in Thailand, unarguably, was a sign in our hotel elevator. It mesmerised us. I'd say it was even better than Watford. (But nothing else was, okay Michael?) The sign was tantalisingly ambiguous: 'Please, no durians in the lift.' More a plea than a command, this wasn't 'No Smoking', it was more of a wail: 'Look inside your heart, can you be so cruel as to bring durians into this, after all we've been through?!' The picture didn't help; it was just a round shape with some triangles on one side. Was this a head? Did it represent people with nutty hairstyles? Had the owners of this hotel been to Leeds? Mum was all for inquiring via crayons and mime but I insisted we didn't, for all we knew we were wading into sensitive cultural waters, asking the Thai equivalent of, 'So who's this Ira guy? He sounds like a blast!!'

Dad found the phrase funny and repeated it everywhere, loudly. It became shorthand for any confusion.

'So how much is a return ticket?' I'd ask.

'Please,' he'd shrug, 'no durians in the lift.'

I tried to shush him but I was curious to see who reacted and how, anything to give me a clue. Old people? Pro-lifers? Veterans of some smallish war that we hadn't noticed? I found pretty much everyone stared at him with a bemused smile, the way you'd greet a pig in a hat, which didn't help, as this is exactly how the British look at him.

We spent days hunting for the Durian people, a shy race, we decided. Until one day dad came running into the hotel room, clutching a prickly thing the size of a rugby ball. He waved it in our faces, too breathless to yell anything more than 'Durian!' He explained that a man had overheard him say his durian catch-phrase. (We all exchanged looks. He had gone out alone, so this was proof that, despite his promises, he does talk to himself in public and loud enough to be overheard.)

His new friend had sold him a durian and dad had run it back to our room, via the elevator. Thus flouting the one rule we'd been openly studying all week; the hotel staff must've thought we had the IQ of a noodle. Now was the moment of truth, why were the hotel staff banning this benign ball? Dad went at it with a couple of chopsticks. He cracked the durian open and we all reeled back. It remains the worse smell I have ever encountered. It smelt like two close friends with stomach flu had shunned bedrest in favour of recreating Two Girls, One Cup. With a dirty cup.

Cowering in the bathroom, pumping frantically on the deodor-ant, we peeked around the door at it and planned our attack. Dad insisted the man had said it tasted lovely. This made sense, you'd only put up with this smell from something that cured cancer or tasted like heaven on a spoon. Otherwise surely all the durians would be shot into space. We wrapped our heads in damp towels and crawled towards it.

The naughty fruit sat innocuously on the floor, as if trying to blame this on the dog. We poked at it with spoons until we'd extricated a bit of flesh each. Then we tried to eat it but it was just impossible. We could not get it anywhere near our mouths. A foot from our nose was the closest anyone could get to it before the dry retching started. We tried to throw it the final few inches at our mouth, but our heads instinctively flinched away.

Eventually we gave up and retreated back to the bathroom, from where we surveyed the regrettable scene. Our lovely hotel room, so expensive that all four of us were sharing it, was now utterly defiled. Lumps of reeking durian scattered the floor, polluting everywhere. We had to dump the evidence. After much debate and blaming dad, we settled for Plan D: smuggling the problem out in little bits, each of us speed-walking through the lobby with plastic bags full of horror. It took half an hour of scuttling through the hotel, smiling politely, murmuring 'good afternoooon'. Over lunch the next day, we all agreed we had preferred the mystery and that we would never search for answers again.

Post-durian, the holiday progressed happily; it was nice to be a four-piece again. Michael's five years younger than me and when I was an adult we had years of picking our way around bothersome juvenalia like bedtimes because there was still technically a child in the house. Now we were all grown-up (physically and legally at least) and the novelty of this still hadn't worn off. We were finally allowed to say bollocks at breakfast, because there was no one left to corrupt. We haven't let any other standards slip, which creates a confusing semantic imbalance, best summed up by mum tutting: 'Use a soup spoon, Dipshit.'

With this to amuse me, I didn't need any extra fun, but on the last day of our holiday I saw a poster advertising an Elephant Sanctuary and said I'd like to go. I expected to be fondly ignored, in usual fashion, but I forgot that on holiday dad becomes a Willy Wonka-ish figure who leaps to fulfil our every whim. It's lovely, but unnerving and there's a definite feeling of relief on the journey home when phrases like 'Two quid!?! You should've drunk water at home' reappear like old friends.

So we all went to the Elephant Sanctuary. My brother was apparently sick of us at this point and so had decided to kill us. Because he bundled us onto the back of mopeds, manned by drivers who didn't acknowledge us, just whizzed off at demented speeds.

Our urge to not die jostled with our sense of politeness. No one wanted to fling their arms around their driver without knowing his name, so I gripped my driver's trousers and steadily wedgied him throughout our time together, probably prompting him to whiz even faster. He leaned forward, I was forced to follow and we engaged in some unwilling high-speed spooning. We overtook dad, who had decided to avoid the whole hips/waist erogenous zone on a stranger and was gripping his driver's arms. I think perhaps, in an ideal scenario, the driver had planned to use those arms for steering but, his struggling limbs and screaming face seemed to say, Life is a rollercoaster, you just gotta ride it.

Mum had really drawn the short straw with a shirtless driver, making any clutching immediately erotic, so she was grasping any bits of the moped that didn't burn her fingers off. As we overtook her I swear I heard her yell 'Seatbelt?' at her driver's naked back. I love her willingness to look Facts in the face then stare so hard that Facts drift out of focus.

Somehow we all reached the Elephant Sanctuary not dead, which prompted some, 'Well hey, how'd ya fancy that?!' type high-fiving from our drivers. Dad's driver mainly. Mine was busy trying to cough up his underwear while mum's was cradling a spanner, pondering how to unhook her from his carburettor. Buoyed by their success one of them offered to come pick us up in a few hours. We confessed that we were very tempted, but we actually lived here at the Elephant Sanctuary now so would never need another lift again. We all looked sad. Thanks anyway!

Dad was still smarting from his failure of the day before, when he had assured us he wanted to go to Ban Phe. It was a fishing port and he liked fishing ports. Michael looked doubtful but didn't want to contradict such confidence. We stumbled around Ban Phe for half an hour, politely gagging into our t-shirt necks and dad announced that he would like to amend his earlier statement. He liked fishing ports with sewerage, in cold countries. The combination of fierce heat and a laissez-faire approach to drainage made Ban Phe the place where Fish and Poo die in each others' arms. Poetic I'm sure but the casual holiday-maker wants to machete her nose off.

Chastened by failure, dad had put me in charge of today's Fun and now here we stood in the Elephant Sanctuary, where we would hopefully see elephants having sanctuary everywhere, possibly swinging from the rafters yodelling the word like massive hunchbacks of Notre Dame. Trouble was, I couldn't see many elephants luxuriating in sanctuary. There were elephants, but they were mainly tied to things while people took photos. I doubt even Katie Price would consider that relaxing. Well, not after the first couple of years. A man beckoned us, so we followed him (we'd be so easy to kidnap) up a ten-foot-high platform.

Employing our Thai language skills (shouting and mime) we established that we were about to ride an elephant. On one hand, that idea nudged hard at my definition of 'sanctuary'. On the other hand, 'Ooooooo! ELEPHANT RIDE!' I can pretend I wrestled with this dilemma for an hour if it makes you feel better but in fact my mind was made up with indecent haste and mum and I readied ourselves to ride an elephant. After which time, my guide assured me, with mime, it would definitely then go and enjoy a bit of sanctuary. Shitloads of the stuff.

An elephant stomped towards us and my mind emptied. It was like meeting my own lung. I'd seen pictures, I'd always been aware of it, but never thought I'd get face-time with it. I was star-struck.

I remember yelling at the TV once when a flabbergasted Martin Clunes met a monkey. 'Say something insightful then!' I'd bellowed 'Be evocative NOW or let someone more articulate meet a monkey.' But now I understand why he'd stammered and stumbled, it is mesmerising to meet a wild animal, especially one as iconic as the elephant.

So I stayed silent with awe. Then stood on it. Which, yeah, did seem a little disrespectful but I made my peace with it. I bounced gently at the knees, thinking 'Shitting hell, I am STANDING on an elephant. Like it's a pub table.' I sat and marvelled at how much better my day trip was than dad's. I looked around for mum but she was still on the platform.

'It's very high,' she remarked in critical tones, as if the elephant was a sofa we hadn't measured up properly.

'Well of course,' I reasoned, 'it's the top of a bloody elephant. Do you want to ride underneath? It's got nipples like stalagtites.'

She dithered a bit more, dad saw an opportunity and shamelessly shoved past to steal her seat.

I really didn't know where this elephant ride stood on my ethical wall chart. (A chart headed 'So . . . Nestlé's evil, right?') I was very anxious that my elephant should enjoy it. Like a gutless punter with a prostitute, it wasn't enough that I got my ride, I wanted my elephant to reassure me she was having a lovely time too. Dad and I agreed that it was very difficult to assess an elephant's emotional state, given that it's an animal made of elbow. Elbow is an inexpressive texture; it's even harder to measure its joy when you're standing on top of it. The only hint of her emotional state was the occasional quivering of her back skin – something I could only attribute to eczema or the sort of sexual ecstasy I'd read about in Daphne Du Maurier's surprisingly raunchy canon. I wasn't wild about either, but settled for sexual ecstasy – at least she was having a nice time, and I don't know, maybe the feel of little feet pattering around on your back is a turn-on; I should lie on a school crossing sometime, test the theory.

As always, when I'm trying to have a magical experience, someone will invariably ruin it. My guide kept pointing things out. I know it's a key feature of the job, but he was a man with only a sketchy idea of What's Interesting. First he said 'Chicken!' and I said 'wow', but my heart wasn't in it. Dad barked back 'Vegetarian!' having learnt the hard way that in Thailand if you show an interest in something there's a chance someone will fry it and whack it on a plate for you. At which point there's nothing to be done but thank them and tuck in.

Since The Incident we played safe and showed indifference towards anything we weren't prepared to have for lunch. Nice kitten? Humph, it's okaaay, we'd shrug, we've seen better. This is my daughter, it's her first birthday today. Really? Well let me know when she learns to dress for her shape. Oh look, some noodles! Gather round kids, admire the noodles, point and smile joyfully at them! Hurray for the noodles!

'Chicken?!' I thought 'So? I'm riding an elephant, an elephant possibly on the verge of orgasm. Nothing is cooler than this.' But he didn't listen to my brain and said 'Look! Potato!' At which point I snapped and said, 'Look, cultural divisions aside, a potato is *never* more interesting than an elephant. Now if I had visited Mr Mud's Mardi Gras of Veg, saddled up a parsnip, urged my reluctant steed around a field and *then* you wanted to point out an elephant, fine. But that is simply not happening.'

He smiled and nodded and for the first time I started to doubt my language skills. The confused silence was thankfully broken by screaming, which I traced back to us. It's still a bit of a blur, but picking through the giggling eye-witness accounts established that the elephant had spotted something she really wanted to eat or fight and she'd charged for it, beneath a low-hanging branch which walloped the three of us to the floor. This finally reassured me that we weren't an uncomfortable weight for her, in fact she didn't even know we were up there! I have never felt so comfortable while nursing spinal damage.

Mum and Michael ran towards us, shoving and yelling over each other in their desperation to say, 'I knew that was going to happen, oh I could just see it coming. This doesn't surprise me in the slightest. This wouldn't have happened in Barcelona.'

Winded, I lay face down on a potato and hoped the elephant would trample them but she was ears-deep in a bush and offering no help. Up close I had to admit, it was a handsome potato. Sign me up for Mr Mud's Mardi Gras of Veg, classic family fun, none of this modern elephant nonsense.

We limped off to point and smile at some noodles till someone fed them to us and dad pondered the consequences of the day upon his bowels. We got onto the subject of tapeworm and, once we got onto it, seemed unable to get off it. We tried to fling ourselves from it but it was going too fast and all we could do was cling on and pray for it to stop. A couple next to us were valiantly trying to have a romantic meal but they seemed to understand English. The girl started flinching every time dad opened his mouth. Welcome to my world.

One man managed to ignore dad, despite being within earshot. He was a German man engrossed in filming his dinner. I understand photographing food – it always seems a shame that beautifully presented food, once eaten, becomes so ugly. But filming it? Surely that's a medium best suited to things that move? I'm not unadventurous but I like my dinner inert; if it starts moving my first thought will be to hit it with a spoon and yell for the waiter, not back-light it and go in for a mid-shot.

This man was filming his dinner with admirable dedication. I only noticed him because he flung his hand high in the air, to race the camera towards his plate and achieve a dramatic crash-zoom on his sweet and sour pork. His family ignored him and kept up a steady bovine munching, despite his attempts to play director. I guessed he'd been forced to develop this exciting camera style when his cast had had enough and refused to betray the slightest flicker of emotion on-screen.

He finally bored of this and swung his camera above his head to capture the ambience of other peoples' lives. All that ambience in the room, he thought, just wasted with no one recording it. Across the room an American man was doing the same. Their cameras paused, staring at each other; two periscopes eyeing each other up, from two kindred submarines. I wanted them to fling their bored families aside and rush into each other's arms and live a long and happy life together, with every single second captured on film. I breathed this romantic wish to my family. They reacted badly. I think some of the poetry got lost in translation, still, it derailed the tapeworm monologue, as I had to deny a fetish for middle-aged tourists.

There was a sticky silence as images of parasitic worms and sodomy danced in our minds. Thankfully broken by mum's summary of the holiday. Thailand was less good than Barcelona but more good than Blackpool. We were unanimous on the Durian's supremacy in the bad smells stakes and the league tables were duly updated.

*   *   *

It was understandable that Michael had decided not to inflict us on Thailand this year and decided to come back and see us, despite his very real fears that mum would stage a *Misery*-inspired maiming on him that kept him from leaving. He wouldn't let her near his legs, which I thought was wise.

After a fortnight we drove him to the airport in a tense silence; the silence of four people crying and refusing to admit it. I was extra-tearful as Michael had had two weeks in which to point out the pathetic lameness of my current situation and hadn't nibbled the bait once. I was so touched. Had our situations been reversed there's no WAY I'd have been that nice about it, a thought that was making my throat very tight.

We waited in the airport for two hours, thanks to mum's enduring love affair with punctuality. There was a lot of silent crying and admiring big Toblerones. Before he headed through the gates Michael turned to me and put his hands on my shoulders.

'You know, I'm sorry but I hope you understand why I went. I just always felt in your shadow,' he said. 'Your scholarships, your sport . . .'

'Netball Captain, Swimming Captain . . .' I added, just to help. 'Swimming for the county, oh God, when I nearly got into that training programme for the Atlanta Olympics!' (Look, he was making a list; I was *helping* . . .)

'Yeah,' he sighed, 'then Oxford . . . a scholarship there as well.' (I did a little 'What Am I Liiike? face.) 'I got so sick of people asking if I was going to follow in your footsteps, I just wanted to go far away and build my own life.'

I patted his ribs (they were eye-level, he is very tall). It broke my heart to think that I had made my little brother so sad. Genuinely, I knew I was achieving a lot of stuff in those days, but none of it was fun. No one could have envied my school years, with their sparsely attended birthdays and lonely hours with my face in a book or a swimming pool. And yet somehow my brother had. I hadn't spotted it, or taken it seriously, mainly because I was busy resenting his popularity, the easy charming way he seemed to sail through life, liked and remembered and welcome wherever he went.

Poor sod, by the time I left school they wrote my name in gold above the bloody entrance. Admittedly it was something they did for each year's most academic student, not a one-off just for me, but I remembered the look on his face when my parents dragged him to visit it. He had the same look when we cracked open the durian.

Ribs aching with hard silent crying, I reached up to hug him tightly and show him how sorry I was and how much I loved him.

'But look at you now,' he mused. My hug loosened. 'Living with mum and dad at your age, doing "comedy".'

(I could bloody well HEAR the inverted commas.)

'It's all a bit of a mess, isn't it? God . . . it's funny how things work out,' he smiled broadly, kissed the top of my head and flip-flopped off through the gate, practically glowing with self-esteem.

Total bastard. Absolute total bastard. But the drama queen in me had to applaud the stylish exit. If our situations were reversed, I would've done the same . . . possibly swivelling back to yodel, 'HA! In your bloody FACE, loser! The tortoise has kicked the hare's ARSE.'

I waited, in case he wanted to do that, but he didn't reappear. A model of restraint, Michael Gustaaf Luurtsema.

Chapter 17

ABLUTIONS

So Michael returned to his exotic life on a Thai island and his house on stilts in the sea, but I wasn't jealous. Not even a little bit, because I got to spend my days around scenes like this:

INT: DINING ROOM – LUNCH

MUM, DAD and NAT are eating soup and sandwiches. Nat's bowl is placed in the centre of a raft of six table mats, to protect the big shiny table and make her feel like a divvy.
The scheme is a success on both counts.

MUM
Remember Natalie's birthday last year?

DAD
Nope.

MUM
We went out for lunch.

DAD
Bully for us.

MUM

In London, at a place called the Duchess?

DAD

(Bored silence)

MUM

Along, just along the road with the Starbucks on.

DAD

(Openly bored, yawns and scratches)

MUM

(With malicious glee, she presses the big red button)
It was a . . . gastrop-

DAD

(Ignites)

A gastropub? Bloody gastropub! I remember, four pounds fifty for a side plate of veg?! And it was TINY! I thought bugger this, I'll bring a carrot next time, nibble it in my top pocket, I'm not paying nearly a fiver for the world's smallest harvest festival. And *she* . . .

Nat stares intently at her soup, trying to ignore the spoon being waggled accusingly at her.

DAD (CONT'D)

. . . *she* wanted oysters, said she'd never had them, always wanted to try them, what did we end up with? Ten quid on soap dishes full of snot that she didn't eat so I had to eat my steak with snot staring at me.

NAT

It flinched when I squeezed lemon juice on it! I'm not eating something that flinches.

DAD

You don't have to chew it.

NAT

I wasn't worried it would outwit me. I reckon I can win a fight with an oyster, particularly if we're fighting in MY MOUTH, I think that gives me home turf advantage. I just felt sorry for it.

DAD

Why, d'it waste ten quid on its lunch too?

Dad isn't tight, but as a family we don't like to be tricked out of money. A cautionary tale in our house is the time our family friend Tim had a haircut Without First Asking The Price. In his defence, I've seen cheeses with more hair, but as he perched in the chair watching his Follicle Technician examine every strand of his hair minutely like he was hunting sneaky nits, Tim started to worry. An hour later we stopped by their house to return a chainsaw (no, I've no idea either) and got embroiled in the story.

We found him languishing on the sofa with a cold compress on his face, moaning softly, 'When they said eight at the desk, I thought it could only end "teen" not "ty".'

His dad swelled with fury at the thought of an eighteen quid haircut, then absorbed the final part of the sentence, deflated and sagged weakly onto the pouffe. I fetched a second moist towelette and they both swooned together. Years later mum still gives this example as the reason why her friend cuts our hair in her kitchen. Even after all this time, the memory of 'that hairdresser' exploiting a loved one makes her lips thin with rage.

'And they pressurised him into hair wax' is now her final say on the matter.

We're not misers but we won't waste money for nothing. Years ago dad used to grow runner beans in the garden. And we used to kick footballs into them by accident. I have vivid childhood memories of racing past those bloody beans, dad in hot pursuit, waving a slipper. (My parents always smacked us with a slipper on the back of our legs. Which has the benefit of hurting like utter fuck but looking like a whimsical parlour game.)

If you eat runner beans when they're small they are juicy and tender. If you leave them to grow they will become tough and stringy BUT much bigger. You will get more bean for your efforts, is all dad heard, and words like 'fibrous' and 'practically inedible' floated past him ignored. So we'd all sit at the dinner table masticating like gloomy cows while mum looked firmly at my brother and I, just daring us to hurt dad's feelings. Dad's stubbornness overrides most of his basic motor functions and so he could subdue the woody mouthful into something the size of a small fist and force it down his throat. My brother and I would do the same but we'd never manage it on the first attempt, it would lodge in our throat, we'd panic and abort the mission, retching it back up for a bit more punishment.

At least the ache in our jaws would distract us from the slipper-sting on our calves after earlier disrespect shown to the Bean. Between sore calves, jaw-ache and horrible lunch, it was three–nil to runner beans.

In the spirit of 'HOW much for a lettuce?! Bugger that,' I discovered dad had got an allotment now, like a proper Dutchman. So far during my Month At Home (sigh), everything had been very tasty, though it refused to conform to Society's aesthetic expectations. Right on!

'What do you grow it in?' I asked. 'Thalidomide?' Apparently this is what veg ACTUALLY looks like, but you wouldn't know, Natalie, as supermarkets insist that all their vegetables look . . . 'Nice?' I offered. 'Good for them.' He shook his head at my naiveté and told me how when he was a kid courgettes looked like poodles and strawberries were the shape of Shakespeare and everyone was happy and healthy. I swear they put LSD in the canals.

*   *   *

But on occasion the Luurtsemas do splash the cash. Well, we laboriously save it up and THEN splash it, but that makes for a less jaunty motto. Moving home had been replete with emotional discomfort for all of us and, after four months, physical discomfort leapt in to join the party. After years of saving, my parents were having their bathroom ripped out and replaced with a new one. Obviously. Without the second stage that manoeuvre is just vandalism and would be frowned upon in the property market. Though I had viewed countless flats where the landlord had ploughed ahead with that scheme anyway.

'Oh, is this crumbling plaster where a sink used to be? How innovative! That will certainly liven up a morning's ablutions.'

I generously supported my parents' right to have a new bathroom, even though I was quite fond of the old one. We moved in fifteen years ago, took one look at the bathroom and concurred: 'Hahahaha. Well, THAT'S got to go.' Then a recession worked its magic, dad lost his job and we all realised that nicotine yellow was a much underrated 'cheerful' colour.

So, fine, if they wanted a new bathroom I supported that. However, I could not condone their methods. At seven in the morning I sobbed myself awake to the noise of big men ripping a bathroom apart. I stumbled out into the hallway in search of answers. No one could give me a good reason as to why this was being done so early, all mum gave me was some chat about putting a bra on.

She prodded me back into my room, where she explained that the next ten days were to be spent bathroom-less and she talked me through various ingenious plans for staying clean. I listened politely, then segued seamlessly from pyjamas to clothes, outlining my plans, which were not to fight the dirt. It's an elemental force, dirt, it's been here for millions and millions of years and will outlast the human race. It's arrogant to think that we can cleanse our bodies of it. Perhaps we should pay Mother Earth the respect of embracing her dirt, hmm? It's taken her millennia to make it, crumbling it down from bigger dirt, I think.

Anyway, the options were Be a Bit Grubby or Wash in a Tiny Sink in the downstairs toilet. A sink that was actually smaller than a flannel. It's a good thing flannels can bend or the system would've been a non-starter. It still felt like too much faff to me and I backed out of this enterprise. I try to be an open-minded person. I frequently fail, especially when it comes to people who are orange or write 'lol', but with my parents I really try to keep my mental saloon doors propped open. Yet sometimes they shove these doors too hard. After the first day of bathroom destruction it was a bit dusty in the house, but we weren't at Miss Haversham levels; there was nothing you could write your name in.

Nevertheless, as soon as the builders left, mum and dad got out the brooms, cloths and vacuum cleaner and cleansed the upstairs thoroughly. They acknowledged that tomorrow would be just as dusty, but 'Natalie, we can go to bed knowing that the house is clean until then.'

I tried to persuade them how little I cared about the cosmetic environment in which I lay my unconscious body, but they would not listen.

This continued for several weeks while our new bathroom was being installed. I tried everything to make them stop this daily cleaning, even saying, 'How do you think the plumber feels when you scrub the house every time he leaves? Dirty and unwelcome I bet. He probably sobs in his van on the way home while his wife gets cucumber slices ready for his poor puffy eyes.' It was a clever tactic, politeness and cleanliness hustle for the top spot in the Luurtsema manifesto, but cleanliness won and I was told to shut up and grab a cloth.

I thought once the bathroom was installed this period of daily scrubbing would cease, but if anything, it escalated. Having something as valuable in the house as the new bathroom sent mum overboard into even more frantic behaviour. This manifested itself in several ways, most notably the day I arrived home from an audition. As a comic I will occasionally be asked to have a go at acting. I usually begin auditions by informing everyone present that I'm untrained, dangerously untalented but a nice person. In my experience this really relaxes a room, fosters a friendly atmosphere and no one feels bad for not giving me the job.

That day's audition had been particularly baffling: 'How's your Bosnian, Nat?'

'How's yours?' I twinkled.

'Fluent.'

'Well, I'll show myself out then . . .'

I think TV casting directors see 'Luurtsema' and expect a more exotic creature than the one that invariably stumbles late through their door. I plodded home to mum thrusting four pints of milk at me. She said, in the strident tones I'd quickly learnt to associate with my imminent misery, 'I've bought that milk you like. It was Reduced.'

'That milk you like' is full fat milk and I quite like it; I didn't have pictures of it on my wall or a hatbox full of grass because I liked the early work. You wouldn't find me blending cheese to try and recapture the magic, I just preferred it to the feeble grey cow tears my parents drank. 'Skimmed' they call it, though the word 'skim' always makes me think of 'scum'. If you're going to name it after one of the ickiest processes it's put through you might as well call it Nipple Dribble. That stuff always looked like a confused farmhand had wanked it out of a dead cow's nose. So I didn't LOVE full fat milk, I just liked it. I like R&B more than dragging a cheese-grater up and down my back then frolicking in a fountain of vinegar; that does not make me an R&B fan. My parents and I waged an unlikely number of battles over dairy – if we went vegan, life would be calmer. Our oldest battle was over the issue of yoghurt.

'What issue?' I hear you cry, in a phlegmy way: 'What issues can surround such inoffensive goo?'

I have never liked yoghurt, milk is nice, cheese is excellent, but yoghurt is the in-between gooey, rotting bit and I can't stand it.

Floating bits of fruit in it doesn't help, it just becomes a deathbed for nice food. Don't sprinkle toasted almonds on a dog turd and think it'll tempt me to pick up a spoon. I will simply mourn the loss of almonds and wonder about your erratic behaviour. And yet every shopping trip we embarked on together, mum and dad would park me in front of the yoghurt section and said: 'Now, which yoghurt do you like?'

I couldn't be less tempted if they'd asked: 'Now, what's your favourite position in which to be strangled by an unknown assailant?'

Obviously I said none of this, I just started grimly chugging my way through milk for fear of seeming ungrateful. Mum insisted I give the full four pints 'my best shot'. My 'best shot' would've been out of an upstairs window, but I didn't share this thought.

I was supping my nearly-off milk amidst a carnival atmosphere, which added to the queasiness. To celebrate the bathroom being finished, mum had invited three mates around for a ceremonial unveiling. I'd hoped for two of them wedged in the bath for the Press and one squeezing out a token poo for posterity. Sadly no. Still, there was always the next lot of visitors we had booked in for later in the week (not the same friends; weirdly being walked around a small white bathroom didn't get much repeat custom).

Mum wouldn't let them in the new bathroom until they had flicked through twenty photos of the old one for comparison. These photos featured me posing reluctantly with all the various bathroom items. Mum and dad kept telling me to 'do it properly' but I was at a loss as to how one posed 'properly' for such a monumentally pointless shot. This remark was not well received at the time.

Mum is a lethal photographer, whenever she sees fun she ruins it. She fiddles with her camera while we cluster around the twitching corpse of the good time we were just having. The atmosphere plummets and in seconds people flit from bogling to yawning. We look grumpy in all our family photos, portraying us as ungrateful bastards, scowling at Christmases, holidays and birthdays, which we're not. We'd been having a lovely time until four minutes before The Fun Assassin finally worked out how to take a photo.

She's not great with technology, this is the woman who once sent me this text: 'I'm in hospital, call me!! Mum.'

I called her again and again and again in a panic, thinking, 'Oh my god I'm an orphan' (I know I'd still have dad but . . .).

By the time she bothered to answer I was melting with fear and she answered, 'What? I'm trying to carry a latte.'

We established two things; mum had NO idea of the slippery nature of tone in a text and she liked the cafe in the local hospital. Who drinks coffee in a hospital cafe, you might ask? Someone who liked a frothy coffee and a slice of life: 'Oo, that looks like a nasty break, blimey is that his wife or daughter? Two sweeteners please . . .'

I broke away from the bathroom tour to tackle another glass of milk. When I returned, mum's mates had run out of things to admire and mum had resorted to demonstrating how she cleaned the surfaces. I walked in on her miming a cloth, saying 'just circular motions, that's all it needs' while they nodded as if this was new information to them. I said how lucky it was mum had showed them this, now they could stop cleaning *their* homes with a brick and jabbing motions. Never again would they 'clean' their possessions into shards and rubble, thanks to mum. She took this quite badly and I returned to my milky troubles.

The new bathroom considerably upped my standard of living, except of course nothing is simple and it brought its own problems to the party. After every shower I was marched back into the bathroom to CLEAN it. Every time. I kept bleating, 'but it's self-cleaning! It creates clean, it doesn't need cleanliness inflicted upon it! If anything, you are insulting its professional pride!' But mum was having none of it and I was forced to mop up clean water from a clean shower with a clean cloth and a tiny windscreen wiper. Have you ever stood naked and shivering, squeaking a tiny windscreen wiper up and down a pristine piece of plastic?

Have you? I really hope you're all answering no, because I was forced to do this repeatedly and every time it felt like the opening scenes of a nervous breakdown.

None of this encouraged me to embrace the Twice Daily showering regime they wanted me to follow. The stupid bathroom was rife with obstacles. I'd creep in there, close the door ('Gently! I didn't pay for a door so you could slam it like an animal!'), pull the cord to turn on the light ('Don't YANK it Natalie!'), then clamber in gingerly. I'd then stand very still under the water, noting all the water splashing off me and onto the wall and the sides of the bath, knowing I'd have to mop it all up in a minute, because apparently in this room evaporation hadn't been invented.

It was already a total palaver, completely supporting my theory that a shower should be a bi-weekly event. But then it got worse, thanks to dad flinging something frankly Bacchanalian into the mix. I think it's clear that the Luurtsemas are not flashy (through lack of funds more than innate restraint), however dad had stumbled across MTV Cribs and seen more than he should've. For he had had underfloor heating installed in the bathroom. That is like a radiator, right, but under the floor. It's mind-boggling. And foot-warming.

When I first heard of this plan I scoffed. I called him Caesar for a day and sarcastically peeled him grapes. (I don't know where that saying comes from; they were minging unsheathed, I don't believe that rich people ever wanted that.) I soon stopped, once I experienced hotfloor and fell in love. I loathe the early part of the day but suddenly found myself waking at eight in the morning to have my feet gently warmed by the bathroom. If the walls massaged me I'm sure I'd become a real go-getter.

Unfortunately I wasn't the only one enjoying hotfloor. The cats discovered it instantly, with their uncanny knack for spotting another bed to add to the database. So whenever the underfloor heating was on (and mum rationed dad to two hours a day, so he didn't get accustomed to happiness) they'd sprawl all over the floor, writhing orgiastically. Which, as you can imagine, really detracted from the glossy look of the new bathroom. Imagine the opening scenes of *Saving Private Ryan*, enacted with relaxed felines. Sure, that casting decision fundamentally changes the tone of the piece, but I still had to wade through bodies.

I got to cement a theory I'd been working on, which was that there were few things more annoying than having a shower, mopping the stupid thing down, drying then packing away the tiny windscreen wiper (because of course in this household even the cleaning utensils need cleaning), then trudging damply back to my room gathering cat hair with my feet, acquiring a horribly Hobbitty look. I'm a big Tolkien fan but there's a time and a place and pre-socks is a bad time for that sort of business.

Emboldened by the new bathroom, mum and dad ventured further into lifestyle improvements. They were possibly trying to upgrade the house to such a level that I felt out of my depth and uncomfortable, and would finally leave. More fool them. I planned to cling on tenaciously, whatever the discomfort. Though dad had developed a new 'joke' of opening the front door with a hopeful look on his face whenever I walked past it. The 'hilarity' soon wore thin and made the house draughty which, considering his mania for not letting heat escape the house, was a sign of how strongly he was committing to the joke.

You may think 'or a sign of how badly he wanted you to leave,' but in our family if someone tells you they want you to leave, you can confidently assume they don't mean it. If we genuinely mean something we NEVER mention it. I don't defend this as a healthy approach to life but it seemed to work all right for us and as long as dad kept telling me to bugger off I felt secure. The day he stopped yelling 'and don't come BACK!' whenever I left the room was the day I would take up residence on a friend's sofa.

Until that day, I decided to stay in the increasingly fancy family home. Mum and dad had bought a motion-detecting air freshener. You may well have seen such things and thought 'such sophistication is beyond my reach'. Yes, I'm sure it is. But don't worry, the

Luurtsemas leap bravely into the unknown so others don't have to.

I understood the theory behind it: activity creates smells, so whenever the gadget sensed movement it would puff out a waft of fragrance. Hate the game not the playa. Unfortunately, in practice it felt like being heckled. Whenever I walked past, it farted out a gust of vanilla and the unspoken accusation that I stank. I had to walk past it regularly and after a day my confidence was shot. Mum found me scrubbing myself in the garden crooning, 'I'm a dirty birdy . . .' If they'd had one of these in Glamis Castle I bet Lady Macbeth would've gone nuts by Act III and the whole play could've boiled down to twenty minutes.

I wasn't the only one feeling uncomfortable with our new lifestyle device. It scared the shit out of the cats who immediately set up a stakeout on the device (I assigned the Estevez and Dreyfuss roles so there'd be no squabbling). Plus, this olfactory twat was by the front door and I had to enter the house silently in the early hours of most mornings. It was not ideal to have to pick my way past Emilio and Richard and this little plastic bastard announcing that I smelt. If this was the future, a world of naked windscreen wiping and being bullied by vanilla, I understand why timid souls hid from it in 'retro' and 'vintage'.

Chapter 18

FUZZY Vs POINTY

Quick question, when exactly does the fun die from life? Is it around twenty-eight? I was starting to suspect so, as I entered the fifth month of my Month At Home and life sank to new depths of dreary. One day I found dad eating a yoghurt over the sink, which is perhaps one of the most depressing angles at which to catch the man that made you.

He heard me sigh, and mumbled through Muller: 'Might as well eat it here, I've only got to wash it up.'

If he was going to go at life with this sort of attitude, he may as well eat all his meals on the toilet. In fact, given this 'mortality' lark, we should all wear backless formal wear and heavy make-up so we're casket-ready whatever the day may bring.

Once he'd finished his yoghurt and washed up his spoon (he didn't move his feet once, it was efficient), I had to listen to him explain in forensic detail why we can't afford a swimming pool. It was hot and I had only idly mused that it would be nice to have one. It would be nice to have lots of things, I don't expect to get them, I just register my desires to the world in case there's a stray millionaire squatting in the hedge.

Earlier that week I'd reached new depths of dull as I'd spent time staring at a bin. My parents' wheelie bins had Union Jack stickers on them and this baffled me. Either the bin men of Watford were being frank about the likelihood of them catastrophically misplacing your bin: 'I'll do my best but I won't lie, it could end up abroad . . .' Or they were expressing their devout nationalism in a way that only the side of our house and 4am would ever appreciate, and I didn't think either of them were registered to vote.

Dad caught me doing this and, in an attempt to prop up my flagging spirits, we had a Chinese takeaway. Mid-week. It's not really our style so I appreciated the breach of protocol just to stop me moping around near the bins. I watched dad scrape a tidy dinner onto his plate: Chicken in Black Bean Sauce, Sweet and Sour Chicken Hong Kong Style ('Ew, they're lumps!' he cried, like a man who'd never met a chicken nugget), noodles and rice. He'd picked at bits here and there, married together a noodle and a 'lump' for one mouthful, united rice and sauce for another, but then clearly decided that this was too time-consuming for the busy man on the go and stirred it all together into one repulsive lump. Much happier, he started shovelling this into his mouth. He caught me staring and got all defensive: 'What? It's all going in the same hole anyway.'

I like to think I'm not a snob (because that's the sort of thing we snobs say) but it's not la-di-dah to dignify your mouth with a name, rather than just a 'hole'. People are replete with 'holes', they're not generic interchangeable thingamabobs. But, I offered, ever the pacifist, shove a nugget up your bum and prove me wrong! He glared at me from behind his dinner mound and we finished our meal in an atmosphere of brittle politeness:

'I'm not going to finish my Coke, perhaps you'd like to pour it over your meal?'

'I am fine thank you. I'm not going to finish my Sod Off, perhaps you'd like to . . .'

'Yes, well, I'm fine too, thanks.'

It may seem unfair of me to write in such detail about dad like this, but I do so in the comfy knowledge that he doesn't read what

I write. I asked him once if he'd ever read anything I'd written about him and he snorted, 'No! Don't need to read it, too busy livin' it.' Which sounded sassy but meant nothing. Accountancy's gain is hip hop's loss.

Dad meant well, trying to drown my gloom in sweet 'n' sour, but mum got to the heart of the matter. She popped home in her lunch break, eyed me up and said 'You're hot and tetchy.'

'Thank you,' I replied. 'You're curvy and controlling.'

She made a small noise I chose to interpret as hysterical laughter, shoved me in the car and drove me to Argos. Of course! A paddling pool, I realised, would make everything better. It was so obvious, I was clearly just a bit overheated; it was nothing to do with the dreary reality of my crap life.

I found a pool I liked the look of – a grown woman and two children could luxuriate in it, the photo assured me. I squinted at this photo; I am convinced they find miniscule yet perfectly proportioned people to pose in these sort of products to make them look roomier than they are. I rented a flat years ago (back when that wasn't an over-ambitious pipe-dream) and after a week of confusion and falling over we realised the landlord had furnished it with cunningly tiny items, which made the flat look bigger, but made us all feel dizzy and gigantic. We'd leave the house so confused I was sure one of us would try to jump the Thames or put a bus in our pocket.

The woman at the till set my mind at rest by saying, 'It's quite big, you realise that?'

I set her mind running down queasily inappropriate avenues with my chirpy reply: 'It needs to be, it's for me, my mum and dad.' Too late I realised I was revealing far too much detail about my life and that everyone had just been treated to a pop-up mental image of three adults crammed squeaking into this pool, dabbing sun block on each other's noses.

I staggered into the house with my giant paddling pool, which was twenty quid in the sale, trivia fans. Dad greeted this news with gleeful gloating: 'You can't MAKE it for that!' Ignoring our lack of manufacturing ability which means, whatever the cost, whatever it is, we definitely couldn't make it. Mum sensed joy in the room and moved quickly to squash it, instructing me to 'clear the floor of the living room and unfold the paddling pool, to check its size'. I was halfway out the back door already and, sensing where this was heading, wailed 'NOOOO! Don't do this! Don't ruin my paddling pool with your boringness. We know how big it is, it says on the box, now let's. Just. Paddle.'

But no. Twenty minutes were then spent unfolding plastic ('Carefully Natalie!') in the living room, ascertaining that yes, bloody hell, it IS a paddling pool, it IS the size it said it was. I feigned surprise that we hadn't unwrapped a child-sized croquet set, as I imagined less prudent families up and down the country were at that very moment reclining on a soggy hoop, tutting 'WHY do I feel so unrefreshed?!'

I grabbed my paddling pool and tried to rush it outside, fill it with water and fling myself in it, but no, it had to be REFOLDED for the three-second journey from living room to garden (Why? Why? WHY?). I scrabbled on the floor, desperately trying to lay it out in time to get it full of air, then water so I could have my fun before I had to set off for my evening's gig.

But no. No, my fun was still not done being thwarted. More thwart hove into view. Mum dangled a key at me. It was the key to the garage, in which I'd find the key to dad's shed (this system was flawed), in which I would find a rake, with which I had to cleanse the lawn before I could lay my pool upon it. I lay face down on the grass, limp with irritation, stating, as calmly as I could, that I LIKED the risk of stones beneath my paddling pool, that it added jeopardy to a paddle. And also that I could vouch for the bit of grass I was lying on being stone-free and was that sufficient assurance for her?

No, it was not.

I stomped off to the stupid fucking garage to get the stupid fucking key to the stupid fucking shed to get the stupid fucking rake, narrating loudly as I went so everyone could appreciate the injustice. I raked the ground like some sort of crazy Stepford Wife cleaning her garden. As I did so, mum hovered. I ignored her. She hovered harder. I sighed and acknowledged her with a polite 'What the fuck now?!' And she explained, taking the rake off me like it was a gun I'd been waving around in a crèche, that it was now getting a bit late to be doing things like inflating pools and having fun, so perhaps we'd continue this tomorrow. I actually quivered with rage.

She then fixed me with a meaningful look and I realised that, in a final indignity, she expected me to refold the paddling pool. I had had such high hopes for an afternoon spent splashing in the sunshine. Instead I found myself neatening flaccid plastic. My fun had descended into origami, which everyone knows is not fun.

As I wrestled with a particularly unwieldy corner I remembered a family holiday years ago when my little brother scampered into the sea with his lilo, sprang a leak almost immediately and staggered out of the waves, wailing, cradling its limp body in his arms. I had felt a painful surge of guilt that I had let the world do this to him. But I was eleven and couldn't express this, so I laughed at him till he cried. Whenever I feel tearful I find I can head off my woe by upsetting someone else. It's a grubby instinct and one that I've failed to outgrow, as ex-boyfriends will testify.

The next morning I woke up to heavy rain and was temporarily immobilised with fury. I could actually HEAR it pattering on my abandoned paddling pool: the world was spitting on my attempts at joy. Once I'd slapped the feeling back into my body I stomped downstairs, filled a huge bowl of Cheerios way too high up and throned myself on the pale-coloured sofa to eat them. Because revenge is a dish best served . . . y'know, I quipped quietly to myself.

Eating cereal spitefully, in an empty house, six feet away from one's deflated paddling pool was not a healthy way to begin the day, as Craine informed me when I called him with the day's whinges. This was a daily call and the earlier I made it, the worse my day. Some days I needed to wait until the evening to have a long enough list of gripes to justify a phone call, other days I was still in my pyjamas as I dialled furiously.

Craine wisely saw that this was time for an intervention. He may not know how to turn the oven off, or why it's so important to lock the front door, but he knows how to cheer me up. And so, he declared boldly, we were going on a safari!! My excitement faded a little in the three hours it took him to travel to me and begin carrying out this scheme, but I was still pretty pumped as we headed off to Longleat: Britain's Africa (For People Who Have Never Been To Africa).

I hadn't been there since I was very young and we had an encounter with a monkey and his flamboyant bottom (a feature on which Mother Nature squandered far too much time. If she'd given the human buttocks this much brainstorming the trouser would never have caught on). This monkey sat on our bonnet, staring dad in the face as he slowly ripped the windscreen wipers off our Datsun Sunny, maintaining eye contact throughout. He seemed on the verge of murmuring, in that soft scary Cockney way, 'All right matey, we got a problem?' He was a monkey with the bum of a novelty soap and the soul of a Kray twin.

As we approached Longleat Safari Park, unwelcome phrases like 'insurance premium' swam around my mind. Craine keeps himself in a very deliberate state of oblivion so nothing ruins his fun. He chuckled and bounced next to me while I fingered my Green Flag breakdown card: 'I'm juuust off the M4, by the lion, any idea how long you'll be, please? Mm yes, lion.'

I managed to push these mundane thoughts to one side as we rounded a hill and discovered giraffes roaming free. They are majestic animals – so poorly designed, like cheap holiday knick-knacks, but they muddle on through. Watching their languid strides prompted one clear thought: they had so much more space than most city-dwellers and they were doing fuck-all with it. Honestly, they had acres of space and no interest in moving around. As someone who's lived in some miserably poky flats, where there's no point crying about it cos you'll only steam up the windows, I was offended. The tigers and lions were particularly inert and required twenty minutes' close study before we were sure they weren't dead. If anything, I thought, keep *them* in a plastic bag.

We were having a lovely time until a camel planted himself in the middle of the road and stared at us malevolently. Suddenly it all got a bit too safari, we wound up our windows and crept past. The camels in Longleat have some serious 'tude: one actually made a beeline for Craine's open window, puckering his lips to spit or snog him. I doubt Craine relished the choice – his attacker was a Bactrian camel and his two humps wobbled most unattractively. I didn't cop a feel but they looked fatty yet gnarled, halfway between bum and toe.

Unfortunately for Craine, I had the ability to disable his window. I had to use this a lot because he is a very annoying person. The sort of person who'll have a window open AND the heating on, then complain he feels weird. I tell him, window autonomy is a privilege not a right. He tells me, he wishes he'd never met me.

Craine was window-down and here was an aggressive/amorous camel charging towards him. Reader, dear reader, I disabled his window and slowed the car to a halt, because cruelty was my hot tub and I liked to soak. Within minutes Craine was a trembling wreck and even the camel seemed to feel the situation had escalated beyond reach. I drove off, reflecting that if the camel did gob on Craine, I would have to clean my car and boyfriend before the day could continue, and that felt like a degree of faff I'd rather avoid.

Safaris are beautiful; you get to look at animals and the countryside without having to walk like some sort of prick. It also meant Craine and I had the privacy to act like idiots. We tried to keep this under control in public, but in our car, nonsense reigned. We have a lovely time together, but it's best we do it without witnesses, like the time we gigged in Switzerland and saw a

Swiss roll. I think he was Swiss, but demanding someone's nationality is a bit Goebbels-Lite, particularly if they're seven, have just tumbled down a hill and you have yelled 'SWISS ROLL!' at them.

There was another reason why it was best we chatted in private. The baby voice was crucial to our relationship. Those cutesy voices, high-pitched and lisping, liberated us to be the bastards we really were:

'Thumtimeth I weally hate you, you demanding wathte of thpace,' I'd coo at him.

'Eddy day I fink oo can't be enny more of a pwick . . . an' den you are,' he'd simper back.

It was nice, like hitting each other with foam-covered baseball bats. All the fun of violence but no tedious A&E queues.

In the privacy of our car we could also openly declare certain animals to be bollocks and then move on swiftly: a refreshingly honest approach that always earned me judgmental looks at London Zoo. There are many reasonable objections to zoos, I acknowledge them all and my only argument in favour of them is that I have two or three jobs, while most animals have none. So if I want to see a marmoset I believe it's only polite that it makes itself available to me.

By this same logic, if a kangaroo found itself in the throes of a rigorous mating season and was seized with an urge to see me (for entirely unrelated reasons I'd hope), I'd graciously make the journey. As it is, we work, they eat and sleep all day and so I think it's their duty to show their faces somewhere within the M25 in return for an easy life and all the admiration they can take. This argument is also applicable to pointless celebrities.

Without witnesses, we held a loud argument about how much zoo keepers got paid. Craine swore blind all zoo keepers were on £20–30,000, I said I thought it was much like comedy, there were probably lots of people happy to do it for free, which seriously weakened your argument for forty grand a year and a company car (but oh, how I try . . .). He scoffed, then a pig-tailed teen in a uniform chugged past on a tractor and I exhaled in quiet triumph.

After all my fretting, my windscreen wipers were safe. Apparently the monkeys had been closed to the public for two years, due to their blood tests returning 'a bit weird' according to a zoo keeper with his flies open. He stood there, hands on hips, thrusting his open fly at our window with every rock on his heels. Jokes about unprotected keeper/monkey sex danced in front of our eyes, waggling coquettishly like Longleat monkeys, begging us to have a go.

I fought the urge to say it, but I could tell Craine was fit to burst. So I thanked our groin-thrusting friend and wandered away from the chat, the way you do at parties when small talk has petered out. However it's much more obvious when you're wandering off IN A CAR; we could all hear my accelerator revving, my clutch coming up, while I tried to look innocent, as if, so sorry, excuse me, my car was dragging me away from this riveting chat. Wish I could stay, but . . .

It was a triumph of a day; we saw amazing animals and there was little to no bloodshed. (There was some but that was just from some otters gnawing the heads off baby chicks. Otter-popularity took a dip in our car.) I know some safari-goers worry about being mauled by a lion but I was more wary of an accidental hit 'n' run on a deer. I'm a very good driver but Craine is an awful passenger and has caused a lot of near misses, thanks to his dangerously affectionate nature; he liked to spring hugs on me out of the blue. I requested that affection be withheld while I drove but sometimes he forgot and terror ensued.

He'd launch affection at me at the worst times, like when we were on a bus screeching to a halt and free hands would've been super-handy to break our fall, or once, memorably, while I was changing lanes on the M4 at eighty miles per hour. I bet he's going to be my future cause of death. Bloody nice of me to stick with him really, but I reason this way I can keep an eye on my looming mortality. Keep your friends close, your fatally clumsy loved ones closer.

One of the most annoying places he'd hug me was on an escalator, swivelling me around and bending me awkwardly into a hug that brought me face-to-face with the person behind him. This was a deeply uncomfortable situation for everyone except Annoyingly Over-Loving Boyfriend. I felt compelled to alleviate the social tension that this position bred, so if I was face-to-face with a man behind him I'd do a come hither face and if it was a woman I'd roll my eyes and look bored, then either way they could amuse themselves by speculating on what a heinous bitch I must be.

Cruel fate dictated that a man with a love of cuddles shackled himself to an unaffectionate shrew. Don't get me wrong, I didn't mind being touched; a tap on the shoulder to warn of a speeding car, fine; a passionate handshake between lovers, how delightful. But I found anything more ambitious blocked my view of the telly, and I was forced to tut and shove.

Craine was such a big fan of hugging I had resolved to honeytrap him into an affair with a koala bear. I'd step in when he wanted to talk about dinner or *Doctor Who*, then I could hook him back up to the koala when I wanted to read unbothered by his 'Love' getting in the way.

We chugged back home in triumph, car intact, no animal bits splattered over the bonnet: a good day. Sadly we returned to exactly the sort of fun-void I had tried to escape. Dad had bought a new TV. Initially, excitement all round, the Luurtsemas rejoiced. In our house TV is like a member of the family, but better, a relative we actually like.

'Uncle Telly, regale us with stories of the war! Or of ditzy gals who love to shop, or of forensic crime-solving.'

But mum insisted the picture on the TV was fuzzy. Dad disagreed, vehemently.

'If anything,' he said, 'if anything, it is too sharp. Painfully pointy.'

I was called in to adjudicate but adjudication only works if people are prepared to listen to my soothing logic, not if they just want more noise to yell over. I became a backing singer to their fruitless jazz bickering.

My point was that as someone who paid four grand to have her eyes surgically lasered to perfection, surely I was best placed to judge Fuzzy Vs Pointy, compared to dad, whom moles would call Speccy. Both he and mum were becoming long-sighted, so mum now read by holding the newspaper at arm's length and squinting at it as if about to make a stirring speech.

Dad was a little more vain and thrust documents away from him in a quick sly movement. A cunning solution, until the day he punched the DHL man in the face: 'Sign here . . . Oof!'

Yet this feeble-sighted pair arrogantly over-ruled me and took the TV back to the shop where they told the shop assistants that the picture was weird.

'I was very fair,' said mum magnanimously, 'I told him, perhaps it was just that the evening's programmes were fuzzy, but just in case . . .'

Craine was finding unexpected advantages to my exile in Watford. In London he would always ask me to drive him places, requests I would reject with a firm but fair expletive before returning to my laptop. Now the prospect of driving him to Paddington station seemed infinitely preferable to watching mum and dad bicker over picture-quality, especially once mum started prattling about 'pixies'.

('Pixels Mum.'

'Oh does it really matter?'

'Only if you want people to understand you.')

So my life was dreadful, but finally Craine had the chauffeur he'd always wanted. One that doubled as a resentful girlfriend.

Chapter 19

A COSY LITTLE RUT

After five months of futile house hunting I had developed a very one-track mind. I couldn't watch a film or TV show without everything fading away to background noise except the real estate. Richard Curtis films became a No-Go area, I feared just a peek at one would unleash all my pent-up bitterness: 'He works in a clearly unprofitable bookshop so how in the name of sanity is he living in THAT house in THAT part of town?!' This preoccupation ruined so much TV for me: Why did they all live in such nice houses? *Arrested Development* was still okay.

In the end I gave up and resigned myself to ogling property shows, leering at other peoples' competence. Keep your Adult Entertainment, pop those nipples back in, I like mine properly adult: 'Look how quickly they got their mortgage approved . . . Kirstie, say it's a Forever home. Say it, say it!' There were loads of these shows, I hoped it wasn't because there were swarms of people like me, sheltering from the economy in their parents' house, scratching that elusive itch by watching *To Buy or Not To Buy* and Nigella licking stuff in her massive kitchen. Broken Britain.

I watched too many of these shows, got drunk one night and signed up online for *Location, Location, Location*. I'm in showbiz, I reasoned, your fortunes can change overnight, look at all those people who became overnight successes! (Temporarily over-looking the many more who didn't.) So probably, I thought, best to proceed with the purchase of a £450,000 Islington townhouse and assume the money would arrive at the crucial moment. I was pretty pleased with this plan, it felt like playing Chicken with Fate and seeing who blinked first.

This self-congratulation lasted until nine the following morn-ing when I awoke to the sound of a ringing phone. A Scottish lady introduced herself as being from the *Location, Location, Location* production team. Hmm. I hadn't actually said my excellent plan aloud to anyone yet, always a litmus test and this wasn't an ideal pitching scenario. In the unforgiving light of day my words struggled to achieve the majestic clarity of the night before. I outlined my initial thoughts, about the vicissitudes of a comedy career and importance of showing Fate who was boss. There was a long silence. I picked a little dried wine from an eyebrow.

'Right,' she kept saying, clearly floundering, 'right.'

'Look, here,' I wanted to say, 'give me your hands, now aban-don reason and JUMP into blue sky thinking!'

I refrained. Over the years I've got better at spotting which things amuse me but no one else, and I keep them internal. So I stayed silent while she struggled. I felt terrible, we were each ruin-ing each other's morning.

She kept stuttering things like, 'Okay, so is your mortgage *in the process* of being arranged then?'

'Huh, "arrange", so that's the verb is it? No.' Well, there's another avenue closed. Thank you, World. Why will no one meet me halfway?

That's okay, shake it off, I told myself, squeaking the wind-screen wiper down the shower tiles. I'm quite thick-skinned, it had stood me in good stead in stand-up, it would carry me unscathed through this too. Years ago, my brother and I had agreed that the best tactic for dealing with the Luurtsemas Senior was to cultivate a sort of mental Teflon. Let most of what mum and dad say and do slide harmlessly off you, leaving behind nothing but residual smears that could be easily wiped away with some shopping on a credit card. Famous people often credit their family with 'keeping their feet on the ground'. Ours took it too far; I was wearing the ground like a pair of socks.

For example: I started a regular voiceover job while living with my parents. I love voiceovers, they're fun and you can do them in your pyjamas if you've got an understanding team. I told dad I'd gone for the meeting, and they had offered me the job while I was on the train home, which I considered flatteringly swift decision-making, though dad's take on it was a thoughtful nod and the suggestion 'probably no one else wanted to do it'.

I agreed, of course that was clearly the case, the job had in fact been offered to me out of a cardboard box near the tube station. If he was wandering past he should have a look, I believe they were waving around the job of Radio 1 breakfast presenter, pleading with commuters: 'Please take it or I'll have to flush it down a toilet. Come on, someone, 'ave an 'eart!'

Thanks to the Teflon, that remark was annoying but not hurtful. Good old Teflon, I'd been applying coats of it for years. I remember being sixteen on a sunny day and feeling good. I'd briefly eased off the ill and mad (more on which later) so I could sit my GCSEs without fainting (Chapter 22, if you really can't wait), and in a breezy mood I donned the year's first summer dress, always a triumphant occasion. I smashed a metaphorical bottle of champagne on my bum and glided downstairs on my maiden voyage. If you put a gun to my head I'd be forced to admit I was looking pretty effing swan-like. I swanned to the back door looking for mum to say 'Ooo' and 'Do a twirl.' But I found only dad, chopping at a tree with an axe, wearing plaid. He must've seen something on TV that gave him ideas – I didn't pry.

He straightened up and stared at me. I stared back, concerned. Oh god, was I dangerously swan-like? Had I reached such levels of womanly loveliness that even my own father's head was turned? With great power comes great responsibility I mused, smoothing down the C&A polyester, which created dangerous levels of static so I stopped before balloons drifted towards me.

He tutted and chuckled. Spit went everywhere. Nevertheless he had a point to make, so he wiped his chin and made it. 'Dear oh dear, you've got your mother's legs.' He pointed dismissively at my legs: 'They're rubbish, legs like bits of string,' he said. 'Shame you didn't inherit my shapely calves,' propping Exhibit A on the tree stump to better flaunt his physical charms. 'Look at the curve on that,' he said in deeply satisfied tones. It was my turn to stare. No young girl should have such a clear picture of what her dad would look like as a lumberjack stripper.

This sounds like I'm lying, I know, but I promise you it's true, and that since I disseminated this story far and wide, he can't clamber into a pair of shorts without overly personal comments. Many men would've backed down in the face of such ridicule but dad thrived on it; he stood firm by his lovely calves, and his right to point out other peoples' shortcomings.

The day he stumbled upon the word 'cankle' his little face lit up and we spent an uncomfortable month piloting him around town while he hosted an ungallant tournament called Spot the Cankle, involving him and any women unfortunate enough to trot past with an inelegant leg. 'There's another one!' was his war cry. 'You can't tell *where* calf becomes ankle can you?'

'No, Dad, but now she knows you're so interested, I'm sure she'd be happy to point it out.'

All of this had toughened me up nicely and I was dealing really well with the ego-bruising period of home-deficiency. Though I was spending a lot of time crying in the car.

One part of my life that I found impossible to integrate into the family home was that I like a good cry. A couple of times a week I like to bawl my eyes out over nothing in particular; it was nice, a little emotional irrigation. But it was impossible to hide, when I cried my face immediately assumed the texture of over-ripe, underfoot fruit. I'd never suit a tempestuous love life, make-up sex is probably nicer with someone whose eyes aren't swollen tightly shut. Mum could spot a blotch at twenty paces and wouldn't accept 'because' as an explanation for tears. To her it was morbid to weep for no reason, even if I assured her I had had a lovely time and it didn't cost anything: the Holy Grail of leisure pursuits.

The only place I had the privacy to indulge in a good old cry was driving between home and gigs. It was perfect really, the pathetic drama queen in me really got off on other drivers seeing me tearstained but dignified, so they could marvel 'what troubles is this poised young woman shouldering while maintaining admirable Lane Discipline?' I had perfected a brilliant brave face, patting my cheeks and sniffing hard, looking straight ahead.

I must stop viewing my life as scenes from a film; it gives me an unshakeable feeling of detachment from major events in my life. Though it was reassuring to discover that mum was guilty of it too. We had had a big barbecue a month ago to celebrate Michael's existence (I'm not bitching, just saying). I'd sneaked off to have a crafty fag behind the garage, forgetting that mum had eyes and a nose and the inclination to use both. She'd caught me brown-handed and, somewhat surprisingly, had slapped my face and marched off. I knew it was a filthy habit but still . . .

I later found her tearfully tossing a salad and a quick chat established that she was more drunk than I'd thought and her slap had only meant to knock the cigarette out of my mouth. When it had made contact with my face she was as shocked as I but, as a fellow devotee of drama, she scorned the indignity of an apology in favour of styling it out: embracing the moment and stalking off, while guests stared.

So I could hardly blame myself if I got my kicks from pulling a Brave Face Complete With Poetic Solitary Tear just when I was at a red light, so everyone could appreciate the moment. Really, the only downside was when I actually arrived at a gig. No one wants a tearstained clown, so I'd have to take a leaf out of mum's book and style it out, bowling into the comedy club bubbling with abrasive cheer: 'Hey guys, guess which idiot forgot she had a Ribena allergy?! Ha ha, look at what it does: blotchy face, pink nose, puffy eyes, croaky voice, yes indeedy, these are the symptoms, that's what this is! Simon, have you had a haircut? No? It looks like you have anyway, let's push on with the night!'

I was really enjoying gigging, mainly for the thrill of being treated like an adult, by people who didn't realise my mum waved me off to work that evening. I tried to keep my 'situation' quiet to preserve my thin veneer of cool. One night I was gigging at the Lyric Theatre, with Richard Herring and Stephen Merchant. We were all chatting backstage, there was an anecdote about Drew Barrymore in the offing (not mine, obviously) and I absent-mindedly unpacked my bag. And suddenly everyone was looking at a Tupperware box in my hands, containing a clingfilmed sandwich, fruit juice, veg fingers and tiny box of raisins: an unmistakeable mum-packed packed-lunch. A heavy silence broke out, with undertones of pity. I broke the tension with a raisin box maraca solo.

Some days, after viewing some especially bad flats, or extra vehement bickering about dishwasher stacking, I did feel a little vulnerable on-stage. On those days I found I was coarser than usual in my ad-libs and chat with the audience – building a little wall of filth to hide behind. That happens, sometimes you get on stage feeling a bit ugly or useless or just plain got-dumped-ten-minutes-ago but unless you've had a chance to write some devastating punchlines about it, you simply have to swallow those feelings down and accept you'll probably meet them again as kidney stones.

Comics have gigged through illness, divorce and all sorts, I knew there was nothing special about my situation, so I slapped a smile on my blotchy face and told no one how I was feeling, except the internet. Blanche DuBois was right, the kindness of strangers can really bolster a gal's feelings.

To add to my woes, I had a run of bad gigs; ones where I died on my arse, where I fostered the sort of atmosphere only a librarian could love and ones where the promoter considered a stage, chairs, lighting and microphone to be needless frivolities. I developed a coping strategy, one that you might find helpful if you too are a stand-up comedian or you do a job where drunken strangers feel comfy yelling abuse at you. Big shout-out to all the night bus drivers and twenty-four-hour McDonald's staff!

Here's my strategy. Popular guide for creepy misogynists, *The Game*, teaches us the value of 'neg-hitting': insulting an attractive woman to erode her self-esteem until she's so miserable she's prepared to consider your repulsive advances. From now on, whenever people yell insults at you, interpret it as determined 'neg-hitting' and *voilá*! They don't hate you, they just fancy you, in a charmingly aggressive way. I must warn you, after some particularly bad evenings you may find yourself swaggering home, drunk on all the attention.

The neg-hitting approach wasn't foolproof and my Mental Teflon was beginning to tarnish, when just in time, the property market took pity on me and presented me with a treat of a flat! This property made me feel brilliant about myself because it was teeming with silverfish. As the estate agent snapped the light on with grimly unconvincing enthusiasm, shoals of insects fled screaming towards the skirting board. Tiernan and Craine were repulsed but I enjoyed the giddy sense of power. I longed to burst into these rooms growling, 'Behold your vengeful God!' and guffawing as awe-struck minions scattered before me. If anything, my plans prejudiced Tiernan and Craine further against the flat.

They persuaded me that we couldn't rent a flat just for the ego-boosting infestations, what if the silverfish migrated? Or God forbid, what if the landlord instigated some basic standards of hygiene? Unlikely, sure, but possible. And I had to admit that even the busiest deity needed a usable kitchen to toss together the occasional pasta. In this flat most of the kitchen cupboard doors swung woozily from their hinges, which gave the room an air of jauntiness I could not share

It reminded me of the opening scenes of Disney's *Beauty and the Beast*. I made a pact with myself, if all this damage had been caused by a cursed Prince and if Chip and his teacup mum were about to pipe up from the mildewy sink and sing some of the classics . . . I still would not rent this flat. I love Disney as much as the next woman but only if she married it with a passion for doorknobs not smothered in necrotising fasciitis.

Thwarted in my early hopes for this flat, I went home, congratulating myself on another three hours and fifteen quid well wasted. Thank god for house hunting, at least it was relieving me of all that excess time and money I was always complaining about. I imagine only crack cocaine burns through your pocket and schedule with such haste, but at least with that there are brief flashes of fun. Plus, if you quit, whatever you do afterwards people will cut you slack and say, 'Yeah, but she used to be a drug addict.'

'That Robert Downey Jr. film is a bit crud.'

'Be fair, at least he's off the drugs.'

'The neighbour's son is pissing in my hydrangeas.'

'Would you rather he went back on the smack, Mr Picky?'

I settled my weary bones on the sofa, thinking maybe I'd just stay there and hide from life until it decided to up its game. I made a pact; I would rejoin adulthood when it stopped being so shit. I could wait. The Freeview Box and I had reached an understanding – it wanted to show me hours of mediocre films and I was happy to oblige. In times of trouble, I turned to mediocrity to soothe my mind. With my self-esteem wilting, amazing things would have made me feel small and useless, whereas rubbish films/books/ modern art were encouraging: 'Give me a free afternoon, bit of Sellotape,' I'd think, 'I could knock one of them together, no problem.'

Mediocre action films were particularly calming during this period. I maintain that a bad romance or comedy is needy; it's a brat lisping, 'Watch me tap danth!' But a bad action film is the solemn child orbiting his cardboard box around the moon; it has its own logic, it doesn't need you.

In an effort to not blame myself for the shoddy shape of my life, I was working on the theory that this house liked to hang onto children. The man we bought the house off fifteen years ago had grown up here, stayed there until his parents died, whereupon he put the house up for sale, moving seamlessly from his childhood home to a retirement home. Even as a child I knew that this was upsetting. Now I think it's downright mad; he missed the whole middle bit of life. His life was a sandwich with no filling, a sad fistful of bread.

It was more heartbreaking to consider that I was the house's latest victim. No wonder my brother moved to Thailand, the little shit fed me to the cursed house to ensure his getaway. 'Take her, not me!' he yelled over his giant backpack, flip-flopping off into the sunset.

Shamefully, I was actually starting to enjoy living there after five and a half months (but hey! Who was counting? Me). I'd finally fashioned a cosy little rut for myself. My parent's house was neater, more fragrant and better stocked than any house I would EVER own. Which only made viewing flats more depressing. The house wasn't palatial, but it was fifteen years of my parents' hard work and everything was Just So.

Cosy though it was, the rut was not without its problems. Mum and dad were starting to seem less odd to me; a sign that I was sliding down the slippery slope of sanity to join them in the hole. Finally allowed near the washing machine, I emptied it one morning and encountered a rogue odd sock. I marched it straight to mum's Odd Sock Box, where its mate was waiting. It gave me an unreasonable amount of joy to reunite them; I used the box lid to add drama, sliding it back slowly, game show-style. I made them embrace then I rolled them up together, neat and reconciled.

I finally understood why dad got so cross when I wore odd socks and why he would warn me in doom-laden tones that when one was on my foot the other would be in the wash, and they would NEVER catch up with each other, are you even listening to me Natalie? Folding the happy couple together into that sock knot that mums do, I finally understood the tragedy of two socks chasing each other round the washing/wearing cycle, doomed never to be together.

The Odd Sock Box seemed mad to me when I first moved home, but after nearly half a year my resistance had been worn down and I was a convert. A sock-box convert who worked nights, lived out of town and never saw her friends any more. So Fine, I thought, that's what Life had planned for me was it? To become a stay-at-home, emotionally stunted oddball whose social life consisted of Asda wine and *CSI*? FINE. So I bought an all-in-one pyjama set (a 'onesi' to aficionados) in the shape of a red panda, complete with tail and hood with face and ears. I was still a weirdo but now this weirdo was warm and cosy.

As you (and the burgundy ball-dress) know, when I write I dress up as if I'm off out to a party. It's an embarrassing confession but I think once I typed the words 'clitoral hood piercing' you and I overstepped some writer/reader boundaries, so you might as well know all my shameful secrets. Email me yours so we're square.

I'm sure our old neighbour thought I was a sex worker, as I'd stay at home all day in silk dresses and stilletos. Admittedly not a very successful prostitute as no one ever visited. 'Poor gal,' he must've thought. 'She's got the wardrobe nailed, but the guys in marketing are really letting her down.' He always gave me a little pursed-lips 'Chin up!' smile when I'd mince out with the recycling.

I dress up to write because it makes me think that I'm about to go to a party. Silk on my skin and feathers in my hair fool me that fun is afoot, it gives me butterflies in my stomach and an unshakeable sense that life is fun and full of possibility and I can plough all this tingly cheerfulness into my writing. As I type this I'm in a feathered mini dress complete with fake fur stole. Once my hair/boobs/eyelashes go up and outwards my spirits follow. It's so much fun being superficial.

However, living with mum and dad brought that fantasy crash-ing down. There was no chance of fooling myself that I might be on the verge of Bacchanalian high jinks. In between the *Neighbours* theme tune and a cat desperate to get its fat gut on my warm Mac, my subconscious refused to be fooled into any sort of optimism and who could blame it? Plus mum and dad hated me dressing slightly inappropriately, even in the privacy of my own bedroom. It 'wasn't normal' they assured me. What if there was a fire? Had I thought of that, rushing into the street in a yellow cocktail dress, the shame! Plus, the creasing . . . look at the creasing.

So I gave up and starting writing in my onesi. It wasn't the perfect solution, I'd get very hot and frequently wake up dribbling into my keyboard. Also it was a bit baggy so I looked like a cutesy serial killer wearing her victim's skin. And, admittedly, the tail did cause me trouble; it was so heavy, like a dead limb hanging off my bum, a souvenir from a limb-scrambling nuclear disaster. Once I'd sown that thought in my mind, going to the toilet in the middle of the night with the old dead-limb banging on my legs was no picnic. It was also near impossible to not dip my tail down the toilet. Of course, once I mentioned this, mum couldn't sleep, tormented by thought of me padding back to bed christening the carpet with my urine-soaked tail.

The weight of my tail meant that when I turned around quickly it became lethal. One sad day, mum called my name, I swivelled, tailed over a glass of orange squash and we 'agreed' that I was not to be a red panda any more. Especially once they found out I had been going to the newsagent in it. (Stupid nosey neighbours.) Funny, I felt no shame striding down the street in it, if anything I felt bold and liberated. But if I was home alone wearing it I couldn't answer the door in it because it seemed somehow furtive, like I'd been 'caught out'. If you're going to dress as a large saggy red panda you've got to do it with a bit of swagger. Swagger that's hard to pull off when you're halfway through the washing up.

I tried to get Craine on board the Emotionally Stunted Train, because if my life was going down the pan I was resolved to drag him with me. That's love, as I understand it. He refused a onesi on the grounds that he was an adult man not a baby. I respected that. So I bought him one in the shape of a shark and he was delighted with the compromise. Fierce yet cosy.

We washed the onesies after a week (because Tail could only evade Toilet for so long) and the washing machine's contents fell victim to centrifugal force. I opened the door to find a bloated killer smirking at me, forcing me to spend an unsettling ten minutes dragging its victims from its guts, like a fuzzy re-enactment of the *Jaws* autopsy scene. As I wrestled a pair of jeans from the bowels of Craine's shark I felt perhaps it was time to stop priding myself on my thick skin. Sometimes it's important to be aware of how the world sees you, say when striding down the street in a onesi, tail held primy aloft like you're late for the Loony's Quadrille.

It seemed fitting that it took a shark to show me this, their skin is so tough it could scrape a person's finger off. (Thank you Discovery Channel daytime programming.) Mind you, sharks probably need that sort of skin, as most people hate them. 'Shake it off', they probably grunt to themselves, 'shake it off', restlessly roaming the ocean, forcing themselves not to dwell on their media portrayal, cos only they know what they're really like, inside.

In many ways a shark would be the perfect house guest for my parents: thick-skinned and similarly incapable of rest. They could flood the downstairs toilet and live together in harmony, with none of the problems I brought to the table.

Chapter 20

WILD CHILD

I was teetering on the precipice of turning into That Weirdo who just lived at home forever. Truthfully, it was a little tempting; the flats we were being shown made me wonder, 'When did my life get so shit?' Was it my life or just life? Was everyone else miserable, was this just what a recession felt like? I thought a recession involved belt-tightening, working a bit harder, not a life so tedious you could use it as anaesthetic.

Something had gone very wrong, I felt like the lone voice of sanity patiently explaining to pointy-toed boys that 'No, I will not pay five hundred pounds a month for a flat that looks like a wet mushroom and no, please don't shrug like a man faced with the deranged whims of a kook, fearful at some point I might climb your leg and beseech "pinch my cheeks like daddy does!" I am the voice of reason here and THIS is good sense.'

Honestly, if a rich old man with his own home and an eye for a bargain had offered marriage at that point my only question would've been 'Are you near a tube?'

What had happened to my young, cool, sexy life? The other night I found that someone had nicked my electric blanket. (Because a person can be hellacool and have poor circulation.) I strode into the parental bedroom to get my stolen goods back. They denied all knowledge but there was an improbable amount of heat emanating from their bed. Either they were lying, or their pants were on fire and it's pretty much the same thing, so I threatened to put my hand under their duvet and check. Dad threatened to wriggle out of his pyjama bottoms, distinctly upping the jeopardy. Stalemate. I returned to my room to plan my next steps in the campaign. And take a long hard look at my life.

I found the longer I stayed at home the more certain oddities crept into my behaviour. I think without friends to point things out, a person can slowly become quite strange. Parents can't be trusted as arbiters of normalcy, they've invariably spent the last forty years being pleasant and paying gas bills and have reached a time in their lives where they want to kick up their heels and lower the tone of the neighbourhood.

I peeled off another layer of my flaking social dignity the day I found myself shopping in my pyjamas. Craine had come to visit, because he loved me and missed me and had a meeting in London the next day. I often questioned how frequently he'd visit if my family home wasn't much closer to London than his. If I pressed the point he'd look blank then proffer 'I love you?' – a useful Ctrl, Alt, Delete out of most arguments I tried to start with him.

Craine had a book that I had stolen from him. He was about to head back to Bath and wanted it back. This seemed outrageous to me. Yes, he bought it, but he was not the reader in this relationship, I was! It's my thing!

I am so good at reading that once in a coffee shop a woman said to me, 'Oh my god are you reading that book or just . . .?!'

I confirmed that I was not a loon who liked to smell paper, I was an awesomely fast reader. She expressed amazement, I did the modest face; we parted on wonderful terms. I still miss her.

So I decided the book should stay with me and I hid it, camouflaging my selfishness beneath adorable blank looks. I'm good at it, but there's only so long you can string it out by feigning ignorance and hiding under a duvet. Craine eventually turned irritable and I had to unearth the book from under the blanket at the top of the wardrobe (the intricacy of the hiding place understandably angered him further. There was real malice aforethought there.)

Craine and dad were heading into London at the same time, so they were going to catch the same train and be forced into conversation for twenty minutes. I mouthed 'sorry' behind dad's head and Craine looked stoic. He was heading into town for an audition that had presented him with very few details except the worrying statement that 'it would be nice to see him topless'. Craine disagreed vehemently, he didn't think that would be nice for anyone.

I wished him luck and dropped them off at the station to catch their train, shaking my head at the strange routines we'd fallen into. I really did feel like everyone's housewife. I'd had to abandon the book mid-sentence so I drove past a bookshop to pick up a copy. Browsing in Waterstones I realised something that really should've been more prominent in my mind. I had leapt straight from bed into the car to drop dad and Craine at the station, pausing merely to fling a cardigan on.

So I was standing, unwashed, teeth furry as kittens, in my pyjamas. As I've said, I'm not a morning person, but this was an awful oversight even for me. I wear pyjamas that I like to think recall Katherine Hepburn at her haughty hottest, but the scrap of self-awareness I have left, lonely and emaciated, wails that it's the look of a bored divorcee out to boink a Jehovah's Witness.

Thank god for the accent, I reminded myself.

While at home my accent had become increasingly 'Watford' but when needed I could still pull out the posh one. And when you're standing in Waterstones in silky jim-jams, smelling slightly, this accent comes into its own. It says, 'I am not weird/disgusting/drunk, I, my good man, am delightfully eccentric.'

I possibly over-egged it, sashaying over to the till, feigning bafflement at the word 'Hi'. Should've leaned more towards 'posh' than 'eccentric', but hindsight is the gift that cannot be rushed. Driving home, I resolved that I had to move out soon, before I started wearing a cat as a hat and chatting to my hands.

Another sign of a fraying psyche was that I had started to sleep-walk again. I hadn't done this in years, not since I was seventeen and anxious about my A-levels, which led to me sleepwalking into mum and dad's room, leaning over dad until we were nose-to-nose and then waiting. He woke up a few seconds later and his screams woke the neighbours. I remembered none of this obviously, and refused to accept any blame. He kept trying to foist blame on me, but I was having none of it.

I guess my stagnant life was weighing on my mind, as I had started my nocturnal wanderings again. There was nothing I could do about this except not sleep naked. Few socially awkward situations are ever alleviated by nudity. I think all my frustrated adulthood was finding an outlet while I slept, as apparently my sleepwalking consisted of pointing and holding forth and generally being more forceful than I was awake. Inside I am a leader of men, outside, a clown with a poor credit rating.

I sympathised with my parents as I'd spent the last few years dealing with Craine's sleep-talking. I had got used to him sitting bolt upright and muttering things that you'd never hear from him awake; phrases like 'yeah, good point, we'll get onto that' and, one memorable night, 'Can I clarify?' All of this delivered in a business-like brisk tone. I discovered he had the subconscious of a hedge fund manager. If I'd kept him constantly sedated he could've been earning me a six-figure salary.

So I was spending my nights striding around and pointing at terrified half-awake family members and my waking hours cradling the limp corpse of my social life. After almost six months back home, gigging most evenings and never seeing my friends, I'd become absorbed into my parents' social life, like an eighteenth-century spinster demoted to Perpetual Tag-Along.

We went to an engagement party together, where I had to bat away lots of 'you next?!' questions/threats. Given that my relationship with Craine had deteriorated into Pen Pals With Benefits, this was the last thing I wanted to think about. To save time I employed one phrase throughout: 'I'm too sexy to be a wife!' It means **nothing,** but if delivered with enough panache it creates the fleeting illusion of charisma, just long enough to squeeze past an interrogator and grab a slice of salami.[13]

Turning up an hour after my parents (you try getting dressed out of a garage. I had to wrestle my bra out of a toolbox), I admired everyone's clothes; they were all smart/casualling the hell out of that social engagement. I had overshot and ended up in Slutty. It'll happen, I am a Watford girl and as such believe the art of stylish dressing is wearing as little as possible without having to hold your hands in strategic positions when you walk. Factor in my aforementioned love of a bargain and I'm often to be found in stockings and crop top, proclaiming 'THREE QUID!!' like a prossie on special offer.

I believe most people are Face or Figure. I cover my face with a fringe and wear hot pants. Guess which I am? Mum disagrees, she holds firmly to the Boobs or Legs maxim and won't accept the happy compromise of One Of Each.

At this party dad had also shot a little wide of the dress code. Thankfully he hadn't landed in Slutty too. I'd hate us to be the sole inhabitants of that sartorial No Man's Land, nibbling vol au vents and rearranging our thongs. I discovered him in a natty grey suit, with a stripy shirt and pink tie, perched on a pouffe nibbling cheese. I turned up just in time to hear someone say how nice he looked, to which he replied mournfully, 'Well, I never get to dress up any more.' Which gave the impression that his handsomeness was his only pleasure in the evening, that attending this party was merely to satisfy his love of a suit.

It also gave the (mistaken) impression that his life used to be all feathers and ballgowns and this evening was a brief escape from drudgery, a chance to peacock around like the old days. Admittedly, he used to have an afro (mum swears the day he cut it off she realised to her displeasure he was shorter than her. But

13 There was a buffet, I wasn't just grabbing at stray flesh like an opportunistic grave robber. If Watford was bedecked with cooked meats ripe for the picking I would be more inclined to love it.

they had married by this point and back then 'misleading hair' was not grounds for divorce).

Of course a pig in a petticoat is still going to roll in mud . . . as the saying very rarely goes. And sure enough, I left him playing nicely with his friends, having a conversation about parties, but it would seem, piecing back through the witness statements, that they strayed from Parties to Booze to Overdoing It to Vomit, and I returned from the buffet clutching my spoils to hear him confiding, 'but sometimes, even when I've got no more sick inside me, I keep retching . . .' and then demonstrating the noise, to an appalled semi-circle.

Dad gets lost in the finer points of tone and appropriate chitchat and will invariably say or do inappropriate things. We alerted him to this little problem years ago, hoping that awareness would help, but now he just said the same awful things, accompanied by a worried frown, and later blamed us for not removing him from the situation. He was getting smaller every year so I reckoned by eighty I'd be able to pop him in a papoose and flee the scene the next time we went to a funeral, he knocked on the coffin and said 'Oak?' in the tone of a man shopping at Wickes.

Years ago I taught him a rule: 'If you're saying it, you probably shouldn't be. So stop, announce that you're on very strong hay fever medication and go sit in the car and wait for us.' Rule for life there. Stick it in your bag for life and you're set.

The next night, in an attempt to shake off the Tag-Along feeling I went Out. I'm not usually a fan of Out, I find In preferable: it's warmer, cheaper, with lower crime rates. But it was my friend's birthday and, while tempted by the offer of sitting quietly at the end of my bed watching me read, she's a firm traditionalist at heart and decided Fun was more appropriate. I acknowledged it probably was time to rejoin the world: my social life was officially dead at this point. I had loaned a friend a pair of heels, a clutch bag to another, doling out the accoutrements of my old life like organ donations from the deceased. I made this point to the girl getting the shoes; she looked sickened but took them anyway.

Feeling slightly nervous, I began my ninety-minute journey from Watford to Fun. I looked very nice. I was aiming to look like a budget Daisy Lowe, for I am a woman of ambition, limited only by looks and finances. Sadly, I was going to London's Soho. I hate Soho after 8 pm, it can go suck its own balls. I'm sure it would make itself queue for an hour for the privilege of doing so, while informing itself that more important people were enjoying the VIP Chill-Out Zone in its anus.

For example, this was how difficult it was to simply enter a wine bar:

Nat: (looking confusedly at a bar too trendy for doors) Hello, how do I get in please?

Doorman: (let's just call him Cock Head for short) Through the door.

Nat: That's very good. (LIE – it was at this point he earned his name) And where's the door please?

Cock Head: Behind me.

(Long pause)

Nat: So . . .? (doing a small mime of a rugby tackle. Classic passive aggression from our hero)

Cock Head: Do you have a reservation?

Nat: An ever-growing list. (he didn't get it, it was quite a subtle joke) Yes.

Cock Head: Let's check that, shall we?

And I was frogmarched in as if I'd rocked up to Downing Street and said, 'Hi, Dave said he'd paint my toenails if I couldn't be bothered, so . . .'

I think if you work nights, like comedians or Cock Head here, it does give you a false sense of superiority. It's inevitable when you're surrounded by staggering drunks and you're managing to keep your shoes on and lunch inside you. Like me, and most people who work nights, I bet he's had a boozy 10 am, but no one sees you whirl around your living room to the opening music of *Frasier* so you can hang onto your snooty attitude.

Before the trendy bar I had met some other friends for dinner in a place called a 'Meat Shack'. (It sounded like an informal abattoir, with mates popping round to hack casually at pigs with whatever came to hand. It didn't exactly get my yummy juices flowing.) Still, sloppy massacre aside, this evening was shaping up to be a social whirl.

'Why Nat,' you're probably saying, fanning yourself with an empty cereal packet, 'I'm a simple person, I cannot keep up with your galloping parade through London's High Society! Just give my love to Lady Gaga and don't let the paps get any up-skirt shots.'

Perhaps it was an ambitious evening, but a few nights before I had watched the beginning of six crime dramas and realised I had seen them all and knew the plots with a forensic detail that would make their pathologist's proud. An upsetting revelation and one that demanded I whack on some heels and paint the town red like a gunshot victim's kidney.

I hadn't realised we were going to a shack devoted to meat, so I was a little over-dressed, but that turned out to be the least of my worries. When I asked our waitress the difference between Spare Ribs and the boldly named Baby Back Ribs, she explained, pointing at *her own ribs* to demonstrate. I'm not a die-hard carnivore, much like my smoking, if anyone criticises me for it I have no defence beyond whining 'it's nice and I like it', and I'm sure many a serial killer has offered up the same argument. But it really did take the edge off my appetite to imagine my waitress carved up and smothered in smoky sauce.

She might as well have said: 'Let me burn my finger a bit, smell that, smell my sizzling meat juices, hang on, I'll try and get a Fear Sweat on, make it more realistic, I'll get Carlos, he's a great actor, he can do the smell of a scared pig in an abattoir SO well, it's yummers!' Encouraged by thoughts of her sliced ribs I plumped for their classic dish: coleslaw.

I staggered home far less drunk than I looked, but a half-hour walk from the train station in heels is quite the task. I opened the front door, tripped over a cat and collapsed on the hall rug. As a result mum and dad insisted on treating me like I was one Babycham from a coma and forced two pints of water down me, while I spluttered, 'I'm not drunk! Ask me my National Insurance number! Okay, hang on, I'll get my wallet.'

Mum often treats me like I'm drunker than I am. I suspect less out of concern, more so she can pretend I'm the reckless wild child she secretly wants me to be. Although in reality she'd quickly tire of driving me to rehab and raking up the condoms.

Mum and I used to work together in a hotel and whenever I'd turn up after a night out she'd take a knowing look into my eyes and tut, 'Nataliiiee . . . your pupils are like pinpricks!'

This would make her sound knowledgeable about The Drugs and would make me sound like a fun groovy drugs-taker. I think mum was titillated by the idea of saying to her mates, 'Natalie takes drugs. Well, you know, London . . .' and looking worldly-wise.

I never minded, as I never really took drugs so I felt blameless. Though years later I realised, while mum was implying I was a hedonist who took pills in nightclubs, actually those drugs cause big pupils. The small pupils she was accusing me of having are more symptomatic of heroin abuse. This was a little wide of the Fun-lovin' Chick label she was trying to slap on me. Though I was bemused by the idea of our colleagues saying:

'You know that waitress with the funny accent?'

'Looks like a budget Daisy Lowe?'

'Who's Daisy Lowe?'

'Never mind.'

'Anyway, apparently she's a skag addict.'

'That might explain her lack of hand-eye coordination.'

Over the years mum and I have gradually accepted that we can't force each other into personalities we'd prefer. There was a setback last year when she gave me a *Mamma Mia!* DVD for Christmas and I imagine she felt the same when I gave her that pestle and mortar. At least I tried. I stared at my present for a while, then politely read the back.

'So a woman doesn't know who got her up the duff, and there's a shortlist of three? If this was in the *Daily Mail* you'd be outraged, but set it to music and you're charmed. I bet she's riddled with STDs.'

When I bought her the pestle and mortar ('So you can grind up spices and make food taste of . . . something?') she unwrapped it and rewrapped it in one fluid move then stuck it back under the tree. She was more gracious when the cat brought her half a twitching frog.

Years ago I tried to rebel, painfully aware that mum's approval made it void. I went to raves and took drugs. Well, I stood in a field with aspirin pumping giddily through my veins. Somehow, drug dealers saw me coming, in my sturdy mac with pockets full of muesli bars ('What time will the rave finish? . . . Right, so it lasts an indefinite period of time and yet there's no catering facilities? Bloody hippies') and sold me headache tablets. They never even bothered to scratch a smiley face on them; I knew from TV that happy pills looked happy even when they were dog-worming tablets.

Subsequently, my late teens were notable for a lot of fresh air and the absence of aches and pains. It would've been lovely, if it weren't for all the strangers hugging me; I could never quite shake the feeling they were after my muesli bars. I couldn't have had a healthier wild child phase if mum had been in cahoots with drug overlords. Which I'm not ruling out; unlike me she is a 'People Person'.

I got ready for bed, returning my bra to the toolbox and resuming my rightful position on the sofa: 'I think we've seen this one. That dining table's drenched in semen, I bet you I'm right. See, dad agrees . . .'

Out is all very well, but I appreciated the joys of In as I discarded my high heels and took my book to bed, where I found that someone had surreptitiously returned my electric blanket. I knew no one could bear to admit fault, so I didn't mention it the next morning, I just greeted both parents with extra cordiality and made myself a tiny bowl of cereal.

Chapter 21

IF THERE'S NO BLOOD, IS IT REALLY SHOPPING?

Whenever friends with a social conscience sigh at people swarming to shopping centres to shovel over cash in the pursuit of elusive emotional and material fulfilment I always exhale gently and murmur, 'I know . . .'

But truthfully?! I am a materialistic child of the suburbs, I think it's a LOVELY way to spend a day and I ache with sorrow for anyone who doesn't know that.

Sunday morning dawned bright and clear. So I was told. I woke up much later, when mum marched into my bedroom like a soldier having a breakdown (in jammies). She looked angry yet excited, I soon realised why. Marks and Spencer were having a sale and she hadn't known! She felt ashamed and foolish, yet now she was armed with this information she was steeled to act upon it. Could I be up and ready within five minutes? If so, move on out people, c'mon, let's go, let's go!

The Marks and Spencer sale was a place where mum and I could have fun, spend time together and celebrate the similar parts of our personalities: our love of clothing, bargains and violence. The first time I shoved a stranger in the pursuit of a three-pound silk dress was in a Marks and Spencer sale and I felt like a young medieval boy finally tall enough to push his father's plough. Mum snatched it out of my opponent's hands before she creased it with her falling body, and I knew then that I had made her proud. Our motto is, if there's no blood, is it really shopping?

We sauntered out into the sales, elbows sharpened for battle, ears on Deaf Mode for peoples' weak cries of 'I was *looking* at that!' I bought a baggy dress for seven quid that should've looked rubbish but didn't. It was the perfect sale purchase, comparable to finding a man who is secretly attractive beneath a horrible beard and 'hilarious' t-shirts. Once you make him shave and buy a cardigan, women will fall at his feet, but it will be too late, for he will be your boyfriend by then. HA! You found a wreck, you renovated it and added value. You are a winner. Kirstie would be proud.

Mum and I rummaged, ate sandwiches, chatted. We had a great time and I knew we were both thinking about how this hasn't always been so tranquil. I was a 'tricky' teenager, and shopping for clothes was a vicious battle, set to a soundtrack of 'Don'tcomeinthechangingroomjustwaitoutside!'

Once I became more normal, mum entered her own Difficult Phase Of Life and we all had to tread carefully around her. Here's a mum-management tip for teenagers: Do not try to make your mum trendy. I understand the impulse, but trust me, it will end in tears and a fifty-five-year-old in jeggings. And this is a certain type of hell that no one needs. Very soon the menopause will do all the hard work for you. It made mine aware of knee-high boots and words like 'silhouette'. Her sleek new look almost compensated for the previous ten months of savage moodiness.

Selflessly, we also brought dad to the sale, even though he was only going to slow us down. We sat outside the men's changing room for half an hour while he tried on an endless collection of identical jeans and we debated the finer points of each. A small girl flounced off declaring, 'Well there's forty minutes I'm never getting back!' I recognised a kindred spirit in the rehearsed quip and offered her a Percy Pig sweet.

The joy of Marks and Spencer is the feeling that you're somehow stepping back into a simpler time, one where people are polite and never surprising, and where 'You' and 'Me' are the only adjectives you need:

'Oh that's so You!'

'Is it? Is it really Me?'

'It's definitely a You dress . . .'

In the women's changing rooms a woman stepped out of her changing room and addressed the room of strangers stretching in their unfamiliar clothes. 'Too short?' she asked, anxiously smoothing some trousers.

We gazed at her hems and chorused 'mmm, a bit'.

'Teetering on an ankle-flapper there,' I offered.

Mum gave me a look that said, 'Why do you do that? Just use the minimum words you need to get your point across clearly.'

I gave her a look that said 'NEVER!'

There was a lovely community feeling that you simply don't get in Topshop. Well, maybe in the toilets, as teen purgers hold each other's hair back, but it's not such a great advert for the brand. I resolved, for my next life crisis I'd seek refuge in my nearest Marks and Spencer changing room.

At the men's changing room the atmosphere was more akin to getting your jabs before war. They didn't make eye contact, and every man had some sort of woman with him for protection.

A young man preened and asked his girlfriend if his trousers weren't a bit tight. 'No,' she chirped. 'It's nice to have them a bit tight there, show the shape of your bum.' A heavy silence descended over the changing room as he crept back to his cubicle, all cheeks blushing pink.

However, dad didn't cover himself in glory either. He hasn't got a flair for dressing himself, and he knows this so he mostly just wears black, reducing the risk of mishap. It does mean he looks like a psychopath, a mime or Ricky Gervais. Or some ungodly combination; a man silently doing That Dance, clutching headless ferrets.

Dad peeked out of the changing room. He edged out stiffly. Mum waited. I waited. We all waited; he had to breathe eventually.

He surrendered with a wheeze and his belly resumed its rightful position – peeking coyly over his waistband as if flirting with his knees. He tested each pair of trousers by lunging on each leg, a move I've never seen him do outside of this situation, while the shop assistants stared at him, clearly thinking 'he'd better buy them now he's crushed his nuts in them.'

'Go for a walk,' mum suggested, as she has from time immemorial whenever anyone in the family has tried on shoes/clothes/ life decisions. He trotted off. Time passed. Then passed some more, as it does.

'Oh,' she said, 'I didn't tell him when to stop.' Without specific instructions of when to return, dad had marched off like a lemming until he reached the edge of the shop, when he confusedly ricocheted back. Sniggers cropped up around us. We joined in, to distance ourselves from him.

After my sterling work as wingman in Marks and Spencer I was allowed final choice and I dragged them both to my new favourite place – the shop that sold dresses for a fiver. They were almost certainly nicked, but that just added to the thrill. As did the way the loud fat Turkish shop-owner treated his customers:

'Hey lady! We don't do that one in your size! No sorry madam, no big sizes. That sort of suits you no? Well,' he'd shrug helplessly, 'I don't know, you look better than when you came in anyway . . .'

He had a hardcore of regulars, me included, who'd take any insult he slung at us for dresses that cheap. I'm sure we all told ourselves, 'Oh it's a cultural thing, a vocabulary misunderstanding.' But you know what? Fat is Fat, as in, 'You are too fat for that dress' and I don't know many countries where women greet that badinage with coy giggles and blooming self-esteem.

He had a loud voice and a permanently open door so the whole street could hear him belittling us, but we LET HIM. We would put up with so much worse; he was the gatekeeper to pretty dresses for only a fiver. You can't get a sandwich lunch for that nowadays! It's as close as I've ever come to having a drug problem and a relationship with my dealer that I'd call 'complicated', blinking through tears to find the drop-down Facebook menu.

Sadly the day couldn't sustain these levels of pleasure and I headed off for my daily viewing of flats. I had concocted a fiendish new tactic – I was considering areas that I really didn't want to live in. My theory: if I didn't want to live there, then other people wouldn't either. And so there would be a spare house for us to live in. My housemates were disappointingly lukewarm on this clever scheme and left me to pursue it alone.

I met an estate agent at her office, made some painfully desultory chat (I am so bad at small talk, I wish I had a dog, we could just look at it and remark upon it, break the ice that way). Together we wandered around another windowless griefhole. Arson would have been an act of mercy.

Seriously, I had never considered windows a luxury item before that year.

'Hmm,' I wanted to say, 'so this is what the last resort looks like.' I fought the urge, no need to get nasty. At least my estate agent was refreshingly honest and she admitted she wouldn't live there either.

I was warming to her, until she confided, 'Of course, it's all terrorist housing around here.' I looked around, the area looked pretty drab but I didn't spot gangs of Jihadis tinkering with bombs on their driveways, swapping chatty tips on the best detonators.

I left her with my email address, including a tiny but crucial misspelling so I wouldn't be troubled by her 'forthright' views on modern Britain. I didn't fancy opening my inbox to 'Well, it's those bloody Mussies that get me . . .'

I went home, popped my feet up and relaxed with a mug of wine. After repeated complaints about how high I filled my wine glass, I had decided that a mug would be a neat way around this endless debate. Then dad started grumbling like a bled radiator about how vulgar I was being. I swung into debate (yelling, really) about my thinking behind the mug and how I was doing my best, when suddenly, out of nowhere, Mother L leapt into the fray and slapped him down like a tiger defending her cub. Hurray! Divide and conquer. A plan with no drawbacks, bar the risk of divorce. To be fair, a man who would list the Pull My Finger game under 'Hobbies and Interests' on his CV really can't be calling anyone vulgar, he left himself very exposed to retaliation and mum pulled no punches.

'Where were you house hunting today?' she asked, to fill the post-fight silence.

I told her, delaying my story of the racist estate agent until I was another mug of wine in and operating at maximum anecdote mode.

'Why are you house hunting there?' mum tutted: 'You need a flat and it's all terraced housing.'

Chapter 22

'FUCK UP EARLY AND FUCK UP BIG'

A last-minute gig cancellation left me with a free evening, which I initially thought I'd spend working in my room. 'Good idea,' said mum, 'yeah, that's a good idea.' Then she hung around the bottom of the stairs enticing me into shouted conversations. In that house, being separated by two rooms and a flight of stairs was never a reason not to carry on a long and involved chat.

I abandoned work once my throat started bleeding and we took up our now customary positions on the sofa. I watched the News while they embellished it with a Director's Commentary: 'Heavy breather, Merkel.' I then sat through an animated debate about people with names like testicles. I blamed Ed Balls for that. Him and a Brian Teste dad swore he'd met at a conference.

I lost patience and announced that we were going to have A Nice Conversation. Mum had spent years trying to get one of these going. By now she'd accepted that the closest we'd ever get was grunted squabbles in the ad breaks, but I demanded we try one now. Mainly to spare me from their debate about whether Andrew Sachs was 'close enough'.

The Nice Conversation put up a plucky fight, but was soon sidelined in favour of Reminiscing, which was a dangerous conversational path, as no one in our family remembered events the same way. We all recounted slightly different versions, featuring ourselves in the lead role and the other three acting like dicks.

Mum was remembering my teenage years, and the day she came home to dad trembling in the kitchen, my brother hiding and me weeping in the living room. Dad 'greeted' her at the front door by clutching her elbows and hissing, 'I didn't say ANYTHING. But then she started crying and it won't stop!!' Good times. (Needless to say, my version of this story began hours earlier when dad decided to point at and catalogue my spots.)

My adolescence is only ever referred to in the tones you'd assign to 9/11 or Lord Voldemort; a sort of 'God protect us, may we never see such times again' kind of attitude. I don't know what they're complaining about, they struck very lucky with me. The pubescent years are a worrying time for any parent, with under-age drinking, gang culture, pregnancies – there's a world of peril and worry out there. Thankfully, while my peers were off drinking and giving blowies in graveyards (I won't name names) I stayed at home and concentrated diligently on my anorexia.

'See ya kids!' I'd wave off my (mostly imaginary) friends. 'Have fun now y'hear? Sniff some glue for me! No, I'm fine; I've got a busy night planned, hiding my dinner in my pockets. Self-harm won't do itself, am I right?! Okay, take it easy . . .'

My parents never had to worry about finding me pregnant or asleep in a puddle of heroin. Granted, they had other, more fiddly problems to contend with, like kidney failure and a weakened heart. But this taught them lots of interesting new medical words and encouraged us to spend time together as a family. In hospital waiting rooms and group therapy. All right, it's no Thorpe Park, but it's all about the quality time, right? Guys?

I had complacently assumed that we were all cool about my former life choices, I mean mum had a shellsuit that I'm willing to forgive and forget, but sadly the milk of human kindness didn't flow both ways. Unlike the M25 (you see, I am learning). However, living together was teaching us more about each other and bringing us closer together, despite our best efforts to resist this by having the telly on loud. Our relationship was becoming stronger than it had been in years, after it had survived the strain of my decade of anorexia.

'Ten years?' you're probably thinking, 'Now, Nat, I know anorexia is a laugh, what with all the unexpected black-outs and a body that looks increasingly like an archaeological dig, but didn't it get a bit repetitive over a decade?'

Not for me, but possibly loved ones found the final eight years a bit samey. With hindsight, there were better ways to spend the nineties, maybe someone else should choose the theme of the next decade. With my track record I'd probably plump for the ebola virus or The Wit and Wisdom of Anne Robinson.

Once I was let out of hospital the NHS gave us weeks of group therapy, so much therapy it crossed the line from generous into insulting. 'Twenty weeks?!' we tutted, 'We're not flinging shit at nuns.'

You'd have thought we'd have aired all our thoughts on this subject during these sessions, but in typical fashion we had ignored the opportunity to learn and grow and treated it as an afternoon of am-dram. We're all decent performers, easily capable of fooling a therapist, without stopping to wonder if we should. It's just so easy to master the language of therapy, especially if you're a shivering bundle of bones with big 'Help me' eyes.

My most useful tool was the phrase 'I have low self-esteem' – a delicate way of saying 'I just don't realise how excellent I am. Big sigh.'

I hope that one day a therapist snaps when this platitude is bleated at them for the millionth time. Just one therapist who flings a beanbag at their patient's head and says, 'You know what?! Maybe you're just not that great. I mean if you think you're a bit shit, why doubt your judgment? Why chalk it up to "low self-esteem"? You're the closest eye-witness; let's just take your word for it, you fucking inadequate.'

But no one ever threw a beanbag at us and so our group therapy passed like a difficult dinner party, with the four of us making nice small talk, distracting our guest from the pie burning in the oven.

We never left therapy stretching and saying 'Well, glad I got THAT off my chest!' but rather 'I think that went well? She seemed to have a nice time didn't she?'

'Oh yes, she was writing in her book a lot, she certainly didn't seem bored. What a good idea to tell her about that time Natalie ate a worm.'

While they conferred, I was usually thinking 'six laughs, I got six laughs out of her. In a very tense atmosphere, so I'll probably count it as eight.'

This approach to therapy didn't exorcise any of our familial woes, it just made us even better at the dinner parties we never hosted and that I wouldn't have eaten. We really honed our ability to steer a therapist's attention wherever we wanted, but never found an outlet to put this skill to use. If we were ever in an old-fashioned sitcom where someone's boss and his narcoleptic naturist friend were coming to dinner on the same night, we would rise to the challenge superbly. It hasn't happened yet but life is long, we can wait. This specific situation will crop up one day; then you'll see something special.

So the counselling did expand our skill sets in new and unusual directions, but was ultimately useless and so I shouldn't have been surprised to find residual resentment clinging to our relationship. It peeked out at rare and unexpected moments, like the morning dad brought me a surprise fried breakfast. Now while this might sound lovely in theory, it's just impractical to have that much saturated fat sprung on you, you need to be in the mood for it first. It's like a surprise sex session, I'm sure it's well meant but do check everyone's keen before you get your socks off. So I managed the toast and beans no problem, but the second fried egg rapidly became a chore.

Dad stood watching me chew for a while, before sighing, 'Great. Anorexic again?' and stalking off for more butter.

We have never discussed the issue, as that simply isn't our way, but I sensed that finally being sane was the only amends they ever wanted me to make. (I assumed this, and didn't check in case they wanted something more, like an actual apology or some financial compensation.)

I felt properly forgiven after six months at home, when our relations had settled into a calm happy rut. Mum and I were driving somewhere to drop something off at someone's house for a friend to pick it up later for their kid's school fete (my parents were always doing shit like this). She said abruptly, 'you were always a nice child.'

We don't go in for compliments in our family so this was an attention-grabbing statement. Previous emotionally demonstrative moments included the time she had patted my shoulder and said 'It *is* good you're so tall. It's a nice thing.'

So I grabbed her compliment with indecent haste and began interrogating it to squeeze out any extra. I feigned deafness so she had to repeat it, then tried a different approach – rejecting the compliment so that it would be proffered again more vehemently. 'Really?' I inquired, 'Really a nice child, even during the . . .?' giving the universal mime of 'nut job'.

'Oh yes,' she assured me, 'I mean, it was horrible, but it never felt like you did it out of malice.'

She was right. I got on with my anorexia assiduously and unobtrusively. If everyone went at their jobs with the quiet devotion that I had gone at mental illness, this world would run like clockwork. Still, this is not to fling flowers at myself as I did get sectioned, self-starvation simply not being The Done Thing, even in the nineties.

I guess if I had to identify a weak point in my Anorexia scheme, and my memory isn't perfect as malnutrition will addle the mind, it was maybe that I didn't know why I was doing it, simply that I must.

I had won a scholarship to private school when I was young and, while I didn't really have any friends, I had a huge library at my disposal and I felt I'd bartered one for the other. The school was amazing, and the school fees reflected this, so my scholarships were worth increasing amounts of money and I had to keep my grades high. I was acutely aware of my tenuous position and desperate not to let go, so I jittered around school like an anxious trader before a constantly looming crash. My accent was also bouncing between my original Watford one and the new posh one I was trying to cultivate. Between seven and fifteen I sounded like Dick Van Dyke's mopey daughter.

I was a painfully shy child, but at twelve years old and five foot eight I was unavoidably conspicuous, despite an impressive stoop. If anyone spoke to me I would blush until my ears throbbed. So I hated the dining hall; a huge cavernous room designed to hold around 800 girls. I was usually too scared to go in there all by myself and almost certainly heading for a tray-dropping, so I'd just hide in the library and read for an hour. The hunger was worth the lack of anxiety.

I was happy to talk to teachers, just not people my age, they were so confusing and always screaming with laughter at things that, to the uninitiated, didn't sound at all funny. They were so alien to me I might as well have been schooled alongside 799 giant lizards.

This continued for months. The daily lack of food made me feel faint, yet I had so much adrenalin racing through me as my body tried to keep the show on the road, I felt invincible. I deteriorated slowly until every staircase became my very own mountain, I could never reach the top without pitching base camp halfway for a rest under the guise of 'What is this thing in my shoe? Best squat down and investigate that! Hmm, how curious, I'll sit here and have a think about the ramifications of the . . . thing . . . on my . . . oh my mouth is so dry.'

I had no plans to foster a model-like figure – I must make

that clear. All the cool girls in school were enviably curvy, with bodies that were an early catalogue of ins and outs. My body went out a bit after my neck, but after that was just an unappealing succession of ins. I tried endless nifty tricks with leggings to foster the illusion of calves, but by my teens I had just given up on my body as it clearly wasn't playing ball.

Back then girls' magazines like *Just Seventeen* or *Smash Hits* had a pretty responsible idea of body image and so all their models displayed proper boobs and bums. In this world my scrawny carcass had no value. And fair enough, I thought, staring at my knobbly knees, only in Butlins in the seventies would these be popular. Ironically I think, I would've been helped by today's media obsession with skinny girls. Just a few peaky waifs in frocks would've been very encouraging, but sadly heroin chic was a year or two away and Kate Moss was yet to pop up with her reassuringly spindly calves. I was stuck staring at Elle 'The Body' Macpherson, wondering how we could possibly be the same species.

I don't think anyone noticed my antics for a while, it was a big school and I was a very unmemorable part of it, while at home I was a shuffling bundle of knitwear, like a jumble sale with feet. Plus there were few outward signs of deterioration.

I remember at Prize Day shuffling light-headed across the stage to collect my medal of academic achievement (I know, private school is weird) and I feared I'd black out, fall off the stage and kill the infant class sat cross-legged below. I made it without fainting, the local dignitary placed the medal round my neck, I smelt lunch on her breath, flinched like I'd been slapped and staggered off-stage dry-heaving.

'People,' I thought furiously, 'why are they so **weird**?'

By thirteen years old I weighed five stone and had resisted all suggestions that perhaps I could make eating a daily thing again? I was offered many opportunities to start eating again, all of which I politely declined, because I had A Plan thank you and you wouldn't understand. So I was taken to Watford General Hospital where, I was told, I was going to be X-rayed. I remember being quite excited by this and trooped along with X-ray facts and questions for the radiographer (which took longer to find in those pre-Google days).

A doctor ushered me into a hospital room, I went in and turned around to see mum and the doctor on the other side of the door, locking me in with awkward smiles (and a key). The smile you give when you pass someone in a narrow corridor.

'Sorry if I've intruded upon you at all.'

'Well, incarceration will impact on my plans a little . . .'

I collapsed on the bed, exhausted from all that turning around, and waited for the next development in an already-surprising day.

Being sectioned wasn't as exciting as it looked on television. I think mum and dad had to sign some forms in another room, but it was hardly *Girl, Interrupted*. Later some doctors came in to take blood and I got genuinely furious, shouting and thrashing about in a rare display of passion.

It was only afterwards, as I caught my breath and inspected my puncture marks, that I thought, 'Now THAT was a bit more televisual!'

Post-sobbing and thrashing I really quite liked hospital. It had surprisingly few rules; anything goes because there was always something more important to attend to than a genial skeleton sauntering around. I was free to loll about in wheelchairs, lashing them together to make the überchair, tugging my old friend the drip trolley behind me. Most days I was an emaciated May Queen, festooned in discarded flowers I'd found along the corridors. There were always loads of them littering the hallways, brought, I liked to think, by people who had a rethink at the last minute: 'Naaaah, they don't deserve carnations. Only encourages them to malinger.'

Many years later I lived down London's Trendy Brick Lane (as it likes to be known) and experienced a similar liberation to this; it was an area so cool it confused itself. All it knew was that looking nice was laughably trad, and so I could buy milk in my dressing gown with my head held high.

The only downside of hospital, apart from the oppressive presence of death and the force-feeding and the fact I wasn't allowed to leave, apart from THAT, the only downside was that it was always uncomfortably hot. It was as if the staff had decided, we-ell . . . the ones we can't cure we'll broil and between the thank you cards and the longpork hot pot, we'll be sitting pretty. I took care not to let them pop a parsley nightcap on me, or tenderly nestle an onion between my cheeks.

I survived the NHS casserole, and I got better and left hospital. Then I got ill again, but not so much that I required hospitalising. Then I got better. Then I was okay for a year, then I stopped eating again and then I started eating again. I could go on, but those were the highlights and there's only boring bits left now.

Someone referred to it as a 'battle with anorexia' the other day and, while the drama-seeker in me sobbingly embraced this term, realistically it's a long boring war of attrition that you fight against yourself. And loved ones can't really be supportive or encouraging, there's nothing to fight, there's no cures, there's just a girl with very cold hands eating lasagna like it's poison. I guess you could wave a little flag at her but it might put her off her stride.

As I said, fuck up early and fuck up big and after that all your other failures will look like small fry. I don't just churn out these thoughtless mottoes, I am living the theory. I'd have to scribble the word mum refers to as See You Next Tuesday over all the walls, get jiggy with Take That's Howard all over the shiny dining room table, scratch it with his various body piercings, spill cereal everywhere and then set fire to everything else with Weetabix Molotov Cocktails before they stop being grateful I'm no longer that douche who starved herself into organ failure.

Chapter 23

LET THE GAMES COMMENCE!

Despite my relative brilliance compared to Teen Nat, mum then hightailed it off to the Isle of Wight on a school trip, and I tried not to take it personally. But she looked offensively pleased to get away. I think she felt bad about leaving us as she filled the fridge with meat. All the meats, even ones like pastrami that you just see in films.

Perhaps she hoped that if dad was distraught at her absence he'd be too meat-stuffed to do anything but cry delicious little gravy tears. And if that didn't help, there was enough raw material there to assemble a meaty replica of her. It was very kind, but meals were like waterboarding ourselves with grease. Within a week we couldn't hear the TV over our breathing.

Mum called several times a day to babble excitedly about zorbing and abseiling and wearing her new sweatshirt and her mate Jennifer the deputy-head having ALMOST EXACTLY THE SAME sweatshirt! But not quite! LOL. She combined these calls with frequent texts, announcing: 'Fencing! Then abseiling and a trip to the beach before bed!' After forty minutes shivering on the front lawn in a fencing mask and bikini, I was forced to accept that these were boasts not promises. I responded in kind: 'Gig to freshers, 150-mile round-trip, three comics to drop off, then a bean-wrap that smells of petrol and bed by 4 am'. Choke on your envy, Mother.

This gig I was boasting about was in Keele. It was a long journey; I fear my jokes have a bigger carbon footprint than a charcoal clown. For the last fifty miles I was hallucinating a cup of tea in bed. To the exhausted London comic, Buckinghamshire, Hertfordshire etc. aren't the home counties, they're the nearly home counties.

When I finally got home I extricated myself from the car and stumbled through the front door. I was feebly wrestling with my shoes (just to get them off, I wasn't suddenly seized with a WWF urge) when dad came to investigate the scrabbling noises in the hallway. I asked him, in my most politely manipulative tones, for some cheese on toast and he had the audacity to step over me, saying 'I was about to go to bed actually.' The standard of parenting round there had declined THE MOMENT mum headed off on holiday, he would never have pulled that sloppy shit within earshot of her.

I said in my saddest tones, 'I'll just sleep hungry then' and trudged upstairs, where I waited, one eyebrow cocked. The eyebrow was not disappointed, he emerged ten minutes later with cheese on toast, but, just to let me know I hadn't won this round, he gave me an obligatory five minutes of how messy my room was, why did I have to be so untidy, had I considered 'growing up' any time soon huh? etc. etc. . . . I ate loudly and drowned his noise out, thankful I hadn't asked for soft food. I'd have had to sing around a soft-boiled egg.

Life at home changed subtly when mum was away. As I was stepping into the shower one morning I saw water glistening on the edge of the bath and thought, 'Oho, Father, THAT'S how we're playing this is it? Let the games commence.' Then I had a shower and didn't wipe down the bath either! Even though it would've been totally slightly moist! This was bad-assery of the highest order, we didn't wipe down the shower post-use AT ALL! Admittedly I spent the next twenty minutes perched in my room, peeking round the door at my damp rebellion. Did evaporation usually take this long? Why wouldn't the water go? Oh sweet Lord what if there was residue? I soon cracked and towelled the hell out of it.

In mum's absence I had some filming to do on a beach, which might sound glamorous but remember what country we live in? Right. I was convinced I'd come away from the experience devoid of nose and chin, sandblasted into a smooth red pebble. By the time I got home I felt decidedly odd. I sat on the sofa[14] while dad happily examined his newest extension leads (they were Special Offer and the man said he'd show him where they were but dad said, no thank YOU, I know this Homebase like the back of my hand and the man was impressed and . . .).

I suddenly felt very sick and faint. As you know, I am terrified of vomit (which leads to the same few inevitable questions, so: YES, in all forms, and no I haven't been sick in fifteen years and yes I go to quite some lengths to achieve that and NO, while we're on the subject, I really don't want to hear a 'funny' story about sick).

Cat sick is bad enough, but the sight of a human puking up is so degrading, it rips bare the horrible truth that we're all just bulging sacks of vomit and excrement parading as something more complex. Forget poetry and art and love, we're dirty animals and that's all we'll ever be and that makes me want to weep and retch. Plus, in my terror I want to run away from the situation, so if the situation is inside me and running isn't a great anti-sickness cure, I'll end up running, crying and retching down the street in the middle of the night. I'm very rarely invited round to the neighbours'. I may not be anorexic any more, but sweet Lord, there's residue.

Another problem soon presented itself in the shape of dizziness, so I slithered off the sofa onto my hands and knees and crawled out of the room. Dad squinted at this through a lustful

14 Pale-coloured. Well, while the cat's away . . .

haze of extension leads and made an incredulous noise. I replied calmly that I felt very sick and was just going to lie down in the bathroom now (if mum was there she would've redirected my crawl towards a less recently decorated piece of the house). He fell quiet and the air around his head went thick.

As I crawled out of the room like a sad green-faced pony, he then decided that a little light conversation about food might help and began 'Oh . . . so you won't want dinner then? I've got a curry out of the freezer, it's got courgettes in and aubergines and chicken . . .' The little pony sped up and shuffled into the bathroom to lie on the floor and think about soap. I think about cleaning products when I feel sick, especially if a stupid man is droning a list of foodstuffs in green curry sauce on the other side of the door.

He meant well but he is SO bad when I am ill. A few months previously I had had a migraine and was lying in my room for a few hours while mayhem reigned in my head. Throughout the day, dad tried to help by yelling through the door things like, 'Huh. You know, I've never had a migraine! Bad, are they? Nat? Bad? What is it, like nausea or headaches or . . . what is it exactly?'

Eventually, not getting much in the way of chat from me, except wails he wrongly attributed to the migraine, he pootled off to go look at twine or whatever he did at the weekend.

There were definite disadvantages to living alone with dad, one of them being that I had to tackle conversations like this single-handedly:

'You know, cats can't drink in public.' This was said over dinner, as if it was nothing.

'What?'

'What?!' (this was me again; my incredulity was such that I queued up and had another go on the What? ride).

'Yes. I stare at the cats for ages and they don't drink. But then when I leave the room . . .' (At this point he made a lapping noise with his gravy. I watched, fascinated.) 'Yeeep, they'll only drink privately.' Work resumed on his little mashed potato volcano (he pours gravy in for lava, I've never seen him approach mash like an adult). Then, without looking up, he concluded: 'Except milk.'

I got suckered in at that point: 'Why milk?'

'I guess cos it doesn't occur naturally, like puddles of water. So the only way a cat could get it would be to . . .'

'Suck a cow.'

'Right.'

We sat in silence, contemplating a cat dangling off a cow's nipples, too prim to sip water in human company, but game for that. Conversations with dad could start to feel like opium dreams. Words like 'so' and 'because' were thrown around haphazardly but they gave the illusion of reasonable thought, nothing more. This was a man who once started laughing uncontrollably. Mum and I stared at him. When he finally recovered, he apologised, wiping a tear from his eye and explaining that he had 'just remembered *Carry On Camping*'. Mum was really going to miss me when I moved out.

Unfortunately, moving out still looked bloody unlikely; the day before I had been party to a flat-viewing where the estate agents made prospective tenants see it in groups of five. There were twenty-seven of us queuing patiently, resembling an uninspired flashmob. It felt like we were going into a museum. The Museum of Badly Laid Out Flats With A Pervading Smell Of Socks. Really, who wants to exit their tiny bathroom, shove through their tiny kitchen and then through a living room full of guests to get to the privacy of their bedroom? Only pervs who like to feel hot fat sizzle on their damp bottom then show the welts to friends.

It was very disappointing, especially after waiting twenty-five minutes to see it, a wait only enlivened by the estate agent in charge of crowd control. It was a difficult job making small talk with disgruntled strangers by a busy road. I sympathised, I was spending a lot of time with new people when house hunting and I didn't have the small-talk skills for it.

In desperation I had started stockpiling Fun Facts to kick-start mutually pleasurable chats. My favourite one was that peacocks don't know they have feet. Due to their anatomy they've never seen their own feet and would probably die of shock if they saw them. The one weak point of this fact was other peacocks' feet. Did every peacock assume all their colleagues had these nasty little growths down there and smugly congratulated themselves on escaping that affliction? How much cognitive ability did the average peacock have? Were peahens different? This Fun Fact was a house of cards, a little light interrogation brought the whole thing tumbling down, so I didn't question it, I didn't want to lose this valuable social crutch.

Sadly before I could line up Old Reliable ('Sorry, did someone say peacock? No? Well, nevertheless . . .'), Mr Crowd Control, King of Chit Chat, stepped up to the plate:

'Suicide bridge right on your doorstep there . . .'

'Lovely,' I said, a little nonplussed. 'I like to see despair from my living room.'

'You know why they call it Suicide Bridge?'

At this point, me and the queue exchanged patient looks. A Swedish man felt the hand of responsibility upon his shoulder and took one for the team:

'Unless we're missing the obvious . . .?'

'Yee-aap . . . people used to commit suicide off it.'

Twenty-seven people looked at the floor, their mouths twitching slightly at the thought of a bridge builder so engrossed in building his masterpiece that he forgot to name it and made a panicked last-minute choice. 'Ur . . . urr . . . Your Mum Bridge? Smell My Finger Bridge? Suicide Bridge!'

To give The King of Chit Chat credit, it wasn't inconceivable that there was an architect called Mr Suicide who struggled for years to name one of his creations after himself. Like the pioneering Dr Death who patented so many new medicines but was never allowed to pop his name on them.

I queued a little longer in merciful silence. Then trudged around the mouldy little crevice on offer ('Oooh, a sink.' I was getting good at this) and wandered back to my car two minutes away. Before I reached the car I received a text message from the estate agent: 'Already had three offers on flat so don't bother unless you're going above asking price.'

I was tempted to splurge ten pence on a frank reply: 'I'd rather live in a fat man's cavity than your sorry excuse for a grotpit,' but I refrained. I saved it in Drafts anyway. It made me feel better. At least my phone knew I was annoyed.

The next day they called me for my feedback on the experience of the house hunt (surely this was a bit needy? They assured me they'd already had several offers on the flat, was it crucial that we all had a lovely time to boot? I'm not a Thai elephant). I toyed with requesting that the queue man rethink his chat but I felt mean and didn't. For all I know he goes home, makes a little mash volcano and regales his poor family with 'facts' about how dogs can't wee when it's windy.

Chapter 24

FAME! I (DON'T) WANNA LIVE (HERE) FOREVER!

Writing about my parents online gave me a couple of ethical twinges during my time at home, especially when strangers offered their condolences and I feared I was sliding into slander. I always politely rebuffed the sympathy because my parents are wonderful, deep down, below their many layers of weird and annoying. Plus, I had no plans to stop writing, it was a useful way to vent, I was enjoying the attention (even if a lot of it still came from children) and when I wrote about them I experienced the giddy novelty of being in charge.

If they had been slightly more internet-savvy, I thought I might be staring at the business-end of a telling-off. A familiar end, one I know better than my own face. I don't think mum ever felt curious about what I was saying, certainly I never found her showing the computer a photo of me and using the loud, slow voice she reserved for foreigners silly enough not to speak English when she deigned to holiday in their country.

Dad was a more dangerous prospect, he totally understood the internet, shopped on there, read reviews of workbenches and everything but his execution of this knowledge was frustratingly slow. He typed with two fingers so carefully you'd assume some idiot had put a Launch Nuclear Missiles button next to the M.

'So, E. Now let's locate the E . . . um . . . "button" . . . ah, there it is: E. Oh, did that . . .? Yes yes, it worked, here is the E upon my "screen". Good old E . . .' While he did this I liked to stand behind him and mime violence to the back of his head.

Seeing me 'doing' the internet every day, mum's curiosity got the better of her and she insisted I Google her. I tried to explain how she could achieve this independently but she reacted like a doctor had lobbed a medical dictionary at her face and slurred 'Sort yourself out, Bleedy.'

So I Googled her while she perched breathlessly next to me, braced for the Googly sensation. I left her to the results, as I suspected 'Luurtsema' would bring up mentions of me as well as her. I've never Googled myself and I doubt I'll ever feel the urge. I wondered how mum would react to the experience. I feared too few mentions would make her feel slighted, too many and she'd be convinced she was being hounded by the press. Thankfully, I returned to find she was gratified by the one mention of her, on her school website.

Nodding at the screen like an old chum, she said 'Just so long as the internet knows who I am.'

'Oh yes,' I agreed, sensing this was all she wanted me to say. 'That's really the main thing here.'

I was relieved that mum hadn't found anything embarrassing on her maiden voyage through Google. My conscience was still needling me though; I never expected so many people to read what I wrote, I thought it would be my friends, perhaps their friends, and the occasional pervert – the usual internet network one attracts. While I was delighted that people liked it, I felt uneasy that people in Canada knew of dad's bathroom habits. I fretted that I'd exposed them to international sniggers.

I confessed what I'd done to Michael, and he presented me with a robust counter-argument, reminding me what utter narcissists mum and dad are. Exhibit A, my middle name is my mum's OWN NAME. My brother's is my dad's. I've never met anyone else similarly afflicted, wasn't it enough that we had the same DNA, surname and Christmas plans? No, apparently not, their name must be two-thirds of ours, leaving us only-one third of originality to play with.

Also, these weren't great names. I tried to think of any names that could've been worse than Gaynor and Gustaaf. (The G in Gustaaf to be pronounced with a phlegmy Dutch sound. Try it. Are you covered in spit? Then you've done it right.) Very few worse names sprang to mind. You'd think that after dragging these daft names around for thirty years, the last thing you'd do is palm them off on an innocent, but mum and dad thought differently.

In the end I still felt bad, so I showed my parents what I'd written about them and let them read through it. I said if there were any parts they wanted me to remove I would do so, happily. Predictably, they skimmed a page before getting bored. They liked it, they said, yes, very much, well done yeah, but it didn't really grab them because 'the cats aren't in it enough'.

I defend my controversial decision to not write exclusively about the cats. For the record, anything that sleeps eighteen hours a day was never going to make a big enough impact on my life to warrant much of a mention.

Sometimes I wish my parents could accept the cats for who and what they are. I have grown to like them, we've had some good times together with bits of string, but my parents are outraged by anything short of adoration.

Every phone call to them concludes, 'Okaaay . . . Well, that's all I had to say. Do you want to speak to the cat?'

'No I do not want to speak to the cat. Thank you.' ('That's fine, we Skype,' never gets the indulgent titters it deserves. If anything, it elicits a rather haughty retort.)

My parents don't like to be reminded of the cats' limitations, the fact that they fall slightly short of being actual human beings. It's like the cats are Magic Eye pictures and mum and dad see so much more in them than I ever can: 'Ah yes, he's hawked up a fur ball because stress goes straight to his guts and he's in turmoil over the long-term ramifications of the Arab Spring.'

Throughout my Month At Home, I learnt to ignore this. I decided never to enter a fight where I was inevitably compared to an animal and found wanting. Any sentence that began with mum cuddling a cat and saying, 'Well at least he doesn't . . .' was not worth sticking around for.

Blog duly read, Mum turned to me and said, 'Now, if you were wondering what to get the cats this Christmas.'

'No,' I clarified, 'I'm really, really not.'

She gave me a look like 'Oh, you kid, but seriously . . .' and told me that the cats would like some more catnip.

Catnip is feline smack, the cats don't need it so much as desperately crave it and would sell their bodies for it if men weren't put off by all the nipples. I'm sure I only had to buy it because Santa can't, not with his record.

I was uncomfortable buying gear for the cats. I was also forgetful and self-absorbed, which was why I spent the twenty-third of December last year scouring the internet for a very specific type of catnip that was their favourite, apparently, though I've yet to meet a junkie with brand loyalty. (Actually that's not fair, I've never asked. I've met several junkies but always skirted around The Issue as I thought that would be what everyone wanted to talk to them about. With hindsight, they probably move in social circles with people with similar lifestyles so it wouldn't have been the tired conversational staple I assumed.)

After I claimed the cats slept too much to have any impact on my life, one of them set about proving me wrong and started sleeping in a way that made my life hell. Despite six months of treating me like a war criminal on a misjudged school visit she had suddenly decided that we were firm friends. From then on, every night was a sleepover. Which would've been fine, except she was some sort of experimental nap-maverick who would try a snooze anywhere, anyhow, in any position she could think of. I had to admire her, as a cat she had surveyed the limited opportunities available to her and thought, 'Well, if all I do is sleep, I shall be a PIONEER in the business of sleep!'

She spent days work-shopping one particular position – 'Sleeping up someone's arm, culminating in a nose-in-ear'. As the owner of said arm and ear, this was a horrible feeling, halfway between a stroke and sexual assault. In her creative explorations she would dominate my bed, sleeping right in the middle and forcing me to sleep in star-shapes around her, like a narcoleptic kid from *Fame* who'd nodded off mid-vogue.

Most nights the only way to settle her down was to hiss '*For . . . Fucks . . . Sake . . .*' at her in tones even she understood. Then, if Craine was around I'd have to deal with the aftermath, which was him miserably prodding me awake to tell me he couldn't sleep. Sometimes a problem shared is not a problem halved, it is doubled and voids any sympathy your loved ones might've had for you.

So the cat proved me wrong: well done cat, you can sleep eighteen hours a day and yet still have a horrible impact on my life. Touché. One–nil to you. My parents were still very hurt by my snub and spent my last month in Watford bringing them to my attention in anecdotal form, or sometimes just parading them past me like a hairy Mardi Gras.

I assumed this was all in the hope that I would immortalise them on the internet; an achievement they had wildly overrated. I showed them some of the least interesting dregs on YouTube to illustrate my point, they stared at the videos in confused silence then looked at me with eyes that cried 'What . . . Why? Is this a thing? A fifteen second video of a man pulling a face? PLUG ME BACK INTO THE MATRIX I DON'T LIKE IT OUT HERE!' I felt bad but they had to learn.

Having blown their minds with YouTube, our week took a further turn for the odd when *The Times* called and asked if I wanted to write an article for them about living at home. I considered myself an expert in very few fields, but there I felt qualified.

They then asked if they could have a photo of me with my parents ('If you think they won't mind?').

I took a deep breath and braced myself for my parent's predictable reactions. I called mum at work and heard her barge through the building yelling: 'Evelyn! Evelyn! Can I have an hour off tomorrow to have my photograph taken by *THE TIMES*?! *THE TIMES* NEWSPAPER. Oh I'm sorry, I thought Evelyn was in this room, as she isn't I suppose my best policy is to march from room to room yelling this information until Evelyn hears it! I can think of no more effective way of requesting an hour off work!'

I heard a couple of her colleagues coo excitedly at the revelation and thought, 'You fools! Don't feed the beast; she will never be sated now! You will have to admire her daily till you die and still she will want more.'

Dad, equally predictably, reacted like it was yet another pleading request from the media for his beautiful face. He graciously allowed them a window of his time, warning me 'I'm not as photogenic as you might think.'

'I must make it clear,' I said, nipping this narcissism pre-bud, 'I NEVER thought you would be photogenic.' I clarified. 'Because of your squashy orange gnome face.'

This was cruel but fair, he is a bit orange, the shade you achieve by dabbing a wet teabag over paper to create Ye Olde Piece Of Papere in one of the more pointless bits of school. He was mixed race remember, not a glamour model; I must reiterate this before you imagine dad with a thong and double E funbags from this point onwards.

There was a hurt silence and a curt goodbye from him and I thought that would be the end of it. But no, dad hung onto his grudges and so, after I'd spent a night driving to Glasgow and back for an admittedly lovely gig, he barged into my room at 7am yelling, 'Get up, get up, get up now or you'll look shit for the photographs!'

Such an annoying way to wake up, especially for a man with the audacity to enter my room in the morning without a cup of tea in hand. To me that's inappropriate. You might as well stride in naked with your hands shoved into a pair of fish.

The photographer came and was liked and approved of. He had a cat that looked like ours and he admired dad's shed. There was a difficult moment when he caught dad caressing some yellow cloths and dad informed him that 'I had a spare half an hour' (implying he was so busy that a fleeting three minutes when he wasn't advising NATO was rare and delightful), 'so I decided to wash, dry and fold some dusters.' And he proceeded to do just that. Our photographer wasn't even up to speed on what a duster was, so this was a mind-stretching few minutes for him, and explains why the eventual photo in *The Times* featured dad carefully folding a duster. Not a classic pose but he really made it his own.

Mum on the other hand was very sad at her photo and all of her chins. She begged me to spread the word that in real life she really only owns one chin and hadn't rented spares for the day; all of which is true. I gently proffered the opinion that perhaps it was just that she didn't suit the kitchen and should stay out of it, like I had to, but this loving piece of helpfulness was shoved right back where it came from.

The day the article came out, I was woken up by mum flinging the paper onto my face. (WHY couldn't these people learn how to wake a person up? I gave them enough practice.)

'Aren't you going to read it?!' she immediately nagged, like I'd spent the morning ignoring it, which was unfair as only a nanosecond before I'd been deep in dreams of home-ownership.

'No.' I said coldly. 'Don't need to read it, I wrote it.' (I won't deny that felt really good.)

My vanity was short-lived and died of neglect, as mum spent the rest of the day fielding congratulations from her capacious social circle. I was asked to pass on some messages of praise myself, confirming my status of mindless conduit. We all seemed to be falling into step with the ideology that Luurtsemas Senior were Comedy Genius and I was less a creative writer than a stenographer, scuttling behind to catch their crumbs of wit. Rather than what I actually did, which was to translate their idiocy into something rational that sane people could stomach.

This attitude had been creeping in for some time, I spotted it when mum fell in a bush and lifted a finger imperiously to command: 'Tell people about this, they will enjoy it. And now help me out of this bush.' We had slipped into odd roles whereby mum was an eccentric monarch and I was the royal spokesperson, braced for Her Royal Highness to issue an edict whenever she felt drollery had occurred. Then I would tug my forelock and scuttle to the internet.

A friend came round to view the article. It was fascinating watching people live without Facebook, they were forever 'popping round' to see things I could've posted online to a thousand people while I was still in my slippers. It felt like the twentieth century round there. Her friend suggested we frame the article, we both poo-pooed this, the friend demanded to know why and we fell silent.

The air hummed with us both thinking, 'There's limited kitchen wall space so to do so implies this is a zenith for Nat, career-wise, and it'll all be downwards from here.'

All right, I doubt mum thought zenith, as being pretentious isn't contagious. But we were both painfully aware of The Scrapbook.

At nineteen I had surprised everyone by winning a radio award for chatting to myself in a cupboard. The local paper covered it, with the headline 'DJ Nat's the Tops!' Like the bed shop Pine Dreams, I was convinced there was a pun in there, but nine years later I still couldn't unearth it, beyond a vague hint at *Top of the Pops*. Tell me if you spot it.

Mum lovingly pasted the article into a pristine new scrapbook. Five years passed. I achieved nothing. The scrapbook took early retirement. But now, proprietarily smoothing *The Times*, I felt she was teetering on the dawn of a new one and I felt a feverish panic to make her proud, with things that could be cut out and pasted. I know, bold words from a homeless twenty-eight-year-old with the early glimmerings of a drink problem.

I just didn't know what to do, my life felt so hopelessly stagnant. After six and a half months I couldn't believe I was STILL living with my parents. I had friends buying houses, getting married and having babies and, while I had no interest in these things, I resented that my life seemed to be going in the wrong direction. At twenty-four I lived in a converted warehouse, earned thirty grand a year and flung my decadent body into taxis whenever I tired of verticality. Four years later I was yelling jokes at drunks, back in the pinny touting Mouthpleasers and, thanks to mum, once again fully appraised of the plot of *Neighbours*. I didn't think finding a house would solve all my problems, but it would certainly be a step forwards.

If my life were a novel or a film, this would've definitely been the point where everything started looking up. If my life was a poem, it was definitely time for a volta. Volta o'clock here. Yes sir-ree, I mused, loud enough for Fate to hear, undeniably I was at a low ebb and it would definitely be a good time for some sort of Big Break, something that would revive my professional pride and perhaps even swell the wallet, giving the house hunting a much-needed boost. That would certainly be a pleasing dramatic arc, maybe enough to poke my lapsed religious beliefs into life. Not that I was trying to blackmail any higher powers, I was just a miserable girl musing loudly, ignoring the stares of passers-by.

And with that, the BBC rang. Proving that the world did listen to my tiny pleas! But that it also had a bitchy sense of humour. The call came from *The One Show*, who wanted to film the Luurtsemas and our stupid situation. It would appear that I had somehow specialised in being a loser. I had become representative of a generation of hacked-off adults back in their childhood bedrooms. I imagined in the future whenever the economy slumped, the housing market stagnated and another generation crawled back to their parents, the news would do a satellite link-up to me 'in the field'. I'd be fifty years old in my childhood bedroom, hugging a teddy bear and pontificating. 'Thank you very much Ms Luurtsema, we'll be talking again a little later.'

'No can do, Andrew, mummy's made spag bol. Skillz.'

I wasn't sure I wanted to flaunt my failure on national television. I didn't think I was a proud person, but around three million people watched the show, and that was potentially a lot of sneering. It was the biggest audience I'd ever played to and I felt uncharacteristically shy.

But, 'If it goes really badly, just change your name and deny it,' suggested dad. A slightly Reggie Perrin approach to life, but a reasonable Plan B, thanks to my super generic face. Plus it was paid work and the old Pride For Cash swap was an ancient tradition performed by generations of comics before me. I was treading in the expensively shod footsteps of many a shamed clown.

The day before the film crew were due to come round mum was staring accusingly at her chin, just daring it to multiply in front of another camera, when I got a phone call from *The One Show*. Apparently, they were going to bring a psychiatrist with them, wouldn't that be fun? As we learnt many years ago, the Luurtsemas don't react to therapy in any helpful way and a filmed session was distinctly upping the jeopardy.

Dad and I agreed to give nothing away 'or she'll make us look like psychopaths,' he warned. 'In fact,' he started warming to this idea, 'maybe we are, because you wouldn't know if you were one, right?'

I said that fascinating though this was, it was precisely the sort of chat he would have to keep internal in front of the film crew and he agreed.

It was vital to get mum on-message as well. We approached her, as she and her one firm chin enjoyed a yoghurt and a spot of TV. She was surprisingly unhelpful, fixing us with a glare and saying 'I'm. Watching. *I'm. A. Celebrity.*' She was craning her neck around us like we were standing in front of the aurora borealis blathering about car tax. She was clearly more interested in enjoying TV than making it, so I just had to hope for the best.

We were all awake early on the day of filming, peeking fearfully through the net curtains for our approaching National

Humiliation. Dad was very quiet, which was always a bad sign and sure enough, he emerged downstairs in a very old, garish purple shirt. This was clearly a premeditated act, he liked the shirt, knew it would be a controversial choice, but it was the shirt he wanted millions of his fellow countrymen to marvel at. Mum was steadfast in her hatred of the shirt, dad equally so in defence. It was a spicy ten minutes and while I also found the shirt bafflingly ugly, I defended his right to wear it. He was always so sartorially obedient; mum bought him a new pair of jeans once a year, relieving the current ones onto gardening duty and demoting the gardening jeans to bonfire night. Because it's nice to have a System.

Sadly my defence didn't help, dad lost the battle and was sulking in a grey shirt ('So boring. Everyone will think I'm boring'). He vented his sadness through facetious comments for the rest of the day. This wasn't the mood in which I wanted him to meet the psychiatrist. She asked dad how long he would fix my mistakes for (a phrase I objected to, but was ignored).

Dad pondered and said, 'Until I'm dead. Then she can please herself.' I knew he meant it lovingly but it came across as genuinely menacing.

The psychiatrist wondered if I really wanted to move out or if I was just happier at home and pretending I couldn't find anywhere. I reassured her this wasn't so, perhaps a little too vehemently, mum and dad looked a bit hurt by the time I breathlessly trailed off.

We then had to do 'noddies': shots of each of us reacting to the others. This was extremely boring, you had to look at everyone for a few minutes at a time, nodding, looking thoughtful, wise and astounded at the perceptive comments they were probably making. Ever since I learnt about these I can't take interviews on TV seriously as I know they've all had five minutes of nodding at each other.

Our noddies took ages because dad couldn't keep a straight face. By which I don't mean that he was giggling, he just had no control over his face. I think he's only got four nerve endings servicing his whole head as he couldn't stop his eyebrows quivering and shooting all over his forehead, while his chin shuddered and his nostrils flared uncontrollably. He managed to subdue everything briefly, but all this kinetic energy had to go somewhere and his ears started waggling. He looked like he was demonically possessed, we all agreed we didn't like it and he should stop immediately.

We filmed for nine hours, by which time dad's face was numb, we'd said regrettable things, and started flicking through the *Yellow Pages* for name-changing services. The cats had reacted badly to the film crew and exiled themselves in a cupboard all day. It took half an hour to prise them out and apologise.

We dragged ourselves to the local pub where dad and I agreed we had more respect for actors we'd previously considered useless, as they managed to keep control of their eyebrows AND chin at the same time. Mum valiantly name-dropped our day's activity to the indifferent bar staff.

'Oh I'm tired . . . you know what's tiring? FILMING.'

'Bar work's pretty tiring too.'

'Hmph.'

No one nibbled the bait and she eventually sat down to her dinner, disgusted that no one had bothered to invade her privacy.

I've never seen the resulting footage on *The One Show*, I think my anxiety would outweigh my pleasure. Dad's colleagues sweetly saved a still of it on his desktop, which he deleted with very ill grace, muttering something about not being as photogenic as you'd assume and so he didn't watch it either. Mum was the only person to watch it and she was delighted with the end result, the house apparently looked spotless and she only had one chin. I think all film reviews should be conducted along this criteria: did the sets look tidy and was everyone's jaw line firm? Then five stars for *Showgirls*!

I spent a week alert for signs of National Humiliation but nothing manifested. People stared at me in the street but that was normal, they were always wondering, 'Is that Sally? It looks like

Sally . . .' I was briefly deluged by Facebook messages and emails from people mocking me for NEVER having left home. I didn't bother to reply to any, I figured if they were baffled by the plot of a five-minute video about a very simple scenario they were unlikely to yield the insightful chat I'd like from a pen pal. Not for the first time, I missed my schoolgirl pen pal.

A friend brought round a souvenir, a photo they'd taken of us on the TV. 'Facebook,' I mouthed at them: 'the internet. Seriously, there is a better way.'

They ignored me, waggled the photo coquettishly at mum and said 'Well?! Time for a scrapbook now?'

Mum held up the blurry photo of a houseplant next to a TV that was showing our faces (even typing this sounds mad, why do they abuse technology like this? It's only trying to help). She looked wary, she'd been let down before, and we agreed that a scrapbook would only be justified by a third achievement and meanwhile she would save these two in an envelope.

At the time of writing there is still no scrapbook. And no one's sure where the envelope is.

Chapter 25

MY WACKY FAMILY OR
SOMETHING EQUALLY DOGSHIT

After a lifetime of identifying myself as the odd one out in my family, six and a half months of studying them up close was shaking my core beliefs. This outsider status I'd always claimed wasn't just me making out I was special, some sort of lone genetic archipelago, we had all agreed on it. But I realised, seeing my parents clearly, as a fellow adult, that they only said this because they were sloppy with the truth in pursuit of a laugh, just like me!

Years ago mum and dad had clearly made a silent pact that tales of my ineptitude were extra funny followed up with a helpless shrug and, 'What bush did we find HER under?' At which point the other one would lean in '. . . and is she too big to shove back in it?' It was a solid gag, played well in most rooms. I was happy to discover that I was actually replete with lots of little family traits, especially my love of lying.

I lie constantly, I think it makes life more fun and interesting. I'm often pulled up on my wildly exaggerated anecdotes as if I've done something wrong when, as far as I can tell, please correct me if I'm wrong, all I've done is give my dull humdrum life experiences a sprinkling of magic, to pass on and cheer *your* humdrum dull life. Well, pardon me. Guess I'll leave the pixie dust at home then Officer.

I learnt this from mum. I'd amble around the shops with her as a kid, listening to her tell stories of recent events, embellishing them with every retelling, like a stand-up comic, feeling out the weak points, cutting unnecessary details and dwelling longer on the bits that got most laughs and/or gasps of horror. By the end of the day we'd return home in triumph, with an impressively well-honed anecdote that bore barely a nodding acquaintance with what had actually happened.

Thank god she was never witness to an incident and had to give a statement. The boring, lumpy truth would've been revealed: 'But I thought you said there were tigers and John Barrowman was there . . .?' her friends would protest, brandishing the *Watford Observer*, and she'd have to scuff her feet a little and admit that well, no . . . a cat and a wheelbarrow.

There's nothing wrong with embellishment, I think telling a good story is an ingrained atavistic instinct, probably to encourage women to keep having babies. Childbirth is clearly awful but at least you can freak other people out with your horror story, it's some consolation.

The reason the human race endures is that look of grim glee on a woman's face as she says to another woman: 'Twenty-seven hours of labour, in the end they had to send a policeman up there to get the baby out.' You'd only go through that shit if you could console yourself with making pregnant women cry afterwards with your stories. And you get a free baby; that usually seals the deal.

Anecdotes of woe are all I have. It looks like conversation, it sounds like conversation, but pay attention and all I've got at a party are tales of doom, retold in a stoic and witty way. I used to work in a little radio station at the Edinburgh Festival every August and found that when your job is sitting alone in a musty box, you develop the social flair of vending machine snacks.

But then one lucky day I was hospitalised with a vicious kidney infection. I remember lying baby-shaped with the pain and thinking, 'This is a nice, take-it-anywhere, anecdote that will see me through the Festival.' And it did! People were interested and sympathetic, they liked the drama and they really liked that it had happened to me not them.

The second year I got another kidney infection, but that was okay because people remembered last year's incident and suddenly our casual acquaintance had History. In the transient social miasma of the Festival my sickly kidneys felt like a tradition. Numbers were swapped, I made friends and it made the burning sensation worthwhile.

Year Three dawned and I was still working in a small community radio station. I've had a meteoric career, just one of those meteors that's been wedged in the earth for thousands of years. I feared ANOTHER kidney infection would highlight the fact I was skiving through three weeks of socialising with just one anecdote. I covered it well though.

Top tip: tell your funny story then glide off, implying that you have spared them a crumb from your feast of chat. Don't linger mutely, flaunting your conversational famine.

I worried unnecessarily because that year my body pulled something very special out of the bag and I went temporarily blind! I had worn my contact lenses too much and when I finally tugged them off I was discovered, feeling my way round a bin, by a friend from Year Two, a relationship that had begun with me telling that year's anecdote. (Good old kidneys.)

I got my eyesight back two days later, and it was discovered I had ulcers on my eyeballs and my eyelids – painful, but totally worth it for a good anecdote. I still dust it off when trapped on the stairs at house parties.

I didn't mind when my parents embroidered me into one of their far-fetched tales, I'm not one of those dicks who when someone tells a story that features me, will feel the need to butt in and say, 'Um, no ACTUALLY I think you'll find . . .' and insert my unwelcome grey 'Facts' into their funny story. Whenever people do that to me, my hand itches to slap. This is why I love stand-up, I tell stories as they should be told, riddled with funny lies and the microphone makes me too loud to be interrupted. Ha. Suck on that, Fact Fans.

There's a family story about my first car, which was a Toyota Starlet several years older than me. It had cost £200 and was previously owned by a man so huge that his constant weight in the driver's seat had left the car with a jaunty tilt. All of which added to the idea that this car was A Bit of A Character; which was lucky, as it was definitely not A Safe Vehicle, nor one capable of reaching thirty miles an hour without sounding like it had screaming banshees in the air vents and poltergeists tormenting the flapping upholstery. It was a car in which it was hard to make a dignified entrance. But one in which you had a good idea of how it would feel to surf a gastroenteritis virus through a lion.

Due to the car's age and general refusal to be user-friendly, the petrol gauge swung the opposite way to my parents' one; something I didn't properly register except to note that in this car, the red bit seemed to mean Full. Why was it red though? I pondered. Probably meant Dangerously Full, I decided and therefore took corners at a sedate eleven mph, careful not to slosh out my petrol into a hedge. I accept now that this was idiotic, which is why I never correct my parents when their version of this story has me running out of petrol, grinding to a confused halt on the M25 and wailing at an AA man, 'But I've got petrol! Too much, the tank's dangerously full.'

There was no need to quibble on the details, the point of the story remained and I had no problem being the butt of their sarcasm.

Six and a half months of co-dependency had honed my parents and I into a well-oiled anecdote-telling machine; faced with a social situation, we would immediately assume team positions, depending on the play.

Story of my stupidity: mum leads play, dad provides sardonic quips and eye-rolling, I back the venture with protests of innocence and how unfair this is, but only in such a way as to keep the narrative moving, I never block play.

Story of dad's stupidity: mum will invariably be the genesis here, remembering a key incident. I run round the back and pick up the story early on. We pass the story back and forth, with dad burbling over the top, 'Well I don't remember any of this at all' (we're so good at this, it's basically jazz). Then, at the end, when NO ONE sees it coming, mum or I will relent and ruffle his head and say something tender. Now he doesn't seem bullied, this sanctions the third party to really abuse him with some vigorous quick-fire piss-taking. Touchdown.

Story of mum's stupidity: the most risky manoeuvre. Basically the weakest team, dad and I, taking on the thuggish Roy Keane of anecdotes (the word thuggish was probably redundant there . . .). An extremely high-stakes game, as mum can flit from giggles to moody at Hadron Collider speeds and she is usually the one driving us home. Very few anecdotes are worth a taxi fare. The only way this game works is if we draft in my brother, the overseas signing.

We're not performers in my family, we're not Put On A Play At Christmas types. I drew a mouse one Boxing Day but that was it. The drawing was viewed and judged 'nice', until dad (correctly) accused me of having traced it. And I never drew another mouse again. Probably would've if I'd wanted to, but frankly the world of rodent-sketching isn't the jacuzzis 'n' cheeses it's cracked up to be. The Luurtsemas performed, but we did so in a sneaky way, by being sassy in public places.

This public sass was one of the more embarrassing revelations from my time with my parents. If we were out in public and we noticed someone listening, a bored teenager whose iPod battery just ran out or perhaps an attentive dog, we would play up to this pathetic excuse for an audience. We'd segue into roles in a sitcom that existed only in our heads called *My Wacky Family Or Something Equally Dogshit* (*MFOSED*, as the imaginary fans called it), and we'd brazenly say things that weren't true to each other to try and elicit an involuntary laugh from a stranger and we wouldn't stop till we got it. And then (and this is probably the worst part) we never mentioned it afterwards, like two teenage girls who snog each other on a night out in a failed attempt to Make Boys Like Them.

As you know, this urge manifested itself particularly strongly in group therapy. I still feel bad about subjecting that therapist to *MWFOSED*. We never completed our sessions, as one day she abruptly announced that I was probably all fixed and didn't have to come and see her ever again. Ever. Please. I suspect she a) never again wanted to be subjected to *MWFOSED* and b) feared her professional efforts were little more than smoothing the duvets on the *Titanic*.

A more socially acceptable version of *MWFOSED* (trust me, it'll catch on. You'll be wearing the t-shirt soon) is our love of market research groups. When I was growing up, we liked to inveigle our way onto a couple a month, for products we'd never heard of but claimed to know intimately. It wasn't for the money – they usually just paid expenses. (Although occasionally a big payer came along. Dad once earned sixty quid chatting about dog food for an hour. Impressive for a man who was only vaguely aware dogs existed. Although, he argued, he dished out cat food daily, so he just imagined that with bigger chunks.)

I think mum did it because she liked to be listened to. She told me once, if I felt unsure, to sit in the middle and I'd never be the first to be asked a question. We looked at each other and knew NEITHER of us sat in the middle, for that reason. We like to be asked things! It makes us feel special and important.

I started doing market researches as a teenager for the pure joy of talking with adults as an equal. If this giddy parity could only be achieved through discussing Golden Grahams in a hotel conference room, then so be it! It was there I shyly honed my wit, without the school friends to practise on.

I only tasted the warmth and joy of making my peers laugh once, one sublime day when that morning's Sex Education class introduced us to Vaginal Discharge ('S'up. Call me V Dissle'). A spot of lunch ('hold the custard') was followed by a geography lesson that insisted we go measure the 'discharge' of a nearby river. I waded into the River Chess, clutching a tape measure, flinching primly from every splash. A perfect bit of mime, treating a river like a massive overly aroused vagina. I milked it for all it was worth, so to speak. My class admired from the river bank. Open-air gigs can be tricky, but I ripped it. I remember a girl collapsing to her hands and knees, her body floppy with mirth. She went back to ignoring me afterwards but we both knew the power I had briefly held over her.

I spent the next ten years chasing the joy I'd found wincing in a river. Until stand-up, nothing got me closer than market research sessions. There I found a bored and receptive audience dying to be amused, which was such an easy gig compared to the group therapy where I'd cut my teeth. I'd sneak quips in here and there, never disrupting the discussion, never annoying the market researcher, just enough to keep a convivial atmosphere bubbling along. I'd go home thinking, 'I got six laughs tonight, and seven scattered titters. Pretty good for a session about own-brand anti-depressants.'

In a market research session you could be whoever you wanted to be. I stand on stage almost every night telling stories, lies and jokes, but I still go to market research for this bit of forbidden escapism. I imagine some people cross-dress at the weekend or take pills and have sex in hay bales. Me, I don't need that much escapism; I just like to tell eighteen strangers that I love a make-up I've never heard of, that the even coverage is crucial for me, a former sufferer of Slap Face, and as a primary school teacher I need to know my sanitary protection won't let me down.

This was the only aspect of house hunting that I liked. It was inviting, when faced with a new living space, to come up with a whole new life to pop within these walls: 'Ooo, a patio, this will be perfect for my literary salons, you know how those poets smoke!' and 'Is this a south-facing living room? Perfect place to relax after another long day of charity work.'

I once mentioned my 'cheese evenings' during a giddy flight of fancy and Craine shot me a repressive look. The cheese evenings did exist, thank you, but it was just me in my pyjamas, with a baked camembert, a spoon and some privacy.

If you say anything wildly perceptive in a market research session the researcher will ask you to stay behind so they can film you saying it to show their client. I was always asked to stay behind, but then, I was determined to be asked. Like a proto Derren Brown I would look for their 'tells', that little smile, that widening of the eyes when I stumbled upon an opinion they'd been asked to look out for. 'Where's the marketing for Pepsi?' I'd beseech them, 'That's what I need to know; I haven't heard anything from them since they set Michael Jackson on fire.'

Occasionally I look at particularly strange products, like the Slanket or the plug hole holder, and feel a twinge of guilt that my years of fraudulent market research participation might be to blame. I have some coconut handwash from the 99p shop (yes, the comedy's going very well thank you, occasionally I treat myself). The label on this handwash entreats me to 'Surprise Yourself!', which feels a little off-topic from a soap. It's also an imperious tone from such a low-cost product. I feel it's overstepped its remit; short of hitting myself around the face with it, drinking it and moving to Minnesota, I don't see what surprises me and the budget handwash can achieve together.

And yet . . . As I type I'm dislodging a memory. Of me, perching in a market research session, nibbling a complementary biscuit and saying something like, 'I just wish I felt more of a personal investment from brands, like they care, you know? Especially from cleaning products, I'm trusting *THEM* to clean *ME*,' while a roomful of strangers nodded; 'Yes, *finally* someone's said what we're all thinking.'

Mum and I once did a market research together and we had to pretend to not know each other, because participants always need to be strangers, to keep the science straight or some such. Unfortunately mum thought ahead and realised that two Luurtsemas in a group would arouse comment. Frankly two in a country causes incredulity, I still suspect granddad invented the name on a boozy whim. So mum wrote her maiden name. Sadly I had also thought ahead and had gone for the obvious Plan B: mother's maiden name. She stared daggers at me for ten minutes while the group chatted pleasantly about how they'd never realised Manning was such a common name . . .

But then the discussion began and the fun soon followed. For the hell of it mum and I had a row about loft insulation. The rest of the group were titillated by our inappropriate hostility and I think the researcher was genuinely touched that we cared enough about the subject for me to point at mum, 'I'm sorry, Gaynor is it? I just find you really blinkered about the benefits of eco-cladding and maybe it's time you stopped mouthing off, listened and learnt, yeah?'

I think we managed to air some genuine mother–daughter frictions and went home in happy harmony (though I had to hide and sneak into the backseat of her car so no one saw us leave together). If I ever need marriage counselling I won't waste my money on a 'qualified professional' I'll just take my hateful/philandering/emotionally distant husband to a market research group and we can battle it out there, under the guise of exploring how we feel about Vosene.

Chapter 26

MESSY XMAS

Reader, we found a flat. Three weeks before Christmas, one dispirited day, six and a half months after we started looking, Craine, Tiernan and I stumbled upon a nice place to live. Out of the blue, there it was. We had told ourselves it would 'just happen' 'one day' 'when we least expected it', all those phrases your mum trots out as your love life lurches from bad to worse and forty looms, twirling a withered ovary. But like her, we didn't really believe it; it was just a thing to say to fill the sad silences.

Hopes weren't high, the estate agent had called this one 'kooky' and we were braced for upsetting scenes. We were by now familiar with 'cosy,' 'basic' and even 'laid-back' (meaning 'the position you'll assume in hospital thanks to the parasites in the carpet'). But 'kooky' was new and we were scared. Crammed in the back of an estate agent's Mini Cooper, we hurtled through Muswell Hill, a leafy suburb of north London, full of opulent houses and we felt confused and sad and squashed. Was he taunting us? What fresh hell was this?

And then we saw our new home; a granny flat perched on the side of a mansion, a cheery little carbuncle that said 'Welcome! My previous tenant has *just* died.' Utterly charmed, we stepped inside. And waited. We had learnt that there was a certain protocol to follow when one found a nice flat. Etiquette demanded that you entered, wiped your feet and then the estate agent checked their phone, said 'No, this one's gone' and dragged you from your dreams.

We stood in the hallway for a minute or two, but nothing happened. Like kicked puppies braced for the boot, we timidly explored our granny flat. The sinks and worktops were low, tiny-old-lady height. Tiernan skipped around delighting at a flat tailor-made for his petite needs. I slouched behind. I didn't mind stooping to wash up, so long as an adorable old-lady-ghost haunted the place. I wanted to be watching TV and she'd scuttle past us to tuck a coupon in a drawer.

'Lovely sunny living room,' the estate agent said, gesturing towards three big windows. Brilliant, we agreed, although 'not much good in a zombie attack', but that was fine, absolutely fine we backtracked under his scorn. We could discuss zombies later; we were clearly in the presence of a man with little tolerance for this sort of chat.

Did I never tell you that one of our points of discussion when house hunting was What Shelter Would It Provide In A Zombie Outbreak? It wasn't a deal-breaker, just a talking point. I probably didn't mention this earlier as I presumed it would erode your sympathy a bit.

Despite its meagre protection against the undead, we wanted this flat. We meekly handed over our deposit, as we were such house hunting pros we took hundreds of pounds with us to every flat-viewing, in the hopes of getting a quick deal. Or mugged. Whatever spiced up the day. We then waited to have our cash shoved back with outraged splutterings about the importance of proper jobs.

Three weeks later, the shoving and spluttering was yet to happen and it was starting to feel cruel. We couldn't live with this hammer hanging over our hopes – just smash them and let's continue with this miserable year! I was too pessimistic to pack, there was no way we were going to be allowed back into the adult world so easily. I was expecting a minotaur to slap me and proffer a riddle.

Mum forced the issue by placing a suitcase on my sleeping body at 7am and then packing it. This was clever, it got increasingly heavy and difficult to ignore. I put up a heroic battle, though, taking shallow breaths and taunting her from under the covers: 'You're doing a lovely job, Mum, look at the crisp fold on that. Military.'

Eventually I felt a rib snap and took that as the starting pistol to my day. Mum had also made a pile of 'things you probably want to throw,' which, it turned out, were just clothes of mine that she disliked. So a selection of hot pants and mini skirts were refolded while she watched from the doorway. 'So . . . keeping that? Oh, I . . . no no . . . just . . . at your age . . . Bit slaggy, no? Okay fine.'

In between sartorial critiques, she had hired a removal van. On the moving-in day we discovered, with some pushing and shoving, that there wasn't enough room for mum, dad, Craine and I to sit up front. Craine was adamant he wanted to go up front, so he could do thumbs-up at real van drivers and feel manly. He was definitely going to call someone 'mate' before the day was out. Dad blamed mum for the seating debacle but gallantly offered to help: 'I'll sit in the back, you dozy cow.'

He clambered into the half-full van, pulled a dining chair into an empty space and sat there, facing backwards, legs loosely crossed.

'Um, really?' we said. 'Like that?'

'Yes, yes, what now?' he snapped. 'Just get on with it and drive.'

'Of course,' mum said serenely. 'Off we go then.'

When she took the first corner at thirty miles an hour, there was some crashing from the back. She didn't say a word, but her mouth twitched. I felt for dad but honestly, he'd known her long enough, couldn't he see that was going to happen? Mum zigzagged an unconventional route towards our new house, circling every roundabout twice, refusing to acknowledge the sobbing and

hammering of little fists. Craine felt occasional spasms of soli-
darity but every time he opened his mouth she raised an eyebrow
and he closed it again.

As a child I hated being dragged into my parents' endless petty
battles, now I'm an adult I'm happy to umpire. When we reached
our new flat dad clambered stiffly down from the back of the van,
bruised chin held high. He looked at mum, nodded at the back
of the van and remarked, 'Yeah, no problem. You wouldn't have
coped with it, but ah . . .' and ran away to cry and bleed.

Everyone's parents were helping us to move, a sign of their love
and desperation to get us out of their homes. The speed of their
unloading was hurtful, Tiernan's dad brought things in at a brisk
trot. By the end of the day everyone was exhausted and sick of
each other: the classic moving house/family holiday/Christmas
feeling.

Our parents ran off, giggling and high-fiving and Craine,
Tiernan and I were left alone in our own flat. We did a quick
conga through the rooms (this took a bit of agility, it was 'cosy' as
well as 'kooky') and then sat, flummoxed. It's funny how quickly
you get caught up in the parental tide of This Is What We're
Doing Today and suddenly we were cast adrift, in our own little
eddy. What should we do? I imagine this is the sort of awkward
tension Romeo and Juliet would've felt if that fake suicide had
worked and they'd ended up married. 'So, finally eh, Jools? Well,
guess I'll go unpack the cups . . .'

I opened up the first box and found smashed glasses and sauce-
pans sprinkled in rice. I quietly cursed the cooking wine from six
months ago. I then caused our first domestic squabble by bypass-
ing unpacking in favour of Gettin' Festive. I strewed tinsel over the
boxes, then rigged up a horrible manky little Christmas tree. It
was so bent over it looked like it was about to puke, but I spruced
up its misery with some baubles and propped it on top of the bin.
This was to make it more visible and pre-empt any attempts to
bin it, as it was already in there.

*   *   *

I was determined to cover myself in glory back in the Real World, but I was staggering towards Christmas with more than my usual incompetence. I was doing well, I had bought half of Craine's nephews' presents (you may point out that Craine should really have done this, but his nephews had taken me aside to say that the increased quality of presents in recent years had been noted and, their faces implied, missed if discontinued). But I'd totally lost track of time while my life was in homeless limbo and, straightening my shitty tree, I was overwhelmed with panic at everything I still had to do.

Giving only half the nephews presents was the worst possible scenario. No presents? Well I'm sorry but I've been ill/busy/dead, IOUs all round. Presents for all? The classic manoeuvre, well done Auntie Nat. But half with and half without? Unacceptable. It's akin to saying 'I have selected my favourites, all the rest begone!' which was not true.

I felt especially bad as one of the gifts I'd got was for a one-week-old baby. Basically a blob with a smile, if anyone could be sanguine re. no present it was surely him, rather than an eleven-year-old mature enough to pretend it's okay but young enough to cry inside.

Mum and dad decided to 'help' and spent the next day in a shopping centre, occasionally calling me:

'Remote control spider?!'

'What?'

(Sigh) 'Remoooote . . . controoool . . .'

'Yes, Mum, I got the WORDS, but without a scrap of context they're naff-all use to me.'

'Would a nephew like one?'

'No. Why would anyone like one? If one of the nephews was staring at spiders thinking "wish I could control that" I'd buy him vouchers for therapy.'

'Can you get that?'

'Vouchers for therapy?'

'Yeah.'

'Probably in America, but not here.'

(Disappointed noise)

'Mum, no one is going to unwrap vouchers for a psychiatrist and be pleased by them. It's a rude gift, something you only buy if you plan to smear it with faeces and push it through your ex-husband's new wife's letterbox.'

Dad was much more practical. He grabbed the phone off mum. (I heard a little tussle.)

'How much do you want to spend on me this Christmas?' he asked.

I pointed out that as he had saved me from the gutter I had no urge to skimp on gifts and he could name his price.

'Well,' said Tiny Tim, 'can I have some new secateurs and a hacksaw because my old one's gone bendy?'

'Yes, where do I get those . . . things you said . . . from?' I asked, in hopeless tones.

'I am holding them,' he announced. 'Just BACS the money to me.'

Good old dad. When people complain about scenarios like this and grumble about where the Spirit of Christmas went, tell them to shut up, it's on a job-share with the Fairy of Getting Useful Presents You Actually Bloody Well Want and the Elf of Not Getting Stuck With Twenty Quid Store Credit in The Button Shack.

Craine, Tiernan and I had three joyful days in the granny flat, eating snacks without plates, not using coasters and generally living the high life. I danced out of the bathroom every morning, thrilled to be emerging from a shower that didn't need a reciprocal wash:

'You scratch my back I'll scratch yours!'

'No, Back-Scratcher. Just do your bloody job.'

I danced a little less once the grouting went brown. And the dance always stumbled into a skid, due to the lack of carpets. We were all having to forget the creature comforts of home and decide that we liked a weak, dribbly shower, that drafty windows were rustic and it was NICE that while we didn't know our neigh-bour's name, we did know what he sounded like on the toilet.

'I'm driving home for Christmas . . .' I crooned to myself, as I drove home for Christmas. There's no better time to sing that (unless you're going to change your name to Ms D. Home for the festive season. If you did I'd applaud your Christmassy attitude). It felt amazing, returning to my parents' home where I didn't live any more. Like a NORMAL person would. Admittedly this was a very recent development but it still felt good.

I was worried that we would have to pretend like we'd all missed each other and this would prove a challenge as mum and dad had sucked a lot of the joy out of Christmas with the executive decision not to cook as 'what's the point without your brother?' Charming. And I wasn't allowed to cook, so Christmas lunch was either going to be crisps or eating out. Despite their festive joy-sucking, it was weirdly nice to see them again. I may even have missed them in my week of regained adulthood. I am wincing as I type this.

I always thought Christmas lunch in a pub was only for relocated witnesses or people who'd lost custody of EVERYONE and broken their TV. But it was actually quite fun. Family friends had a raucous table of fourteen, while we perched nearby on a table of three that advertised our lesser fertility. 'Tangled tubes,' I mouthed at passers-by; no point being ashamed.

Mum's friend Helen had adult chicken pox, so dad led a cheery singalong of 'Shingle Bells', which was great. I told you, he's a brilliant drunk. Helen didn't agree obviously, she suckled furi-ously at her tube of Bonjela (did you know chicken pox can go to the gums? Me neither. Fascinating, though not the pre-dinner chat I would've chosen).

Watford covered itself with its usual inglory; I went to the toilet at one point and discovered an older lady having a whiz with the door open. Unfazed, she welcomed me with, 'Don't mind me, love, I'm just having a French Piss!'

'Oh,' I stammered, trying to look unshocked (but really, how scummy would my life have to be that a pissing woman with Christmas knickers wrinkled round her ankles didn't raise an eyebrow?). 'So is that what they do in France?'

I may have been repulsed but I was learning facts. Facts that were a little undermined by her reply: 'Prob'ly. Dirty buggers.' And there's the joy of xenophobia. Doesn't matter how low your life slumps, you can always think 'pfft, well at least I'm not *French.*' I think this explains Jeremy Clarkson.

Getting home was tricky on icy roads and port, especially with Drunk Mum in tow. Drunk Mum had a hard-to-love habit of trying to cover up her inebriation by pointing out everyone else's. She sneered at me, 'You're too pissed for this road,' like a mumsy bouncer, then fell flat on her arse in a snowdrift. Dad laughed himself into a crouching position, as did I, while she lay in the middle of the road, slurring regally 'I MUST tell Helen about this, fetch my phone.'

'Helen. Guess where I am. Oh. Yes, that's right.' Helen could still see us from the pub, where she was sipping Baileys and watching the carnage. She felt no urge to help, which was fair enough after three verses of Shingle Bells.

It was another lovely day out with my parents, the sort I didn't remember having before my Month At Home. I'm sure we used to bicker more about petty things and I'd always stomp home in some sort of resentful fug. Living together seemed to have rubbed our corners off. I was probably a bloody circle by this point.

Although the first few months home had been infuriating for all of us, we seemed to have finally arrived at a sort of noisy domestic harmony. Forced into close proximity again, our relationship had withered then unexpectedly bloomed, like a dead orchid revived by a spell in the bathroom. (Old Chinese Proverb.)

I am now facing Britain's economic woes with a lot more hope. Sure, quality of life is probably going to continue this slow nose-dive, we're going to live in smaller, crappier places, while bankers spit on us out of limos, *but* we'll end up with much better family relationships! Remember that as you tuck your cousin Barry into the clingfilm drawer and check on Uncle Bert in the loft. Perhaps we should all embrace an Eastern family dynamic, where several generations of the same family live in one big house together. I think this could be great, like a big commune without the hassle of group sex. Unless your family is really fit, then it's up to you.

A worldwide economic crash will give everyone the gift of filial joy. Happy families will hang out together in massive gangs of thirty and forty (while we are stuck with our infecund three and a photo of Michael). It will be like the old days when you were born somewhere remote, fancied the vicar, married your cousin and never had to introduce yourself to anyone. I'm only half joking.

I'd like to finish this book on a positive note and that's the best I can do. If you're the sort that favours neat endings and Happily Ever Afters, I'd advise you to stop reading at this point. Let's disregard the sea of negatives and focus on the positive. Like declaring 'Oh man, this nuclear winter makes for the best sunsets! And I don't have to share them with *anyone*! (maniacal lonely cackle).' Let's ignore Real Life and how, only one month later, it sat its fat arse on the freshy painted Perfect Life of Nat and Craine . . .

EPILOGUE

I spent six and a half months obsessed with finding a new home. My previously wonderful existence had been put on hold while I was homeless. But once I found a new place to live, I was ready to saddle up the old Perfect Life again, sling Craine on the back and trot off into the green sunset.

If we've learnt anything through this book, however, it's that when I lavish all my attention on one thing, the results are often lamentable. Previous obsessions have included an Olympic swimming career, academia and a life independent of food, and I think the results speak for themselves. I succeeded in none of these and picked up some heinous collateral damage in the shape of no friends, a miserable sibling and sectioning under the mental health act. And so it was this time. I found a flat, went to get my Perfect Life out of storage and it wasn't there any more.

Over those six months, while I thought my adulthood was safely in suspended animation, not everything was hermetically sealed and aspects of my Perfect Life had been rotting. Sure I had acquired impeccable cleaning skills, an intimate knowledge of all the various *CSI: Someplace* shows and a wardrobe full of five quid dresses, but something had been quietly deteriorating. And after a couple of months in the new flat, Craine and I split up.

We actually split up when I was halfway through writing this book and it felt cruel to keep telling you stories that would endear him to you, knowing how this story was now going to end. You and I were whooping it up, sledging downhill into a snowdrift, and only I knew that that snowdrift was full of frozen turds and razor blades. I should've told you stories of Craine being a boring arsehole, to make this ending less sad, but sadly these stories did not exist.

It was a very loving break-up, fear not Craine-fans; I've had soups less warm and comforting. But it did mean that, after a month of longed-for domestic stability, everything fell apart again and parents and onlookers sighed. It's like teaching your kid to ride a bike, and the little tit WON'T STOP falling off it. I assured everyone that I wasn't doing this deliberately and I really, really wanted to ride my bike like the other kids.

Once she had got her foot in the door, the Fuck-Up Fairy decided that she liked it there and she was going to stay. So she lingered around long enough to reveal that the new flat was riddled with damp. We only discovered this once it had spread to our lungs and we started fainting in the shower. Suddenly the once-risible Hornsey group shower idea seemed a lot more safety-conscious. One to break your fall, one to call for help. If you can't retrieve your ex's floppy wet body from the shower while you cough into his hair then really what's the point in love?! I believe Adele sang that one.

The Fuck-Up Fairy lingered a little longer still, flinging her shitty dust around, and a few weeks later we learned that the windows didn't protect us against zombies *or* burglars. We learned this lesson twice within a month, just to be sure. Burglars each time, sadly for the sake of exciting anecdotes. This lesson hit me the hardest as I have always believed that insurance is the refuge of pessimists and wimps.

At least, Craine and I consoled ourselves we didn't have to go through the heartache of dividing up our possessions now. We took half a Crime Reference Number each and sang a tearful Auld Lang Syne around the less dusty patch where the telly used to be.

Somehow in the break-up I got custody of the flat. I didn't remember petitioning hard for it but somehow I had won.

'Well done,' Craine said, 'Good for you. I love you, but not in that way!' as he scampered away from our moist, ransacked home.

'Um, My Workplace-Appropriate Footwear?'

'Yeah?'

'The bus stop is that way, my Auntie's Workplace-Appropriate Footwear.'

'Of course. Thank you, November's Egg 'n' Cress.'

So, after a failed attempt at amphibian living, Tiernan and I are house hunting again. We are now a streamlined house-hunting team, no longer held back by possessions, love or full lung capacity, I joked grimly to Tinman Dooby as we went into an Estate Agents where they now knew us by name. Like *Cheers* without all the hope. Dooby responded with a hard stare that I chalked up to pre- and mid- and post-Traumatic Stress.

I was trying to stay chipper but Tiernan wasn't fooled. He sighed one evening and said, 'You're going to drink your way through the sadness aren't you?'

I confirmed that he was absolutely right, that was the plan, and he went to clear the clutter out of the hallway. When I get home drunk I like to enter the house dramatically, sometimes yelling 'Bam!' I don't know why. This is extra dangerous when I'm carrying some looted furniture, which is more often than you'd think. I have a fetish for drunkenly raiding skips for furniture; at 3am half a filing cabinet looks suspiciously like the only thing missing from my life. But in the morning I remember all the other things.

So goodbye Perfect Life, it's gone now; that carrot I had dangled at myself for the last six months as an incentive to keep going is now a sicky chutney that entices no one. It's damage control time. I am no longer in my happy loving relationship, though I am the proud owner of some sort of Victorian lung problem that my GP finds fascinating. And there's always my career spent mainly in motorway service stations. Plus Ol' Silvery Jim has had a party, invited some mates, and they show no signs of leaving. Should've killed him when I had the chance, now I'm outnumbered.

I'm so glad mum finally persuaded me to start making lists, that cavalcade of crap looks even more unpalatable written down.

But I am determined to not end up in Watford. Shove the filial love and growing closer, I **will not go back**. I've only just got my posh voice back – it took ages to shake off my real accent again! Any time I got excited I'd squawk like a guttersnipe. Now the real me is safely tucked away again, behind the facade of this lady who knows all the different types of mushrooms and definitely doesn't still shoplift when she's in a funny mood. No way, not this lady!

When you next hear from me, in perfectly modulated RP tones, life will have careered off down one of several routes:

1. I'll be in a new flat and everything will be great, just peachy. (Come on Option One: 'Gimme an O . . .')
2. I'll have given up and embraced my soggy destiny by growing cress behind my knees.
3. I'll be inviting you to turn this book into a Fighting Fantasy-style quest, where you flick back to the first page and go through all the adventures again, screaming every word aloud in despairing tones. Onlookers won't thank you, but it'll be a cheap and accurate sequel.

I fear I'm always going to spend my life scrabbling forward inch by inch into adulthood until something snaps and I ping back to adolescence. That's a sobering thought. Perhaps I'll do this for years, until one day the elastic in my umbilical bungee rope will perish like an old pair of pants and I'll finally be an independent human being, with just some saggy flaccid rope dangling between me, mum and dad (admit it, you're touching yourself again aren't you? You're only human . . .).

This overstretched metaphor will become a nostalgic keepsake, impotent now but always handy for a bit of impromptu skipping. And I'll leave you with that harrowing mental image, as I bet they won't let me put it on the book cover. Plus, gotta go, there's a structurally unsound maisonette by a busy road that's just come on the market! I know, I thought it was just a rumour too. I'm looking forward to bumping into Craine at the viewing.

Whenever I imagined my adult life, I never thought it would feature so much mould and retracing my steps. Though it's still way better than my teens, so at this rate of improvement I can't wait for my thirties! All I need is a roof over my head and enough body weight to keep my vital organs going and I'll consider the next decade a resounding triumph.

Start badly, improve slowly; I'm sticking by this motto.

ACKNOWLEDGEMENTS

I'd like to thank all of these people for their various help. Basically if you were nice to me between January and September 2010 you should be on this list, but I am forgetful so you possibly won't be. I'll leave a gap for you to fill your name in, it'll still count.

My manager Alice Russell and everyone at Avalon. If I named you all, this book would never fit in a reader's bag but I am truly grateful to you all, especially Alex Sayer.

My editor Fenella Bates and everyone at Hodder (Ciara Foley and Lucy Zilberkweit in particular) who make me feel so welcome and GIVE ME FREE BOOKS. I still can't get over this. I have a devoted Cupboard Love for you all.

The coven: Kate Quine, Maz Moore and Chloe Morgan.

My Jigs Tom Craine and Dan Antopolski.

Tiernan Douieb

The Craines: Angela, George, Michael, Joy, Tim, Jonty, Ben, Matthew, Robert, Kate, Kym, Jolien, Barnaby, Noel, Ally and Tilly.

The Douiebs: Liz and Brian.

Let's have a round of applause for the catering team: Georgie, Graham, Oliver, Pauline, Ian and Ann.

Paul Byrne

James Hingley
Tom Lamont
Chris Daniel
Stuart McGurk.
Ben Mallaby

All the comics who humoured my 'I'm an AUTHOOOR' dance. It was obnoxious and made long car journeys longer, thanks for not tipping me out onto the hard shoulder.

Cheap red wine. My friend and enemy.

Twitter. Ditto.

The baristas at Cafe Nero and Starbucks in Muswell Hill. I eked out an espresso for eight hours a day every day and you never slapped me round the head with a muffin. Your restraint was appreciated.

And mum and dad, ta for everything, sorry for everything.